Boston Red Sox: An Interactive Guide to the World of Sports

Tucker Elliot

Printed in the United States of America.
Copyright © 2011 by Tucker Elliot.

All rights reserved. No part of this publication may be reproduced, stored in a retrieval system, or transmitted in any form or by any means, electronic, mechanical, recording, or otherwise, without the prior written permission of the author.

This title is part of the Sports by the Numbers series, which is a trademark owned by Daniel J. Brush, Marc CB Maxwell, and David Horne.

Cataloging-in-Publication Data is available from the Library of Congress.

ISBN: 978-0-9826759-8-4
First edition, first printing.

Cover photo courtesy of Adam Belson.

Black Mesa Publishing, LLC
Black.Mesa.Publishing@gmail.com

www.blackmesabooks.com

Contents

Introduction	1
The Legends	5
The Rookies	25
Cy Young Worthy	45
The Batting Champions	65
Defining Moments	85
The Most Valuable Players	107
The Sluggers	127
Winning Pitchers	147
The Closers	165
Walk-off	185
About the Author	207
Acknowledgements	209
References	211
About Black Mesa	213

For Travis, Cayden, and Gracie, who saw their first Red Sox game together.

"This is the greatest story Baseball ever told."
— *Tim Kurkjian, on Boston's victory in the 2004 American League Championship Series*

Introduction

THE FENWAY FAITHFUL are fully aware how painful and tragic some of the most compelling moments in baseball history are, precisely because many of those same moments defined Red Sox fandom for 86 years. That curse is over, however, and a new era is upon us. Boston celebrated the miracle that was 2004, the validation that was 2007, and today, its fans look ahead unafraid, unburdened, expecting nothing short of greatness, but able to withstand the inevitable heartache, any letdowns that await, knowing that all franchises share in great moments from time to time but the truly great franchises, such as ours, have more than a moment—*much more.*

We have a legacy.

A legacy that began with the first world championship in baseball's modern era and that continues to grow in the 21st century, as Boston became the first club to claim two titles in this new millennia. It is a compelling legacy built on the talents of legends, some of the greatest this game has ever known. It is a legacy defined by individuals who stretch the limits of our imaginations through feats that verge on the inexplicable. It is a legacy that casts a long shadow on this game, our national pastime, for it is impossible to separate the history of the Red Sox and the history of baseball—without Boston, any telling of baseball's history would be incomplete. This team is the legacy of Mr. Yawkey, who brought honor and prestige and a desire to compete back to Fenway. And this team is our legacy—the fans who persevered, who loved the Red Sox even when the club let us down.

This book is a tribute to that legacy.

In the coming pages you will read about the greatest numbers in franchise history—those that were retired in honor of our greatest legends. And the biggest names from every era are all here: Young, Speaker, Cronin, Ruth, Williams, Doerr, Pesky, DiMaggio, Yastrzemski, Fisk, Rice, Evans, Lynn, Clemens, Boggs, Ortiz, Varitek, Ramirez, and Pedroia, just to name a few.

Every Hall of Famer from Red Sox history is in this book—as is every award winner, the greatest performances in franchise history, the postseason triumphs and heartaches, the fan-favorite players who never became stars, all the glory, the passion, and emotion that the greatest moments in Red Sox history evoke are all here.

A thousand numbers await you, and they all tell the story of the Boston Red Sox. The format is unique, intriguing, and compelling, because as baseball fans we all love the numbers, and in these pages the numbers celebrate records, lore, trivia, personalities, anomalies, championships won, championships lost, the good and the bad, and all that is great about baseball and the Boston Red Sox.

Now sit back, reminisce, and enjoy.

Tucker Elliot
Tampa, FL
March 2011

Ted Williams—Boston's greatest legend.
(Courtesy National Baseball Hall of Fame Library, Cooperstown, NY)

"I wanted to be the greatest hitter who ever lived. A man has to have goals—for a day, for a lifetime—and that was mine, to have people say, 'There goes Ted Williams, the greatest hitter who ever lived.'"
— Ted Williams, Hall of Fame Legend

Chapter 1

The Legends

BASEBALL'S AMERICAN LEAGUE began play in 1901 with eight franchises as charter members, one of which was the Boston Americans. Hall of Famers Jimmy Collins and Cy Young led Boston to 79 victories for the second best record in the league's inaugural season. It was a good year, but there were even better years to come—and of course, some heartbreaking, gut-wrenching, agonizingly painful years as well.

Such is the history of the Boston Red Sox.

This is the team that boasts some of the absolute greatest moments in baseball history. The first World Series game and the first perfect game in baseball's modern era both took place at Boston's Huntington Avenue Grounds—and for both of those games Cy Young was the pitcher. Ted Williams' 6 for 8 performance on the season's final day in 1941, his 4 for 4 performance with two home runs during the 1946 All-Star game at Fenway Park, and on September 28, 1960, the last home run of his career—in his final at bat. Carl Yastrzemski won the 1967 Triple Crown—the last of the 20th century. Fred Lynn won Rookie of the Year honors and the Most Valuable Player Award in 1975. Carlton Fisk created one of the most enduring images in sports history with one magical swing in the 1975 World Series—one made possible by Bernie Carbo, who earlier in the game tied the score with his second pinch homer of the series. Dave Henderson came through with a game-saving homer against the Angels when Boston was down to its last strike in the 1986 League Championship Series. Roger Clemens struck out 20 batters in a game—twice. Pedro Martinez tossed six hitless innings in relief against Cleveland to clinch the 1999 Division Series—after the Indians scored eight runs on seven hits in the first three innings. Big Papi hit 54 home runs in 2006, eclipsing the franchise record held by Jimmie Foxx since 1938—and, Jason Varitek became the first player in baseball history to call four no-hitters when Jon Lester tossed a no-no against the Royals on May 19, 2008.

This is the team that won baseball's first World Series in the modern era in 1903, and that claimed five titles before the New York Yankees won their first pennant in 1921. This is also the team that endured 26 world championship celebrations in the Bronx before winning title number six. Hall of Famers Waite Hoyt, Herb Pennock,

Red Ruffing, and Babe Ruth all began their careers in Boston, but they were all traded or sold to the Yankees, and it was for their exploits in the Bronx that they earned legendary status.

This is the team that witnessed Ted Williams' .406 season and two Triple Crowns, but saw him place second in Most Valuable Player balloting behind a Yankee all three seasons. Wade Boggs won five batting titles with Boston, but he won his only ring with the Yankees. Roger Clemens won three Cy Young Awards and a Most Valuable Player Award with Boston, but he won *both* of his rings with the Yankees.

This is the team that won three World Series titles in four seasons from 1915-18, but this is also the team that lost the first one-game playoff in league history in 1948, lost a double-digit lead and a one-game playoff in 1978, and lost Game 7 in the 1946, 1967, 1975, and 1986 World Series'.

And this is the team that suffered an 86-year nightmare—victims of Enos Slaughter in 1946, Bob Gibson in 1967, Joe Morgan in 1975, Bucky Dent in 1978, Bill Buckner in 1986, and Aaron Boone in 2003—before experiencing the miracle that was the 2004 postseason.

It was a miracle, but it was also redemption.
Redemption for all the Red Sox legends and four generations of fans who never tasted victory in the World Series—guys like Williams, Pesky, DiMaggio, and Doerr, Yaz, Pudge, Rice, Dewey, and Lynn.

Johnny Pesky wrote the following in *The Boston Red Sox* by Milton Cole and Jim Kaplan: "I looked up in the heavens and I thought of Mr. Yawkey. And Cronin. Eddie Collins. Ted was the first one I thought of. I thought about Ted and I thought about Dom and I thought about Bobby . . . I shed a few happy tears and I'm unashamed of it. We felt like a bunch of children, just so elated with such a good feeling. You've been around here all these years, and you see fans pouring into that ballpark all these years, and rooting so hard for you to get a base hit or strike out the opposition. I'm glad we won, because of the fans. I've been in the game my whole life, and never won a World Series."

All of those moments are in this book—but we begin with the legends: Bobby Doerr, Joe Cronin, Johnny Pesky, Carl Yastrzemski, Ted Williams, and Carlton Fisk, the retired numbers honored by the Boston Red Sox, these are among our favorites in chapter one. You will also find some astounding performances—among the best in this chapter are Roger Clemens' 20 strikeouts in 1986, Jon Lester's clincher in the 2007 World Series and his no-hitter in 2008, and Tony Conigliaro's 1965 home run title.

Now leading off . . .

1 The number of World Series titles (1) it takes to make your childhood dreams come true. Boston won the first title in the modern era of major league baseball, defeating the Pittsburgh Pirates in 1903. The franchise has won seven titles through 2008, and counting: 1903, 1912, 1915, 1916, 1918, 2004, and 2007.

2 The number of postseasons (2) for Carl Yastrzemski. He is the franchise leader with 3,308 regular season games—a total that is also the second highest in major league history—but he got to play only 17 games in the postseason. Boston won pennants with Yaz in 1967 and 1975, but lost the World Series in seven games both times.

3 The number of times (3) a Red Sox player has won the Triple Crown in batting: Ted Williams (.356, 36 HR, 137 RBI) in 1942, Ted Williams (.343, 32 HR, 114 RBI) in 1947, and Carl Yastrzemski (.326, 44 HR, 121 RBI) in 1967.

4 The jersey number (4) retired in honor of shortstop Joe Cronin. He spent 24 seasons with the club in some capacity—player-manager, manager, or general manager—and his 1,071 managerial wins are a franchise record. Cronin was elected to the Hall of Fame in 1956.

5 Dwight Evans won (5) consecutive Gold Gloves from 1981-85. He was dangerous at the plate and in the field, using his canon of an arm to cut down runners from out in right field. Today, fans show up hours before game time to watch players take BP—but back in the day, one of the biggest pre-game draws was watching Evans and Jim Rice play long toss (no arc here, frozen ropes only) from one corner of the outfield to the other. Evans' eight career Gold Gloves are a franchise record.

6 The jersey number (6) retired in honor of shortstop Johnny Pesky on September 28, 2008. Pesky became the first player in franchise history to have his number retired without being a member of the Hall of Fame, but it was an honor 57 years in the making and long overdue. Baseball Commissioner Bud Selig issued a statement saying, "I am truly pleased that No. 6 will overlook Pesky's Pole from the right field façade forever." Pesky tossed out the ceremonial first pitch in Boston's final game of the season after a video tribute to his life and career with the organization.

7 Wade Boggs surpassed 200 hits (7) consecutive seasons. He hit .349 as a rookie in 1982, but he did not qualify for the batting title because he only batted 338 times (Willie Wilson won the title with a

.332 average for the Royals). Boggs then got 210 hits in 1983 and won his first batting title, and from 1983-89 he surpassed 200 hits every season and won five batting titles.

8 The jersey number (8) retired in honor of outfielder Carl Yastrzemski. He was elected to the Hall of Fame during his first year of eligibility in 1989 with his name on 95% of the ballots—and with his enshrinement at Cooperstown he became the first Hall of Fame player to be a product of Little League Baseball.

9 The jersey number (9) retired in honor of Hall of Fame outfielder Ted Williams. He is a baseball legend—and in 1982 Red Sox fans voted him the Greatest Red Sox Player of all-time.

10 The number of RBI (10) for shortstop Nomar Garciaparra against the Seattle Mariners on May 10, 1999. He hit three home runs—including two grand slams—and his RBI total tied a franchise record shared by Fred Lynn, Rudy York, and Norm Zauchin.

11 Hall of Fame legend Babe Ruth hit (11) home runs in 1918. Fans associate monstrous numbers with Ruth—and rightfully so, because he is one of the biggest names in all of professional sports history—but it took only 11 big flies to give Ruth his first career home run title as the dead ball era was drawing to a close.

12 Heinie Wagner got (12) hits for the New York Giants in 1902. He was a 21-year-old shortstop who signed, played 17 games, and was released by the Giants in a span of 17 days. It took him four years to get back to the majors, but once there, he tallied 141 steals for the Red Sox—the fourth highest total in franchise history. Ten years after his release from the Giants, Wagner and the Red Sox beat New York in the 1912 World Series.

13 Buck Freeman hit (13) home runs in 1903. The outfielder won his second home run title that season—and it was also the third consecutive season that Freeman led the club in both home runs and RBI.

14 The number of seasons (14) for second baseman Bobby Doerr. He played every one of them for Boston, and in honor of his Hall of Fame career the Red Sox retired his number one jersey.

15 Don Schwall won (15) games in 1961. He earned Rookie of the Year honors after completing ten of his 25 starts. Schwall actually started the season in the minors and did not make his big league debut until May 21, but once in Boston he came out of the gate so strong that he managed to play his way onto the All-Star team. Schwall lost 15 games in his sophomore season, and he never made another All-Star team or won more than nine games in any other season.

16 Dave Morehead was tagged for (16) losses during a dismal 1965 season that saw the Red Sox lose 100 games. The club began play on September 16, trailing the Twins by 37 games and having lost four of five during their current homestand, so it was not a surprise that only 1,247 fans came out to Fenway to see Morehead (and his 9-16 record) vs. Cleveland. Two hours and nine innings later, Morehead fielded a comebacker off the bat of pinch-hitter Vic Davalillo to close out a 2-0 victory—and, a no-hitter.

17 Ted Williams hit (17) career grand slams. He is the toughest batter to get out in major league history. It was never fun for opposing pitchers to have to face him, but that was never more true than it was when there was nowhere to put him—and his grand slam total is only one of the many franchise records that he owns.

18 Roger Clemens pitched (18) complete games in 1987. He led the league and set a career high as he was on the mound to finish exactly half of his 36 starts that season. Clemens was dominant for the second year in a row as he struck out 256 batters, won a league best 20 games, and captured his second consecutive Cy Young Award.

19 Bill Mueller hit (19) home runs in 2003. He was not a massive power guy—his total that season set a career high—but he got three of them and a piece of history in one game on July 29, against the Texas Rangers. Mueller hit a solo shot in the third inning, a grand slam in the seventh, and another grand slam in the eighth. He was only the 12th player in history to hit two grand slams in one game—but Mueller, who was a switch-hitter, became the first player in history to get one from both sides of the plate in the same game.

20 The number of strikeouts (20) for Roger Clemens against the Seattle Mariners on April 29, 1986. "I watched perfect games by Catfish Hunter and Mike Witt," said manager John McNamara. "But this was the most awesome pitching performance I've ever seen." It also set a major league record—one that Clemens equaled against the Detroit Tigers on September 18, 1996, in a game that was also his last victory as a member of the Red Sox.

21 Mike Greenwell hit 22 home runs in 1988—with home run number (21) coming during his first at bat of a home game against Orioles pitcher Jose Bautista on September 14. Greenwell was just getting started. He doubled in the fourth, tripled in the sixth, and batted in the eighth needing a single to hit for the cycle—and he got it.

22 Jim Lonborg won (22) games in 1967. It was the only 20 win season of his career, and his total also led the league and earned him the Cy Young Award. Lonborg, who was selected to the Boston Red Sox Hall of Fame in 2002, is the actual player seen in the picture behind the bar on the popular sitcom *Cheers*.

23 Jon Lester faced (23) batters during Game 4 of the 2007 World Series. His 2006 rookie season was cut short due to cancer—he was diagnosed with anaplastic large cell lymphoma. Lester beat the cancer, fought his way back to the majors, posted a 4-0 record down the stretch in 2007, and then gave up only three hits as he beat the Rockies in the title-clinching game of the World Series. In the off-season, Lester was honored with the 2007 Tony Conigliaro Award for "overcoming adversity through the attributes of spirit, determination, and courage."

24 Roger Clemens won (24) games in 1986. That total tied Babe Ruth for one of the ten best in franchise history, and it gave Clemens the first of his major league record seven Cy Young Awards.

25 Jim Rice got 18 hits and (25) total bases in 24 games in 1974. The legendary slugger made his major league debut that season on August 19, going hitless in two at bats, but reaching base for the first time after getting hit by a pitch in the eighth inning. Two days later he got a pair of singles for his first hits—and over the next 15 seasons he was a powerful force to be reckoned with. He amassed 4,129 total bases during his career—the third highest total in franchise history.

26 Ernie Shore retired (26) consecutive batters against the Washington Senators on June 23, 1917, after entering the game in relief of Babe Ruth during the first inning. Technically, he combined with Ruth on a no-hitter. The truth, however, is that Ruth faced one batter, walked him, argued with the umpire, and was ejected from the game. Shore came on in relief, the base runner was cut down trying to steal—and Shore proceeded to retire every batter he faced.

27 The jersey number (27) retired in honor of catcher Carlton Fisk. He became a part of postseason history when he hit a dramatic walk-off home run to force a Game 7 against the Cincinnati Reds during the 1975 World Series. Pudge never won a ring, however, so when the Red Sox won the 2004 World Series the franchise awarded him an honorary ring in recognition of his Hall of Fame career.

28 Boston banged out (28) hits vs. Florida on June 27, 2003. The offense scored 14 runs on 13 hits in the first inning alone, with newly acquired Johnny Damon hitting a double, a triple, and a single. In that inning, Boston got ten consecutive hits at one point, and Marlins pitchers threw 91 pitches and were on the mound for 50 minutes. It took 59 pitches and two relievers before the Marlins got the first out. The final score was 25-8. Damon became just the second player in baseball's modern era to record three hits in one inning. Gene Stephens was the first, and he also did it for Boston, collecting three hits in a 17-run inning against Detroit back in 1953.

29 Babe Ruth hit (29) home runs in 1919. It was a major league record—but of course he shattered that total in each of the next two seasons with New York. Ruth also posted a 9-5 record as a pitcher for Boston in 1919. His 29 home runs came in only 432 at bats—but on the mound he faced 591 batters and gave up only two long balls all season.

30 Dustin Pedroia came up one game short of a (30)-game road hitting streak in 2008. On August 10, Pedroia hit a first inning double against the White Sox to reach 29 games—a mark last achieved by a member of the Red Sox in 1913, when Tris Speaker hit in 29 consecutive road games. Pedroia went 0 for 4 the next day in the series finale, but he left for home with a tidy .328 road batting average through 61 games.

31 The number of at bats (31) for Mike Greenwell in 1985. He was a 21-year-old outfielder who got a cup of coffee in September, 1985—and all he did was put his first three major league hits out of the park. Greenwell went on to tally 1,400 hits during his career. He never achieved the superstar status many thought he would, but he retired with the tenth highest hits total in franchise history.

32 Tony Conigliaro hit (32) home runs in 1965. He was a 20-year-old outfielder in his sophomore season when he became the youngest home run champion in league history. Conigliaro was only 22 when he surpassed 100 career home runs in 1967—but that same season a fastball from Angels' pitcher Jack Hamilton struck him in the face on August 18. It was a devastating blow that nearly took his life, and though he did play again, it effectively ended his career.

33 The jersey number (33) for catcher Jason Varitek. He became only the third team captain in franchise history (Carl Yastrzemski and Jim Rice were the first two) after Boston's 2004 championship season. Varitek was a three-time All-American at Georgia Tech and the 1993 *Baseball America's* College Player of the Year, and he was the first player in Georgia Tech history to have his jersey number retired—also 33.

34 Smoky Joe Wood won (34) games in 1912. His total led the league and set a franchise record—one that is as close to unbreakable as a record can possibly be. He was 34-5 that season and pitched 344 innings during 43 games. He was only 22 years old when he set the record, but by his mid-20s his arm was a complete wreck—so he became an outfielder instead. He played six more seasons, and closed out his career by hitting .297 with eight home runs for Cleveland in 1922.

35 Jimmie Foxx hit (35) home runs in 1939. He hit 15 fewer home runs than he did the previous season, but his total was still the best in the league. Foxx, who won the Triple Crown in 1933 while playing for Philadelphia, was also second in the league with a .360 average and eighth in the league with 105 RBI.

36 Ted Williams hit (36) home runs in 1942. It was the second consecutive season that he led the league in home runs. He also won the batting and RBI titles—giving him the Triple Crown, and earning him Major League Player of the Year honors.

37 On May 19, 2008, Jon Lester took the mound against the Kansas City Royals for career start number (37)—and he tossed a no-hitter. Lester made 130 pitches, 86 for strikes, 44 for balls, but none of them resulted in a base hit by the Royals offense. He induced 11 groundball outs, five fly outs, and two line drive outs, and he notched nine strikeouts. Only 24 years old at the time, Lester has beaten cancer, clinched a World Series, and thrown a no-hitter.

38 Cy Young pitched (38) complete games in 1901. It was the second highest total in the league, which was an anomaly, because Young led the league in almost everything else that season. He won the pitching

Triple Crown after posting 33 wins, a 1.62 earned run average, and 158 strikeouts.

39 Jim Rice hit (39) home runs in 1983. It was his third and final home run title. The perennial All-Star, who spent his entire career with Boston, is a member of the Boston Red Sox Hall of Fame and the Ted Williams Museum and Hitters Hall of Fame.

40 Dom DiMaggio hit a career high (40) doubles in 1948 and he led the club with 127 runs. DiMaggio never led the league in doubles, though he was the team leader twice (1942, 1951) and he was among the top ten league leaders six times—and he closed out his career with 308 doubles, one of the ten highest totals in franchise history.

41 The number of save opportunities (41) for rookie Jonathan Papelbon in 2006. He converted 35, including 20 straight to begin the season. Papelbon posted a 0.92 earned run average with 75 strikeouts in 68-plus innings—and for his efforts placed second in Rookie of the Year balloting.

42 The jersey number (42) retired in honor of Hall of Fame legend Jackie Robinson. The Boston Red Sox proudly joined Major League Baseball in retiring Robinson's number 42 jersey in 1997 on the 50th anniversary of his major league debut with the Brooklyn Dodgers. Robinson broke baseball's color barrier when he took the field on April 15, 1947, and in 1962 he became the first African American elected membership into the Baseball Hall of Fame.

43 Manny Ramirez hit (43) home runs in 2004. He hit two more than teammate David Ortiz to win the league home run title. Manny also led the league with a .613 slugging percentage and he drove home 130 runs. He was only third in league MVP balloting—but the ring and Most Valuable Player Award he picked up in the 2004 World Series more than made up for it.

44 Hall of Fame legend Carl Yastrzemski hit (44) home runs in 1967. It was a career high and the only time that he led the league in home runs—and it coincided nicely with his league leading RBI total and his second of three career batting titles. Boston also won the pennant, but lost the World Series to the Cardinals. Yaz said after losing the series, "If I have a choice between a pennant and a Triple Crown, I'll take the pennant every time." He got both in 1967, and he won another pennant in 1975, but he never won a ring.

45 Manny Ramirez hit (45) home runs in 2005. At the time it was the fourth highest total in franchise history, but it was only the third highest in the league that season, and only the second highest on the club behind teammate David Ortiz.

46 Jim Rice hit (46) home runs in 1978. He won his second consecutive home run title on the strength of a career high total. It was the second highest total in franchise history at the time, and it remains among the top five.

47 David Ortiz hit (47) home runs in 2005. He lost the home run title to Alex Rodriguez, who hit 48 for the Yankees. Big Papi did lead the league in RBI and extra-base hits, but despite his monster numbers he also came in second behind A-Rod in league MVP balloting. Rodriguez, after being told he won the Most Valuable Player Award over Ortiz, said, "I would certainly trade his World Series championship for this MVP trophy."

48 The number of batters (48) faced by Babe Ruth during Game 2 of the 1916 World Series. The Red Sox met the Brooklyn Robins (later they became the Dodgers) in the Fall Classic, and after winning 6-5 in Game 1, Boston sent Babe Ruth to the mound for Game 2. In the top of the thirteenth, with the game tied 1-1, Robins' pitcher Sherry Smith came to bat with two outs and the potential winning run on second. He hit a fly ball to left that was caught by Duffy Lewis to end the threat. The *Boston Globe* described the play in much more dramatic fashion: "Tearing along as if it was a case of life or death, he made one final reach while twisting his neck like a seagull and managed to reach and hold the ball." Smith and Ruth both tossed complete games, but it was Ruth and the Red Sox who came out on top, winning 2-1 in 14 innings. Boston won the series four games to one.

49 Boston trailed the Yankees by (49) games when play began on September 5, 1927. It was a disastrous season, but on that day New York was in town for a doubleheader and there were so many fans at Fenway that they had to be seated on the outfield grass in a roped off section next to the fence. The attendance was estimated at 36,000—just over 10% of the 305,275 in attendance for the entire season. Boston won the first game 12-11 in 18 innings, but lost the second game 5-0.

50 Hall of Fame legend Jimmie Foxx hit (50) home runs in 1938. He became the first player in franchise history to reach the 50 home run plateau.

51 The number of doubles (51) for Joe Cronin in 1938, Wade Boggs in 1989, and Nomar Garciaparra in 2000. Hall of Fame members Cronin and Boggs both led the league for the second and final time of their respective careers when they posted 51 doubles—but Garciaparra was second in the league behind the 57 doubles for Carlos Delgado of the Toronto Blue Jays. All three players share a total that ranks among the top ten season efforts in franchise history.

52 Josh Beckett faced (52) batters during the 2007 American League Championship Series. He gave up only nine hits in two starts and 14 innings of work, and he defeated Indians ace CC Sabathia twice. The Red Sox won the pennant, and Beckett won the Most Valuable Player Award for the series.

53 Hall of Fame legend Tris Speaker hit (53) doubles in 1912. It was the first of eight seasons that he led the league in doubles. Speaker is baseball's all-time leader with 792 doubles, and the 53 he hit in 1912 set a franchise record that lasted until 1931. His total remains among the top ten in franchise history.

54 David Ortiz hit (54) home runs in 2006. Big Papi led the league in addition to breaking the franchise record held by Jimmie Foxx since 1938. He also led the league in total bases, walks, and RBI, and was second in slugging—but he only placed third in MVP balloting behind Justin Morneau and Derek Jeter.

55 The number of games (55) for Hall of Fame second baseman Bobby Doerr in 1937. He was a 19-year-old rookie who got 33 hits and scored 22 runs. He hit only .224, but the next season he was a regular, and the season after that he was a star. Doerr closed out 14 seasons in Boston with 2,042 career hits—a total that ranks among the top ten in franchise history.

56 Nomar Garciaparra led the league with (56) doubles in 2002. He became the first player since 1931 to surpass the old franchise record of 53 that Tris Speaker hit in 1912. Nomar was sidelined by injuries for much of 2001, but he rebounded just fine in 2002, and did even better in 2003—seeing as he married soccer legend and three-time Olympian Mia Hamm that year.

57 The number of strikes (57) for Pedro Martinez vs. Cleveland during Game 5 of the 1999 Division Series. Martinez was the starter in Game 1 of the series, but he was battling injuries and left the game after throwing 58 pitches in four innings of work. Boston lost that game, and the next, but then won two straight to force a winner-take-all contest in the best-of-five series. Martinez had not pitched since Game 1, but with Game 5 tied 8-8 in the third inning, Jimy Williams sent his ace to the mound. Martinez tossed 57 of 97 pitches for strikes—and tossed six scoreless, no-hit innings, as Boston won 12-8.

58 Buck Freeman legged out (58) triples for the club from 1902-04. He was second in the league with 19 triples in 1902, and third in the league with 20 triples in 1903, but his 19 triples in 1904 gave him the highest total in the league. Freeman's totals are the second and third highest season efforts in franchise history.

59 The number of triples (59) for Carl Yastrzemski from 1961-83. His career high was nine triples in 1964, but he averaged three triples for every 162 games he played—which is the exact total he hit in 1965. It just so happens that one of his three triples that season came against the Tigers on May 14, the same day he smacked a pair of home runs, a double, and a single, that when added to his triple gave him the cycle, a 5 for 5 performance, and five RBI.

60 The number of extra-base hits (60) for Hall of Fame legend Tris Speaker in 1913. He was only third in the league, but his total included 22 triples—a franchise record that still stands almost a century later.

61 The number of errors (61) for Hobe Ferris in 1901. He was the first second baseman in franchise history. His errors total from that inaugural season is a franchise record and the second highest in history for an American League second baseman.

62 Smoky Joe Wood gave up only (62) earned runs in 1911—despite pitching 275 innings. That works out to a very cool 2.02 earned run average that was third best in the league. He only gave up 7.38 hits per nine innings for the second best ratio in the league—a number that was helped by his performance on July 29, when he pitched a no-hitter against the St. Louis Browns.

63 The number of earned runs (63) scored against Babe Ruth in 1916. He was on the mound 323 innings and he faced 1,300 batters—both numbers were the third highest totals in the league. Ruth, who led the league with nine shutouts, also posted a league best 1.75 earned run average that is among the top 15 in franchise history.

64 Boston gave up (64) runs during 17 extra-inning games in 1969. They outscored their opponents 71-64 in those games—posting a respectable 10-7 record while giving the fans some free baseball. It was a frustrating season, however, because no matter what the club did they were never able to get near Baltimore as the Orioles ran away with the division, and that frustration was never more real than it was in a game against the Seattle Pilots on May 16. Boston had just gone 6-1 on a West Coast swing, and was starting a homestand with the lowly Pilots. The first game went extra-innings, and the two clubs combined to score 11 runs during the eleventh inning. The final score was 10-9, but it was Seattle that scored six runs in the eleventh and Boston that scored five—and the Red Sox lost when Carl Yastrzemski struck out to end the game.

65 Jimmy Collins hit (65) triples for Boston. The Hall of Fame legend led the club with 16 triples in 1901, but his career high 17 triples in 1903 was only second best behind the 20 for Buck Freeman. Collins hit 116 triples during his career, and the 65 he hit for Boston ranks among the top 15 totals in franchise history.

66 Hideo Nomo tossed (66) of 105 pitches for strikes against the Baltimore Orioles during a contest at Camden Yards on April 4, 2001. He struck out 11 batters and led the Red Sox to a 3-0 victory by tossing a no-hitter in his very first start with the club. It was the second career no-no for Nomo, who tossed his first one in the N.L. as a member of the Dodgers.

67 Earl Webb hit a franchise record (67) doubles in 1931. He hit only 155 doubles during parts of seven major league seasons, and he never hit more than 30 in any other season. The outfielder played for five teams during his short career, but he spent more time in Boston than with any other team. His career highs for runs, hits, doubles, RBI, walks, average, on-base percentage, slugging percentage, and total bases all came in 1931—but two years later his career was over.

68 The number of strikes (68) for Tim Wakefield against the Texas Rangers on April 20, 2008. Wakefield tossed 86 pitches in eight innings of work, and he was around the plate all night long. He gave up seven hits and five earned runs, but he also struck out five and didn't walk anybody—and when the Red Sox rallied for a 6-5 victory, Wakefield earned career win number 170. The Elias Sports Bureau reported that of his 170 career wins, it was only the second time that he pitched at least eight innings and didn't walk anybody.

69 The number of innings (69) pitchers Cy Young and Bill Dinneen combined to throw during the 1903 World Series. Boston used only three pitchers in the best-of-nine series: Young, Dinneen, and Tom Hughes. Dinneen tossed four complete games, Young tossed three complete games, and Hughes made one start—but Hughes lasted only two-plus innings before Young came out of the bullpen and tossed seven innings in relief.

70 The number of pitches (70) for Yankees starter Chase Wright against Boston on April 22, 2007. In the bottom of the third with two outs and the bases empty, and in a span of just ten pitches, Manny Ramirez, J.D. Drew, Mike Lowell, and Jason Varitek hit four consecutive home runs against Wright. It was only the fifth time in baseball history that a team hit four consecutive home runs—but it was the second time for Drew, who was also the second of four Dodgers to hit consecutive home runs on September 18, 2006. The odds of J.D. Drew hitting the second of four consecutive home runs on two separate occasions was calculated by Boston College professor of mathematics Dr. Nancy Rallis, who put the probability at 1 in 14.3 million.

71 Carl Yastrzemski scored (71) runs in 1961. It was a banner year for Maris and Mantle in the Bronx, so few people outside of Boston took note of the 21-year-old rookie out in left field for the Red Sox. Yaz, of course, became a legend in his own right. He scored a franchise record 1,816 career runs—one of the top 20 totals in baseball history.

72 The number of hits (72) for Harry Hooper in 1909. He was a 21-year-old rookie who broke into the majors by playing alongside the legendary Tris Speaker in the outfield. Hooper was so good on defense that former manager Bill Carrigan once said, "The best outfield trio I ever saw? That's easy—Speaker, (Duffy) Lewis, and Hooper, and the greatest of those was Hooper." Hooper could swing the lumber too—he is among the top ten in franchise history with 1,707 hits.

73 The number of games (73) for relief pitcher Tom Gordon in 1998. He was so good out of the bullpen that season that noted Red Sox fan Stephen King wrote a best-selling book titled *The Girl Who Loved Tom Gordon*. He posted a league best 46 saves, and earned the A.L. Rolaids Relief Man Award.

74 Steve Lyons attempted (74) steals during nine major league seasons—but it was an attempt on June 5, 1986, that he is remembered for. Lyons was thrown out trying to swipe third with two outs in the ninth inning—down by two runs—and Wade Boggs at the plate. Boggs was hitting nearly .400 and the potential tying run was on first. Boston lost to Milwaukee 7-5, and three weeks later Lyons was traded to the Chicago White Sox.

75 Hall of Fame outfielder Harry Hooper hit (75) career home runs. His total might seem low, but then he also began his career during the dead ball era. Hooper still managed to hit some memorable shots. He became the first player in history to lead off both ends of a doubleheader with a home run when he performed the feat in 1913. Two years later, Hooper became the second player in history to hit two home runs during one World Series game.

76 The number of games (76) for relief pitcher Heathcliff Slocumb in 1997. His first 49 games were out of the Boston bullpen, but after posting an 0-5 record with 34 walks in only 46 innings—not to mention, a 5.79 earned run average—the Red Sox Faithful were glad to see him go. Slocumb was traded to Seattle, where he went 0-4 with a 4.13 ERA in his final 27 games that season. This was definitely one trade that worked out well for the club, because in exchange for Slocumb we got Derek Lowe and Jason Varitek.

77 Hobe Ferris hit (77) triples for Boston. The English born second baseman hit ten or more triples five times from 1901-07, and was among the top six league leaders four times. His total with the club is among the top ten in franchise history.

78 The number of games (78) for Juan Beniquez in 1975. He was a key utility guy for the club that season, playing all three outfield positions as well as third base and DH on occasion. He also gave key production at the plate. Beniquez hit .291 with just two home runs, but on consecutive days during a six-game road winning streak in June he beat the Tigers with an extra-inning triple and an eighth inning home run.

79 Jim Rice hit (79) career triples. He led the league with a career high 15 triples in 1978, but then again, he led the league in almost everything that season. Rice was among the top ten league leaders in triples four times, and his career total is among the top ten in franchise history.

80 The number of strikeouts (80) for Pedro Martinez during the postseason from 1998-2004. He made 11 starts and two relief appearances during Boston's playoff appearances in 1998-99 and 2003-04, and he posted a 6-2 record. Perhaps the most memorable start for Martinez came vs. New York in Game 3 of the 1999 League Championship Series. The match-up was dubbed "Cy Young" vs. "Cy Old" because Roger Clemens was on the mound for the Yankees. Boston was down 0-2 in the series and facing a must-win situation—and Pedro delivered. Seven innings, two hits, no runs, and 12 strikeouts. Clemens got shelled—lasting only two-plus innings before getting yanked, as Boston won 13-1.

81 The number of extra-base hits (81) for Ted Williams in 1947. His total was the highest in the league—as was his total of 32 home runs. Williams ranks among the top 20 in baseball history for both extra-base hits and home runs.

82 The number of hits (82) for pitcher Slim Harriss during nine major league seasons. He was a .145 career hitter, but for the Athletics in 1923 he hit only .066 after collecting just four singles in 61 at bats. That same season, Harriss actually hit a double against Red Sox pitcher Howard Ehmke that nearly left the yard on September 7. The ball ricocheted off the wall and Harriss cruised into second—but he was called out because in his excitement he completely missed first base while on his way to second. That erased the hit—what would have been the only hit of the game for Philadelphia, as it turns out—and Ehmke completed the 4-0 shutout with a no-hitter.

83 The number of extra-base hits (83) for Ted Williams in 1946—the highest total in the league. He was pretty non-discriminate in that he punished opposing teams equally, but St. Louis probably would have disagreed with that assessment, especially on July 21, when in a game against the Browns, Williams hit for the cycle for the only time in his career.

84 Bob Watson came to Boston in a trade with the Houston Astros in 1979, playing (84) games for the Red Sox before signing with the New York Yankees in the off-season. On September 15, 1979, he had a particularly good game against the Orioles when he went 4 for 5 at the plate and hit for the cycle. It was an especially notable performance because Watson, who in 1974 scored run number 1,000,000 in baseball history, became the first player in baseball history to hit for the cycle in both leagues.

85 The number of extra-base hits (85) for Ted Williams in 1949, Nomar Garciaparra in 1997 and 2002, and David Ortiz in 2006. They share one of the ten highest totals in franchise history—but Williams is the only one who led the league when he posted his 85 extra-base hits. Nomar came in second in 1997 and fifth in 2002, and Ortiz came in second in 2006.

86 The number of years (86) the Red Sox Faithful suffered after tasting victory during the 1918 World Series. The narrator in the classic movie *Fever Pitch* got it right: "Eighty-six years of banging our heads against the Big Green Wall—but we finally did it."

87 The number of hits (87) for Frank Malzone in 1965. He was an All-Star third baseman who placed second in Rookie of the Year balloting in 1957 when he got a career high 185 hits. Malzone was nearing the end of his career when he struggled to a .239 average with his 87 hits in 1965, but he closed out his days in Boston with 1,454 career hits—which put him among the top ten in franchise history.

88 The number of extra-base hits (88) for David Ortiz in 2005 and again in 2007. Ortiz led the league in extra-base hits three times in four seasons from 2004-07.

89 Hall of Fame second baseman Bobby Doerr hit (89) triples. Doerr led the league with a career high 11 triples in 1950, and six times he was among the top ten league leaders. His career total is among the top ten in franchise history.

90 Jim Tabor hit (90) home runs for Boston. He was a 22-year-old rookie in 1939 when he hit four home runs in a doubleheader against the Philadelphia Athletics. Tabor hit three of his home runs in the second game, two of which were grand slams. He was just the second player in history with two grand slams in a single game—and of the first 12 players who accomplished this feat, four of them did so for the Red Sox: Tabor, Rudy York, Nomar Garciaparra, and Bill Mueller.

91 The number of extra-base hits (91) for David Ortiz in 2004. Big Papi led the league, but he came up one shy of the team record 92 extra-base hits for Jimmie Foxx in 1938—and he also came up two home runs shy of the 43 for teammate Manny Ramirez in the battle for the league home run title.

92 Harry Hooper came to bat (92) times during World Series games. He used them well, scoring 13 runs and posting a .293 average during 24 games. Hooper was the only player who was with the club for the 1912, 1915, 1916, and 1918 World Series titles.

93 Boston scored (93) runs in 20 games against Philadelphia in 1923, but gave up only 67 runs while posting a 13-7 record against the Athletics. Boston, however, had a losing record and was outscored head-to-head by every other team in the league that season, as the club won only 61 games. It makes sense then, after looking at the numbers, that the best performance of the season for a Boston pitcher came against Philadelphia. Howard Ehmke, who won 20 games to account for nearly a third of the season total for the club, tossed a no-hitter against the Athletics on September 7.

94 Mel Parnell won (94) games during a five-year stretch from 1949-53. Parnell, who is a member of the Red Sox Hall of Fame, began that stretch with a league best 25 wins in 1949, and in 1953 he posted 21 wins for the second highest total in the league. He won only five games total the next two seasons, however, and by the end of 1955 it was apparent that his career was coming to a close. He stayed on for one more season—and on July 14, 1956, Parnell and all of Red Sox Nation were glad he did, as he tossed a no-hitter against the Chicago White Sox.

95 Boston won (95) games in 2005 and tied New York for the best record in the division. The club spent 89 days in first, but because New York won 10 of 19 games head-to-head, Boston placed second in the standings behind the Yankees for the eighth consecutive season. The Red Sox settled for their fifth Wild Card, but got swept by the White Sox in the Division Series.

96 Boston won (96) games in 2007. Terry Francona managed the club to a 96-66 record for the club's first division title since 1995. Boston swept the Angels in the Division Series, rallied past the Indians in the American League Championship Series, and then swept the Rockies to win the seventh World Series title in franchise history.

97 On April 27, 2002, Derek Lowe tossed (97) pitches in a complete game shutout against the Tampa Bay Devil Rays. He threw 66 pitches for strikes, and of those, opposing batters took 39 cuts against him and put the ball in play 21 times. He got 13 groundball outs, eight fly outs, and notched six strikeouts—and posted a no-hitter.

98 The number of times (98) shortstop Rico Petrocelli walked in 1969. He set career highs in walks, runs, hits, doubles, home runs, average, on-base percentage, slugging percentage, and total bases that season—and for the only time in his career, he posted fewer strikeouts (68) than walks. Petrocelli is ninth in franchise history with 661 career walks—and he is fifth in franchise history with 926 career strikeouts.

99 Boston held a nine-game lead over the Yankees after the first (99) games of 1995. Boston improved to 60-39 with a win on August 13, but one year earlier on that date the club had trailed New York by 17 games. One of the key reasons for the turnaround was Tim Wakefield, who joined the club in the spring after he was released from Pittsburgh. Wakefield got the win on August 13, after which his season numbers stood at: 17 games, 14-1 record, six complete games, 131 innings, 98 hits, 79 strikeouts, and a 1.65 earned run average. Boston went on to claim the division title, and Wakefield placed third in Cy Young balloting.

100 The Cy Young Award balloting share (1.00) for Pedro Martinez in 1999. He was a unanimous selection, gathering all 28 first place votes in the balloting. Martinez earned the award in spectacular fashion after winning the pitching Triple Crown that season—he led the league with 23 wins, a 2.07 earned run average, and 313 strikeouts.

Hall of Fame legend Carl Yastrzemski.
(Courtesy National Baseball Hall of Fame Library, Cooperstown, NY)

"I remember in 1961, when I was hitting .220 after the first three months of my baseball season, doubting my ability, a man was fishing up in New Brunswick. I said, 'Can we get a hold of him? I need help. I don't think I can play in the big leagues.' He flew into Boston. Worked with me for three days. Helped me mentally. Gave me confidence that I could play in the big leagues. I hit .300 for the rest of the season. I'd like to thank Ted Williams—ladies and gentlemen, no man is an island. He must have a support system which without he cannot function."
— Carl Yastrzemski, Hall of Fame acceptance speech

Chapter 2

The Rookies

YAZ WAS RIGHT, of course. Baseball players do need a support system to help them function—but that is never more true than it is when a player is a rookie, when he gets that first taste of big league action, when the expectations are high, the margin for error is low, the pressure to succeed is enormous, and your team is one of the most successful franchises in all of sports. The standard for excellence in Boston is exceptionally high, considering the numerous legends throughout baseball history who have called the Red Sox their home team, which is why one of the unique attributes of the Red Sox organization is so vitally important: Boston's greatest legends have always maintained close ties with the club once their playing days are over.

Yaz illustrated perfectly the benefits to this in his Hall of Fame acceptance speech. Derek Lowe and Curt Schilling were veterans when Boston won the 2004 World Series, but they were quick to recognize Johnny Pesky by name—and for good reason. Pesky last played for Boston in 1952, but his close ties to the organization since his career ended in 1954 are legendary. His presence was so great, among rookies and veterans alike, that Lowe and Schilling understood that the championship belonged to Pesky just as much as it did to the guys on the playoff roster.

Perhaps this is why so many rookies have excelled for the Red Sox.

Boston's first Rookie of the Year recipient was Walt Dropo (1950). Other recipients include Don Schwall (1961), Carlton Fisk (1972), Fred Lynn (1975), Nomar Garciaparra (1997), and Dustin Pedroia (2007)—and they are all in this book, but in chapter two we meet rookies Dick Radatz, Dom DiMaggio, Clay Buchholz, Wade Boggs, Carlton Fisk, Ted Williams, Carl Yastrzemski, and Charlie Zink. Radatz saved 24 games as a rookie in 1962, earning the nickname The Monster because he was so feared out of the bullpen—but his career took an unexpected twist after tinkering with his delivery. DiMaggio made his debut as a 23-year-old outfielder in 1940, and while his brother Joe dominated the national stage, Dom's place in Red Sox history was cemented over the course of a decade during which he was one of the team's best players.

Buchholz began his career in fine fashion, tossing a no-hitter in his second major league start. Wade Boggs got off to a quick start as well—he had the highest average in the league in 1982, but he did not win his first batting title until the next season because he did not have enough at bats to qualify as a rookie. Carlton Fisk not only won the 1972 Rookie of the Year Award, he also won a Gold Glove.

Ted Williams set a major league rookie record for RBI in 1939—and then there is Yaz, who struggled to get going in 1961, but thanks to Williams, Boston's all-time hit leader finally got on track.

And then there is Charlie Zink.

Zink toiled in the minors for seven seasons before getting to start one game for the Red Sox in 2008—and he became only the third pitcher in baseball history to be staked to a 10-0 lead in his big league debut. But could he hold that lead long enough to get a W?

The answer is in chapter two—along with some great performances by Boston's pitching staff in the 2004 World Series, a flawless season at first base for Kevin Youkilis, a very happy birthday for Nomar Garciaparra, and a dominating postseason for Josh Beckett.

As we head to the second...

101 The number of games (101) for Moose Solters during his 1934 rookie season. The outfielder played only 125 games total for Boston during parts of two seasons before he was traded to the St. Louis Browns for Ski Melillo during the 1935 campaign. He put up some good numbers too—surpassing 100 RBI three consecutive seasons from 1935-37. His best day in a Red Sox uniform, however, came on August 19, 1934, against the Detroit Tigers, when as a rookie he hit for the cycle.

102 The number of RBI (102) for first baseman Bill Buckner in 1986. It was the second season in a row he surpassed the century mark in RBI, and his offensive output was a major reason Boston won both their division and the American League pennant. Of course, he is best remembered for his fielding error that gave Game 6 of the 1986 World Series to the Mets. Boston went on to lose the series, and the club released Buckner in 1987, just nine months later.

103 Bobby Doerr scored (103) runs in 1950—the only time in his career he surpassed the century mark. His total was not high enough to rank among the top ten league leaders, although he did crack the top ten in runs during three other seasons. The Hall of Fame second baseman is also among the top ten in franchise history with 1,094 runs.

104 The number of saves (104) for Dick Radatz as a member of the Red Sox. His nickname was The Monster because he was feared by opposing teams that trailed late in the game against Boston. Radatz was a phenom as a rookie in 1962, posting a 9-6 record out of the bullpen with 24 saves and 144 strikeouts. He came back in 1963 to post a 15-6 record, 25 saves, and 162 strikeouts; then in 1964, he posted a 16-9 record, 29 saves, and 181 strikeouts. He began to lose his stuff in 1965, however, after tinkering with his delivery on an off-speed pitch, and by 1966 he was so ineffective that he was traded to Cleveland.

105 Boston won (105) games in 1912. Player-manager Jake Stahl hit .301 for the winningest Red Sox team of the 20th century—and the club went on to beat the New York Giants to claim the 1912 World Series title.

106 Tris Speaker hit (106) triples for Boston. He hit a franchise record 22 triples in 1913. Speaker hit 222 career triples for one of the top ten totals in baseball history, and his total for Boston is the second highest in franchise history.

107 The number of times (107) Ted Williams walked in 1939. He was a 20-year-old rookie who hit 31 home runs and struck out only 64 times all season—and he went on to draw a franchise record 2,021 free passes during his career.

108 The number of games (108) for Dom DiMaggio in 1940. He was a 23-year-old rookie outfielder who hit .301 and scored 81 runs on the season. DiMaggio picked up 126 hits as a rookie, and his production only got better as he matured as a player. He averaged 195 hits per 162 games he played during a full decade with the club—and his 1,680 career hits is the eighth highest total in franchise history.

109 The number of runs (109) Dwight Evans scored in 1987. He set career highs in average, home runs, and RBI that season as he placed fourth in MVP balloting—and it was also the fourth and final time that he surpassed the century mark for runs in a season. Evans is third in franchise history with 1,435 career runs.

110 The number of total bases (110) for Wade Boggs in 1999. It was his final major league season and he was a member of the Tampa Bay Devil Rays. Boggs hit only two home runs all season, but his second, the final of his career, was also hit number 3,000 for the Hall of Fame third baseman. He is the only player in history to reach that plateau on a home run. Boggs is among baseball's elite because of his Red Sox career—and the 2,869 total bases he accumulated for Boston is the sixth highest total in franchise history.

111 The number of hits (111) for Dwight Evans in 1990. The new decade signaled the end of an era in Boston, because for the first time since 1974 Evans and Jim Rice were not roaming the outfield together. Rice retired after 1989, and the 111 hits Dewey got in 1990 were the last of his career in Boston. He moved on to Baltimore after the season with 2,373 career hits—the fourth highest total in franchise history.

112 The number of times (112) Dwight Evans walked in 1982. Evans hit .292 that season and he led the club in walks—a combination that produced a league leading .402 on-base percentage.

113 The number of strikeouts (113) for All-Star pitcher Tex Hughson in 1942. He posted a 22-6 record as he led the league in wins and strikeouts—although his strikeout total has the distinction of being the lowest league leading total in franchise history. Hughson made the first of three consecutive All-Star teams that season, but he missed 1945 while serving in the army during the war. He returned to win 20 games in 1946, including the game that clinched the pennant.

114 The number of games (114) for Lou Clinton in 1962. The right fielder came to bat only 398 times, but when he got the chance to play, he produced. He hit .294 with 18 home runs and 75 RBI—and on July 13, against the Kansas City Athletics, he had the best offensive day of his career: 5 for 7, four runs, four RBI, and he hit for the cycle.

115 The number of pitches (115) for Clay Buchholz against the Baltimore Orioles on September 1, 2007. In only his second major league start, the 23-year-old rookie faced 30 batters and threw 73 of his pitches for strikes—and tossed a no-hitter. He struck out nine, including Nick Markakis for the final out of the game. Buchholz became only the 21st rookie during the modern era of baseball history to pitch a no-hitter, but he became only the third pitcher to do it during his first or second major league start. Bobo Hollomon tossed a no-hitter for the St. Louis Browns during his major league debut in 1953, and Wilson Alvarez tossed a no-hitter for the Chicago White Sox during his second major league start in 1991.

116 The number of batters (116) faced by Babe Ruth during World Series play. He made three starts in the Fall Classic and posted a perfect 3-0 record. Ruth gave up only 19 hits and three earned runs, despite pitching 31 innings. He also set a record by throwing 29 2/3 consecutive scoreless innings during his three postseason starts. Ironically, Yankees' legend Whitey Ford broke Ruth's record in 1961—the same season his teammate Roger Maris broke Ruth's home run record.

117 It took (117) pitches for Derek Lowe, Bronson Arroyo, Alan Embree, and Keith Foulke to combine on a four-hit shutout against the St. Louis Cardinals—and clench the first World Series title for the franchise in 86 years. Lowe got the Game 4 start in the 2004 World Series, and he responded by tossing seven shutout innings while giving up just three hits. He threw 54 of 85 pitches for strikes. Arroyo and Embree both worked in the eighth, and Foulke closed it out in the ninth.

118 The number of hits (118) for Wade Boggs in 1982. He was a 24-year-old rookie who hit .349 on the season and placed third in Rookie of the Year balloting. Boggs then produced seven consecutive seasons with at least 200 hits. He left Boston after 1992 with five batting titles and 2,098 career hits.

119 Dutch Leonard gave up only (119) hits during 125 innings of work in 1918. He was limited to only 16 starts, as he gave up a large part of the season serving in the military during World War I—but he made good use of his time on the diamond, especially on June 3, when in a start against the Detroit Tigers he tossed his second career no-hitter.

120 The number of RBI (120) for Bobby Doerr in 1950. It was the sixth and final time he surpassed the century mark, and he also set a career high. Doerr closed out his career with 1,247 RBI for one of the ten highest totals in franchise history.

121 The number of RBI (121) for Carl Yastrzemski in 1967. It was the first time he surpassed the century mark in RBI, a feat he accomplished five times during his career. His total also led the league and set a career high. Yaz closed out his career with 1,844 RBI—five more than Ted Williams—for a franchise record.

122 The number of RBI (122) for outfielder Jackie Jensen in 1958. It was a career high total and the second of three times he led the league in RBI. Jensen earned the Most Valuable Player Award that season on the strength of his strong play, but at the height of his career—he surpassed the century mark in RBI five times from 1954-59—he abruptly retired because major league teams began to fly from city to city, and he could not overcome his fear of flying.

123 The number of RBI (123) for Dwight Evans in 1987. His total set a career high and led the club—and when he picked up RBI number 51 on the season, he became only the fifth player in franchise history with 1,000 RBI. It was only the second time in 16 seasons that Evans surpassed the century mark in RBI, but he did it again in 1988, and once more in 1989. His career total of 1,346 RBI for Boston is among the top five in franchise history.

124 The number of home runs (124) Jim Rice hit from 1977-79. He posted totals of 39, 46, and 39 during that three-year span. He also batted .315 or higher and surpassed 200 hits in all three seasons—making him the first player in baseball history to have three consecutive seasons with at least a .315 average, 200 hits, and 39 home runs.

125 The number of RBI (125) for Yankee legend Joe DiMaggio in 1941. It was the only Triple Crown category that Ted Williams did not lead the league in that season. Williams won the batting title with a .406 average and he hit 37 home runs to win that title as well. Williams also led the league in on-base percentage, slugging percentage, OPS, runs, walks, and times on base—but with 120 RBI, he came up five short of the Triple Crown. DiMaggio also won the Most Valuable Player Award.

126 The number of RBI (126) for Mo Vaughn in 1995. He once told a reporter, "I consider a man on first to already be in scoring position." He definitely made good on his quote in 1995, as he led the league in RBI and took home league MVP honors—although it was also the only time in his career that he led the league in a category other than strikeouts, a dubious feat that he accomplished twice.

127 The number of games (127) for Joe Cronin in 1934 as a member of the Washington Senators. He was the player-manager for

Washington and one of the best shortstops in the league, but he was also the son-in-law of Washington's part-owner and team president Clark Griffith. Tom Yawkey, the new owner in Boston who was trying to restore prestige to the franchise, decided he wanted Cronin to be the player-manager for the Red Sox in 1935—so he paid Clark Griffith $250,000 and Griffith agreed to ship his son-in-law up north to Beantown.

128 Wade Boggs scored (128) runs in 1988. It was the fourth consecutive season that Boggs won the batting title and led the league in OBP, but it was the first time he led the league in runs.

129 The number of triples (129) for third baseman Larry Gardner. His career total is among the top 100 in baseball history—but the 87 he hit as a member of the Red Sox is the fifth highest total in franchise history.

130 Jimmie Foxx scored (130) runs in 1936 and again in 1939. His total was the seventh best in the league in 1936, and the third best in the league in 1939—but in both cases, his total is one of the top ten efforts in franchise history.

131 The number of games (131) for Carlton Fisk in 1972. He was a 24-year-old rookie who made 15 errors that season in 933 total chances for a .984 fielding percentage—and won a Gold Glove. Fisk, who played until 1993 and caught more games than any player in history, never won another Gold Glove.

132 Mo Vaughn received (132) points in the 1996 MVP balloting. He placed fifth behind Juan Gonzalez, Alex Rodriguez, Albert Belle, and Ken Griffey, Jr. in the balloting—this despite 44 home runs and a career high 143 RBI, a total that tied him with Jimmie Foxx for one of the ten best totals in franchise history.

133 The batting average (.133) for Cardinals' sluggers Albert Pujols, Scott Rolen, and Jim Edmonds during the 2004 World Series. They combined to hit 122 home runs with 358 RBI during the regular season, but they were unable to solve Boston's staff with baseball immortality hanging in the balance. Rolen was 0 for 15, Edmonds just 1 for 15, and Pujols 5 for 15. They did not hit a home run—and collectively they had one RBI.

134 Ted Williams scored (134) runs in 1940. Teddy Ballgame led the league for the first of six times in his career. Six of the top ten season runs totals in franchise history belong to Williams—and his 1,798 career runs are second only to Carl Yastrzemski (1,816).

135 The number of games (135) Kevin Youkilis played first base in 2007. He got 1,080 total chances on defense while playing first but did not make a single error. Youkilis was flawless all season, and earned his first career Gold Glove.

136 Tris Speaker scored (136) runs in 1912. He was a 24-year-old center fielder when he won the Most Valuable Player Award and set a franchise record for runs that lasted until 1938, when Jimmie Foxx scored 139 times.

137 The number of at bats (137) for Hugh Bradley in 1912. He was a seldom used first baseman who hit just .190 on the season. Bradley's only homer that year came on April 26, but as it happens, that home run was also the first ever in Fenway Park history. It was only the second home run of Bradley's career—and his last.

138 The number of pitches (138) for Roger Clemens on April 29, 1986. He used them to strikeout a major league record 20 Seattle Mariners. Catcher Rich Gedman said afterwards, "When he has that kind of stuff it's really not difficult to call the game." Clemens threw 97 strikes and only ten balls were put into play.

139 The number of RBI (139) for Jim Rice in 1978. It was the first time he led the league in RBI, a feat he accomplished once more in 1983. Rice surpassed the century mark eight times, but his 1978 total set a career high. He closed out his career with 1,451 RBI for the third highest total in franchise history.

140 The number of innings (140) for relief pitcher Bill Campbell in 1977. He led the club and was third in the league with 69 relief appearances. Campbell was 13-9 and led the club in wins despite not starting a single game all season. He also saved 31 games and earned the A.L. Rolaids Relief Man Award.

141 Ted Williams scored (141) runs in 1942. It was the third consecutive season he led the league in runs, and he did it with the third highest total in franchise history. Williams is among the top 20 in baseball history with 1,798 career runs—and his name is next to the three highest season totals in franchise history.

142 Ted Williams scored (142) runs in 1946. He led the league with the second highest total in franchise history in his first year back after serving as a pilot during World War II—and he picked up his first career Most Valuable Player Award as well.

143 The number of RBI (143) for Mo Vaughn in 1996. He won the 1995 Most Valuable Player Award, and then backed up his hardware by raising his average from .300 to .326, his hit total from 165 to 207, his home run total from 39 to 44, and his RBI total from 126 to 143—but in 1996 he only placed fifth in MVP balloting. The four players ahead of him in the balloting were: Juan Gonzalez, Alex Rodriguez, Albert Belle, and Ken Griffey, Jr.

144 The number of hits (144) for first baseman Jake Stahl in 1910. He spent eight-plus seasons playing major league baseball—mostly with Boston—but his best offensive numbers came in 1910, when a league best ten of his hits left the park.

145 The number of RBI (145) for Ted Williams in 1939. He set a major league record for rookies. Williams also scored 131 runs in only 149 games, and his strong play earned him a fourth place finish in MVP balloting behind some pretty elite company: Joe DiMaggio, Jimmie Foxx, and Bob Feller.

146 The number of singles (146) for Johnny Damon in 2005. Damon led the club in singles, but he also led the club with a .316 average, 197 hits, 18 steals, and six triples.

147 Rich Gedman set a career high with (147) hits in 1985. The catcher and long-time fan-favorite put together a solid season—he made his first All-Star squad, and drove in a career high 80 runs—but in a game against the Blue Jays on September 18, he put on the best offensive display of his career. He made an out in his first at bat, but then homered, tripled, and singled in his next three at bats. Just a double shy of the cycle when he came to bat in the eighth, he got it done—and his stats for the day: 4 for 5, two runs, and seven RBI.

148 The number of RBI (148) for David Ortiz in 2005. He led the league for the first time in his career. Ortiz lost a close MVP race to Alex Rodriguez that season, prompting the *Boston Globe* to write, "By any measure, there has been no player more valuable to the Red Sox over the past two seasons than David Ortiz. He has proved his value at the plate, as the best clutch hitter in the team's history by any reasonable measure."

149 The earned run average (1.49) for Smoky Joe Wood in 1915. It was his final season in Boston, and he posted a 15-5 record and led the league with an ERA that remains among the top five in franchise history. Wood was the baseball coach at Yale University three decades later when his good friend and former teammate Babe Ruth, who was dying, came to visit. Wood and Ruth can be seen in a now famous picture taken with the captain of Yale's baseball team at the time—George H.W. Bush, who went on to become the 41st President of the United States.

150 Ted Williams scored (150) runs in 1949. His total set a career high and a franchise record, and it was also the sixth and final time he led the league in runs. Williams, who won his second Most Valuable Player Award that season, just missed a third Triple Crown. He led the league in on-base percentage, slugging percentage, OPS, total bases, doubles, home runs, RBI, walks, and extra-base hits—but lost the batting title and the Triple Crown because without rounding his .3427 average came up just short of the .3429 average for batting champion George Kell.

151 Mel Parnell received (151) points in the 1949 MVP balloting. He placed fourth behind teammate Ted Williams, who won the award, and Phil Rizzuto and Joe Page of the Yankees. Parnell quipped earlier that season after the Red Sox beat the Browns 21-2 on June 24, "Boy, I hope they get me 21 tomorrow." He did win the next day, 13-2, and he won a lot more besides that, as he led the league with 25 wins.

152 The number of hits (152) for Bobby Doerr in 1944. He wasn't slapping the ball around either—Doerr was hitting for power. He led the league with a .528 slugging percentage on the strength of 55 extra-base hits. On May 17, Doerr gave a prolific demonstration of his power when he hit for the cycle against the St. Louis Browns.

153 Boston hit (153) home runs in 1957. That total was second among eight teams in the league, trailing the 166 hit by the Kansas City Athletics. Ted Williams led Boston with 38, a total that placed him second in the league behind Roy Sievers of the Washington Senators.

154 Mo Vaughn struck out (154) times in 1996—the third highest total in the league. He never got cheated at the plate though, and when he made contact all bets were off. Vaughn went yard 44 times and his 370 total bases was also the third highest total in the league.

155 Carl Yastrzemski got (155) hits during his 1961 rookie campaign. He was only getting started, of course. Yaz led the league in hits twice (1963, 1967) and was among the league's top ten leaders seven times. He piled up 3,419 hits by the time he hung up his spikes. His total is easily a franchise record, and it is the sixth highest total in baseball history.

156 The number of times (156) Ted Williams walked in 1946. His total set a franchise record that lasted for exactly one year. He walked 162 times in 1947, and then tied that mark again in 1949. Eight out of the nine highest season totals in franchise history for bases on balls belong to Williams.

157 The number of hits (157) for Dustin Pedroia after a 5 for 6 performance against the Rangers on August 12, 2008. The second baseman also scored five times as Boston won a wild 19-17 game against Texas—and the Elias Sports Bureau reported that Pedroia became the first player in franchise history to collect five hits and score five runs in the same game. Pedroia got ten hits total in the series against Texas, which left him tied with Rangers' second baseman Ian Kinsler for the league lead with six weeks to play.

158 The number of strikeouts (158) for Cy Young in 1901. It was the second time in his career that he led the league in strikeouts. Young also led the league with 33 wins, the second highest total in franchise history.

159 The number of RBI (159) for Ted Williams in 1949. His total led the league and set a career high, and it was also his eighth consecutive 100 RBI season. His streak was broken in 1950 when he picked up 97 RBI, but he got those in only 89 games. Williams closed out his career with 1,839 RBI for the second highest total in franchise history.

160 Hall of Fame outfielder Harry Hooper hit (160) triples—and a franchise record 130 of those triples came for Boston. Hooper was among the top ten league leaders seven times with the club from 1912-20.

161 Bruce Hurst gave up (161) hits in only 117 innings in 1982. He was a 24-year-old lefty in his first full season—and he struggled to a 3-7 record in 28 games. He got better though, much better. Hurst was 18-6 in 1988, his last season with the club, including a 13-2 record at Fenway Park where he gave up exactly 129 hits in 129-plus innings.

162 The earned run average (1.62) for Cy Young in 1901. He led the league with the fourth lowest ERA in franchise history. Young is tied with Ray Collins, who also posted a 1.62 ERA for Boston in 1910—but Collins was only sixth among league leaders.

163 The number of games (163) for Jim Rice in 1978. He played every game during his MVP season—and because Boston and New York were tied after the 162-game schedule was complete, the one-game playoff for the division title made Rice the first player in franchise history to play 163 games during one regular season.

164 Ernie Shore posted a (1.64) earned run average in 1915. The towering righty logged 247 innings but gave up just 45 earned runs—and posted the sixth best ERA in franchise history. The top five season efforts are: Dutch Leonard (0.96, 1914), Cy Young (1.26, 1908), Joe Wood (1.49, 1915), Cy Young (1.62, 1901), and Ray Collins (1.62, 1910). Of the top six, only three actually led the league: Leonard, Wood, and Young (1901).

165 Larry Gardner stole (165) bases in his career—including 134 as a member of the Red Sox. He stole a career high 27 for Boston in 1911, and his career total with the club is among the top ten in franchise history.

166 Boston pitchers gave up (166) runs during April, 1996. The club only scored 120, and the result was a disastrous 7-19 record in the first month of play. Kevin Kennedy managed the club to 85 wins despite the poor start, but that was only good for third in the division as Boston failed to repeat as division champs.

167 The number of consecutive errorless games (167) played for Carl Yastrzemski. He is the only player in A.L. history with 400 home runs and 3,000 hits, which makes it easy to forget just how great an outfielder Yaz was. He won seven Gold Gloves though, and in 1977 he tied a major league record by posting a 1.000 fielding percentage.

168 Carl Yastrzemski stole (168) bases in his career. He even stole a career high 23 bases in 1970, but he was also thrown out attempting to steal 13 times that year. Yaz, who never ranked among the league's top ten leaders for steals, was among the league's top ten leaders for being caught stealing in three different seasons—but its all good, as his career steals total is among the top five in franchise history.

169 The number of hits (169) for Ted Williams in 1951. It was the last full season for Williams before he returned to active duty during the Korean War. Williams led the league in on-base and slugging percentage, total bases, walks, and times on base, and he was among the top five leaders in hits, runs, home runs, RBI, and extra-base hits—but he placed just 13th in MVP balloting.

170 The number of hits (170) for Bob Johnson in 1944. The All-Star outfielder was at the end of his career, but it was his first season as a member of the Red Sox. He did okay, too. He was sixth in the league in hits, second with 65 extra-base hits, and second with 106 RBI. His best offensive game that season came on July 6, against Detroit, when he hit for the cycle and led Boston to a 13-3 victory.

171 Jackie Jensen hit (.171) for the Yankees in 1950. He later became an All-Star and MVP recipient for Boston, but as a 23-year-old rookie he won the 1950 World Series with New York. Jensen earlier won the 1947 College World Series playing for the University of California, only to become an All-American running back who competed in the 1949 Rose Bowl. He was the only athlete in the 20th century who competed in all of these events: the College World Series, Rose Bowl, East-West Shrine Game, Major League World Series, and the Major League All-Star Game—and his wife was a two-time Olympic medalist in diving.

172 Johnny Pesky hit a career high and league leading (172) singles in 1947. He also led the league with 207 hits—but for the only time in his career, none of his hits left the yard. His singles total though remains the second highest in franchise history.

173 Rube Foster gave up (173) hits during 182 innings of work in 1916—but while tossing nine shutout innings against the Yankees on June 21, Foster did not give up any hits. His no-no was the first of two that season for Red Sox hurlers, and the first ever at Fenway Park. It also began a streak of three consecutive seasons a member of the Red Sox staff tossed a no-hitter—a record that was later tied by the Cleveland Indians, and then broken by Sandy Koufax and the Los Angeles Dodgers.

174 The earned run average (1.74) for Pedro Martinez in 2000. He posted an 18-6 record and easily had the lowest ERA in the league. Martinez won his third Cy Young Award, but check out how the players who placed two through six in the balloting did in terms of

ERA: Tim Hudson (4.14), David Wells (4.11), Andy Pettitte (4.35), Todd Jones (3.52), and Roger Clemens (3.70).

175 The number of RBI (175) for Hall of Fame first baseman Jimmie Foxx in 1938. His total is a franchise record and is tied with Lou Gehrig for the fourth highest total in major league history—and it earned him his third and final career MVP.

176 The number of hits (176) for George Scott in 1975. The former Red Sox first baseman put together a career year for the Milwaukee Brewers, hitting .285 with 36 home runs and 109 RBI. He got one very painful hit that season against his former club, as well. On July 2, he ruined a no-hit bid for Boston hurler Rick Wise with a two-out, ninth inning homer.

177 The number of times (177) Mark Bellhorn struck out in 2004. The switch-hitting infielder, who is a native of Boston, led the league in strikeouts and set a dubious franchise record at the same time—but in all fairness, he also hit three postseason dingers in 2004 (and added another 17 strikeouts) and won a ring.

178 Dustin Pedroia went 4 for 4 to lead Boston to an 8-0 victory over the Chicago White Sox on August 29, 2008, moving him past Ichiro Suzuki for the league lead with (178) hits and a month left to play in the season. He increased that lead the very next day, when he again went 4 for 4 and led Boston to an 8-2 victory over the White Sox. It was the seventh time in 2008 that Pedroia collected at least four hits in a single game, but it was also the 53rd time he collected at least two hits—and according to the Elias Sports Bureau, Pedroia became the first Red Sox player since Pinky Higgins on June 21, 1938, to go 4 for 4 in consecutive games.

179 Roger Clemens gave up (179) hits in 1986. That worked out to a tidy 6.34 hits per nine innings of work for the Rocket. His ratio led the league, and it remains among the top five in franchise history.

180 The batting average (.180) for Joe Rudi in 1981. He was a three-time All-Star and twice a runner-up in MVP balloting while playing for Oakland from 1972-75, during which time Rudi was playing so well that Red Sox owner Tom Yawkey tried to buy him in an effort to bolster a Boston offense that was led by young phenom Fred Lynn. The transaction was blocked by the league commissioner, however, and by the time Rudi finally made it to Boston he was well past his prime and he got just 22 hits and six home runs in 49 games—after joining the Red Sox as part of the deal that sent Fred Lynn to California.

181 The number of hits (181) for Pumpsie Green from 1959-62. He was the first African American player to take the field for Boston, though Earl Wilson was actually the first to sign with the club. Green made his big league debut on July 21, 1959, exactly one week before Wilson made his debut. Green saw limited playing time during four seasons, with his best numbers coming in 1961, when he hit .260 with six home runs.

182 The batting average (.182) for the Philadelphia Phillies during the 1915 World Series. Boston scored only 12 runs during the five-game series, but pitchers Rube Foster, Ernie Shore, and Dutch Leonard combined to give up just nine earned runs and 27 hits during 44 innings of play—and the Phillies scored just ten runs total. Boston won the series four games to one.

183 The number of hits (183) for first baseman Pete Runnels in 1962. He set career highs in hits, doubles, home runs, average, and slugging percentage. Runnels also hit a home run during the 1962 All-Star Game. He hit .326 on the season and won his second batting title in five years, but the Red Sox traded him in the off-season to Houston.

184 Jason Bay hit .293 during (184) at bats with Boston after joining the club in the Manny Ramirez trade in 2008. Fans anxious to see how the former N.L. Rookie of the Year would hold up in his first career postseason were quite pleased with his performance vs. Anaheim in the Division Series. Bay hit a two-run homer to rally Boston to a 4-1 win in Game 1, he hit a three-run homer in the first inning of a 7-5 win in Game 2, and he scored the winning run in walk-off fashion in the series-clinching Game 4. Bay hit a series best .412 with a .882 slugging percentage.

185 The number of hits (185) for All-Star outfielder Dom DiMaggio in 1948. That was the sixth highest total in the league. DiMaggio hit .285, was second in the league with 127 runs, and fourth with 40 doubles.

186 The number of hits (186) for Ted Williams in 1942. He was not shy about speaking his mind on any subject, least of all baseball—and he once famously said, "If there was ever a man born to be a hitter, it was me." He was right, and he proved it 186 times in 1942 as his hits total led to a .356 average, 36 home runs, 137 RBI—and the Triple Crown.

187 Wade Boggs hit a franchise record (187) singles in 1985. Boggs led the league with one of the ten highest totals in baseball history, and only five players in the league had as many hits that season as Boggs had singles: Don Mattingly, Bill Buckner, Kirby Puckett, Harold Baines, and Phil Bradley.

188 Grady Little led the club to (188) victories during two seasons as manager—good for a .580 winning percentage. He also led the club to six more wins during the 2003 postseason, but it was a decision he made during Game 7 of the League Championship Series vs. New York that likely cost Boston a seventh victory and a trip to the World Series—and that almost certainly cost Little his job as well. Pedro Martinez tossed seven innings at Yankee Stadium and Boston clung to a 5-2 lead going into the bottom of the eighth—but inexplicably, despite a bullpen ready to go and obvious signs that Martinez was beyond tiring, Little sent his ace back to the mound. "He had enough left in his tank," Little said later, but the events as they transpired certainly did not support that conclusion. Martinez gave up three consecutive hits with one out, and the potential-tying runs were in scoring position when Grady finally made a trip to the mound—but he left Martinez in to face Jorge Posada, who promptly tied up the game and set the stage for Aaron Boone's heroics in the eleventh.

189 The number of hits (189) for Carl Yastrzemski in 1967. His total was the highest in the league for the second time in his career. Yaz also won his only career home run title when he hit a career best 44 on the way to his Triple Crown.

190 Jim Rice averaged (190) hits per 162 games during 15-plus seasons in Boston. He got a cup of coffee and 18 hits in 1974, and then in 1975 his 174 hits and 22 home runs earned him second place in Rookie of the Year balloting behind teammate Fred Lynn. Rice got 2,452 hits before he hung up his spikes—the third most in franchise history.

191 The earned run average (1.91) for Luis Tiant in 1972. Boston signed Tiant after he was released by the Twins in 1971. He was only 1-7 though, as his injury-plagued arm took away his once dominating fastball, which made what he did in 1972 all the more remarkable. Tiant completely reinvented his repertoire, using all sorts of motions to deliver one junk ball after another. The result was a 15-6 record that included a streak of seven consecutive complete game victories (four of them shutouts) and the best ERA in the league.

192 Charlie Zink made (192) minor league appearances before getting a chance to pitch in a major league game. His debut finally came on August 12, 2008, and the Red Sox hitters sure made him feel welcome. David Ortiz hit a pair of three-run home runs—*in the first inning*—and Boston scored ten runs in the frame to stake him to a 10-0 lead. Zink only needed to get through five innings to earn the victory, but after becoming just the third pitcher in major league history to be staked to a 10-0 first inning lead during his major league debut Zink only got one out in the fifth before it all fell apart. He was charged with eight earned runs and got a no-decision, though the club won 19-17.

193 The earned run average (1.93) for Roger Clemens in 1990. It was the first of three consecutive seasons that he led the league in ERA. Clemens posted a 21-6 record and also led the league with four complete game shutouts, but he placed second in Cy Young Award balloting behind Bob Welch, who was 27-6 for Oakland. Welch and the Athletics also swept Boston to claim the pennant in the postseason.

194 Ted Williams got a career high (194) hits in 1949. He also won his second MVP after belting 43 home runs for a career high. It is almost impossible to believe that Williams never got 200 hits or even led the league in hits—but then again, he also averaged 143 walks per 162 games, which severely limited his opportunities. He still retired as the franchise leader with 2,654 hits, a total that has only been surpassed by Carl Yastrzemski.

195 The number of hits (195) for Patsy Dougherty in 1903—which means if you get asked the following question while playing Boston Trivia, "Who has a higher career best hits total with Boston: Ted Williams, or a guy named Patsy?" the answer is, well, a guy named Patsy. That same Patsy was the first guy to bat in the World Series for Boston, leading off Game 1 of the 1903 World Series; he hit the first World Series home run for Boston; he was the first guy in baseball history to hit two home runs in one World Series game; he was the first guy in baseball history to win a pair of World Series titles; he led the league in hits and runs in 1903; and Patsy Dougherty, on July 29, 1903, became the first player in franchise history to hit for the cycle.

196 The earned run average (1.96) for Bruce Hurst during the 1986 World Series. He tossed eight shutout innings for a 1-0 victory against the Mets in Game 1, and then he came back with a complete game 4-2 victory in a must-win Game 5. He was one out away from a World Series ring—and he had already been selected as the series MVP—when the Mets staged their gut-wrenching two-out rally in the tenth inning of Game 6. Hurst took the mound in Game 7, and he held a 3-0 lead in the sixth inning before he finally tired and gave up three runs. New York went on to win 8-6, and the Mets Ray Knight won Series MVP honors.

197 The number of hits (197) for Nomar Garciaparra in 2002. On July 23, Nomar got three of those hits in spectacular fashion against Tampa Bay. Playing on his birthday (he turned 29 that day) Nomar hit a two-run home run in the third inning—but then his teammates batted around, bringing him back to the plate where he hit a second two-run shot in the same frame. Boston scored ten times that inning, but in the fourth the fireworks really got going. Nomar batted with the bases full, and with the crowd singing "Happy Birthday, Nomar" in the background—he hit a grand slam.

198 The number of hits (198) for Jimmie Foxx in 1936. He was a 28-year-old first baseman playing his first season for the Red Sox after coming over in a trade from the Philadelphia Athletics—and he led the club in virtually every significant offensive category. Foxx belted 41 home runs and 81 extra-base hits on his way to a franchise record 369 total bases. He broke his own record two seasons later when he posted 398 total bases.

199 The number of total bases (199) for Fred Lynn in 1980. His production was down dramatically from the previous season. Lynn posted 338 total bases, 39 home runs, and 122 RBI in 1979—but went yard only 12 times in 1980 with 61 RBI, exactly half his total from the previous season. He was still a dangerous hitter though, as he proved to the Minnesota Twins on May 13, when he hit for the cycle and accounted for ten of his total bases on the season in that one game.

200 The number of innings (200) for Josh Beckett in 2007. He led the majors in wins with a 20-7 record—and then went 4-0 in four starts during the postseason. Beckett placed second in Cy Young Award balloting behind CC Sabathia of the Cleveland Indians, but it was Beckett who beat Sabathia and the Indians twice in the American League Championship Series. Beckett lost the Cy Young Award, but he got a ring and earned Red Sox Pitcher of the Year honors.

Boston Red Sox Cy Young Recipients:
- *Pedro Martinez (2000)*
- *Pedro Martinez (1999)*
- *Roger Clemens (1991)*
- *Roger Clemens (1987)*
- *Roger Clemens (1986)*
- *Jim Lonborg (1967)*

Boston Red Sox Strikeout Champions:
- *Pedro Martinez (2002), 239*
- *Hideo Nomo (2001), 220*
- *Pedro Martinez (2000), 284*
- *Pedro Martinez (1999), 313*
- *Roger Clemens (1996), 257*
- *Roger Clemens (1991), 241*
- *Roger Clemens (1988), 291*
- *Jim Lonborg (1967), 246*
- *Tex Hughson (1942), 113*
- *Cy Young (1901), 158*

Boston Red Sox Pitching Triple Crown Champions:
- *Pedro Martinez (1999), 23 wins, 2.07 earned run average, 313 Ks*
- *Cy Young (1901), 33 wins, 1.62 earned run average, 158 Ks*

"Connie Mack, who has seen more ball games than any other American, living or dead, always considered Young's perfect game against Rube Waddell in 1904 the greatest exhibition of pitching ever performed."
— *Tom Meany, award winning sports journalist*

Chapter 3

Cy Young Worthy

BASEBALL'S BEST PITCHERS are honored yearly with an award that bears the name Cy Young. It was created in 1956 as a tribute to Young, who died the previous year, and it is a prestigious award because it elevates the recipient to an elite class, a select club with only a few members, so exclusive that some of baseball's biggest names have been left out—which is exactly as it should be when you consider Young's legacy.

Young made 815 starts, completed 749, won 511, and pitched more than 7,350 innings—all major league records.

Boston won 79 games in 1901, but Young was the winning pitcher 33 times. Boston won 77 games in 1902, but Young was the winning pitcher 32 times—and he won 119 games in four seasons from 1901-04.

He was on the mound for Boston's first home game at Huntington Avenue Grounds on May 8, 1901. He was on that same mound for the first World Series game in baseball's modern era on October 1, 1903—and again on May 5, 1904, when he tossed baseball's first perfect game of the modern era.

No one else comes close.

In this chapter our favorite numbers are about those Red Sox pitchers who have been found worthy of the Cy Young Award.

Jim Lonborg was the first Boston pitcher to be so honored when he won the award in 1967. He led the league in wins, strikeouts, and . . . hit batsmen.

Roger Clemens was the second (1986), third (1987), and fourth (1991) pitcher to win the award for Boston, claiming three of his record seven Cy Young Awards while playing for the Red Sox. Clemens was the first Red Sox pitcher to win the award in consecutive seasons, and Pedro Martinez was the second.

Martinez won 23 games and the pitching Triple Crown to earn his first Cy Young Award in 1999. He won only 18 games in 2000, but his numbers in every other category were better than the previous season, and for that he won his second Cy Young.

Cy Young is also in this chapter—for a truly astounding number.

And so are Mel Parnell, Tex Hughson, Lefty Grove, and Joe Wood—guys who posted Cy Young worthy numbers, but in the pre-Cy Young Award era. Parnell, Hughson, and Wood are all members of the Boston Red Sox Hall of Fame, and Grove is a member of the Baseball Hall of Fame.

Wood led Boston to a world championship in 1912, Parnell is one of the winningest pitchers in franchise history, Grove won four earned run average titles with Boston, and Hughson was a two-time 20-game winner—all stories found in chapter three, along with some other great pitching performances: Big Bill Dinneen in the 1903 World Series, Hideo Nomo keeping a Boston streak alive, Jesse Tannehill, Cy Young, and Dutch Leonard tossing no-no's, and Luis Tiant carrying the load in the 1975 postseason.

Also in this chapter is pitcher Jose Santiago—one of our favorite numbers in this book, he did something extraordinary during the 1967 World Series.

Find out what it was here in the third...

201 The number of starts (201) for Pedro Martinez during seven seasons in Boston. Martinez posted a 117-37 record from 1998-2004 and won two Cy Young Awards. His 117 victories rank among the ten highest totals in franchise history.

202 The number of total bases (202) for Tom Brunansky as a member of the Red Sox in 1990. The club traded Lee Smith to get Brunansky from the Cardinals. Brunansky was a slugger, and he hit 15 home runs with 71 RBI in only 461 at bats as Boston battled Toronto down the stretch for the division title. On October 3, the season's final day, the title was still up for grabs when Brunansky hit an RBI triple (to surpass 200 total bases for Boston) and scored a run to help Boston take a 3-0 lead against the White Sox. He then made a game-saving catch on defense, robbing Chicago shortstop Ozzie Guillen of extra-bases with the potential tying runs on base and two outs in the ninth. Boston won 3-1, clinched the division, and made the Toronto vs. Baltimore game meaningless.

203 The number of hits (203) for Wade Boggs in 1984. His total was the second highest in the league, but he led the league with 162 singles—a total that remains among the top five in franchise history.

204 Trot Nixon hit (204) doubles for Boston from 1996-2006. Nixon hit 20 or more doubles seven times—including a high of 36 in 2002—and his total is one of the top 30 in franchise history. He also hit ten more doubles for Boston during postseason play, including three in the 2004 World Series.

205 The number of hits (205) for Johnny Pesky in 1942. He was a 22-year-old rookie who led the league in hits. Pesky also led the league with 165 singles—one of the top five totals in franchise history.

206 The earned run average (2.06) for Bill Dinneen during the 1903 World Series. Cy Young was the first pitcher to take the mound in World Series history, but the Hall of Fame legend lost Game 1 to the Pirates 7-3. Boston sent Big Bill Dinneen to the mound in Game 2 and all he did was toss a three-hit shutout to even the series. The *Pittsburgh Post* wrote of Dinneen, "He was the whole shooting match, for shooting he did, with a vengeance." Dinneen started and took the loss in Game 4, but he came back to win games six and eight for a 3-1 record in the best-of-nine series.

207 The earned run average (2.07) for Pedro Martinez in 1999. It was the best number in the league, and he won the pitching Triple Crown after posting 23 wins and 313 strikeouts. Martinez won the Cy Young Award, and he nearly became the second Red Sox pitcher to win the Most Valuable Player Award. He received the most first place votes in the MVP balloting, but he placed second overall because two writers felt pitchers should not qualify for MVP consideration and left his name off the ballot completely.

208 Johnny Pesky led the league with (208) hits in 1946. He led the league in hits as a rookie in 1942, but then he missed all of 1943-45 while serving in the military. Pesky then led the league a third time with 207 hits in 1947—meaning his first three seasons with the club he led the league in hits.

209 The number of hits (209) for Nomar Garciaparra in 1997. It was a league best total, and one of the ten best in franchise history. Nomar also led the league with 11 triples and was second in the league with 85 extra-base hits—all during his rookie season.

210 The number of hits (210) for Wade Boggs in 1983. He won his first batting title when he posted a .361 average, but he was second among league leaders in hits—a feat he accomplished five times during his career.

211 The number of extra-base hits (211) for Butch Hobson from 1976-79. He busted out for 30 home runs and 112 RBI in 1977. Hobson was sixth in the league with 68 extra-base hits that season, and he placed among the top ten league leaders in doubles, home runs, and RBI as well.

212 The earned run average (2.12) for Ernie Shore from 1914-17. He was 58-33 during four seasons in Boston, and his ERA remains one of the top five in franchise history. Shore was traded to the Yankees in 1918, but he was one of the few players from Boston who did not find success there. He was 7-10 in two seasons with the Yankees.

213 The number of hits (213) for Dustin Pedroia in 2008. He tied Ichiro Suzuki of the Seattle Mariners for the league lead in hits, but his .326 average fell just short of the .328 average for batting champion Joe Mauer of the Minnesota Twins. Pedroia also led the league with 118 runs and 54 doubles.

214 The earned run average (2.41) for Jon Lester during September, 2008. The young lefty was 4-1 in September as Boston battled Tampa Bay down the stretch, and for his performance he earned American League Pitcher of the Month honors. Lester continued his dominance into October, pitching 14 innings vs. Anaheim in the Division Series without allowing an earned run. Lester got the win in Game 1 and a no-decision in Game 4, but Boston won the series in four games.

215 The number of total bases (215) for Dwight Evans in 1981. His total was the highest in the league during the strike-shortened season. Dewey piled up some pretty impressive numbers that year—leading the league in home runs and times on base as well—but he also posted some big numbers for his career. Near the top of that list are his 4,230 total bases—the fourth highest total in franchise history.

216 Boston scored (216) of their major league best 1,027 runs in 1950 against the St. Louis Browns. The Red Sox were 19-3 against the Browns—and gave up only 115 runs during those contests. The biggest rout was on June 8, when Boston pitcher Chuck Stobbs drew four walks—as a batter—in four consecutive innings, Red Sox leadoff batter Clyde Vollmer came to the plate eight times in eight innings, the club scored 17 runs in one inning and tallied 58 total bases for the game, and won by a final of 29-4.

217 The number of innings (217) for Pedro Martinez in 2000. He gave up only 128 hits, but faced 817 batters. Martinez posted an 18-6 record as he won his second consecutive Cy Young Award for Boston and the third overall for his career.

218 The number of games (218) Smoky Joe Wood pitched for Boston. He completed 121 of 157 starts—including 28 shutouts—but he also made 61 relief appearances from 1908-15. Wood posted a 117-56 record during his tenure with the club, and when he left, only Cy Young had more wins for Boston. Today, his 117 victories place him in a tie for sixth with Pedro Martinez in the franchise record book.

219 Roger Clemens gave up (219) hits in 1991. It may sound like a lot, but batters were no more eager to face Clemens that season than they were any other time—which is the same as saying they would just as soon not have to bat against him at all. Clemens faced 1,077 batters and struck out 241—and won his third career Cy Young Award.

220 The number of strikeouts (220) for All-Star pitcher Hideo Nomo in 2001. He led the league in strikeouts during his only season in Boston. It was the third consecutive season a member of the Red Sox staff led the league in strikeouts—Pedro Martinez did it in 1999 and 2000, and Martinez went on to make it four straight for the club when he led the league again in 2002.

221 Boston scored (221) runs in August, 1950. The team scored 1,027 runs that season—easily the highest total in the league—and August was their second most productive month behind June. August was also the month Boston made a run at the pennant, posting a 24-6 record that included a 16-1 run to end the month. In that run Boston rallied from a 7-0 deficit to beat Cleveland 11-9, and then the very next day they rallied from a 12-1 deficit to beat Cleveland 15-14. The team could flat produce on offense, but in the end they lost the pennant by four games.

222 The earned run average (2.22) for Pedro Martinez in 2003. He posted a 14-4 record after giving up just 46 earned runs in 186 innings of work. Martinez placed third in Cy Young Award balloting, but he led the league in ERA for the fifth time in his career.

223 Bobby Doerr hit (223) home runs. The Hall of Fame second baseman hit a career high 27 home runs twice (1948, 1950) and seven times he was among the top ten league leaders. Doerr once referred to luck as "a lot of practice and a lot of work." He obviously created his share of luck with that exact formula—and as a result his career home run total is among the top ten in franchise history.

224 The number of home runs (224) for Bobby Grich from 1970-86. He hit only nine for the Angels during 1986, his final big league season—but he got a very memorable big fly courtesy of Red Sox outfielder Dave Henderson during Game 5 of the 1986 American League Championship Series. With two outs in the sixth, Grich hit a long fly to center field that Henderson chased down at the warning track—but as he banged into the wall, his glove tipped backwards and sent the ball out of the park for an improbable home run and a 3-2 Angels lead. Henderson got a shot at redemption though—and in the ninth, with Boston down to their last strike in the series, Henderson hit a two-run blast that gave Boston the lead. Then when the Angels sent the game to extra-innings, Henderson got the game-winning RBI in the eleventh. Boston rallied to win the series after trailing three games to one—and Grich never made it to the World Series, losing all five championship series he played in.

225 The earned run average (2.25) for Cincinnati Reds reliever Rawly Eastwick during the 1975 World Series. He was the #1 reliever all season for skipper Sparky Anderson, and he was terrific all postseason as well—so it was not a surprise when Anderson brought him in to face pinch-hitter Bernie Carbo in Game 6 with two on, two out, and the Red Sox trailing 6-3 in the home half of the eighth. Carbo, a former first-round draft pick by the Cincinnati Reds, went deep as a pinch-hitter in Game 3 of the series—and he did it again against Eastwick, tying the game, and setting the stage for Carlton Fisk's heroics in the twelfth inning.

226 The earned run average (2.26) for Pedro Martinez in 2002. It was the lowest number in the league, which contributed significantly to his .833 winning percentage—easily the highest number in the league.

227 The number of strikeouts (227) for Pedro Martinez in 2004. Martinez was second in the league for both strikeouts and strikeouts per nine innings, and he placed fourth in Cy Young balloting during his final season in Boston. In 217 innings he actually gave up 94 earned runs—that works out to a 3.90 earned run average, by far his highest mark during his tenure with the club. He was still 16-9, however, and when he left Boston, he did so with a 2.52 ERA over seven seasons—one of the ten best in franchise history.

228 The slugging percentage (.228) for pitcher Jose Santiago. He hit .173 over eight seasons and 162 career at bats. Only seven times did he get an extra-base hit—six doubles and one home run—but on

October 4, 1967, he hit a home run against Cardinals' Hall of Fame legend Bob Gibson during Game 1 of the World Series.

229 The batting average (.229) for White Sox third baseman Lee Tannehill in 1904. He went 0 for 3 against his older brother and Red Sox hurler Jesse Tannehill on August 17, in a game that Boston won 6-0. Good thing, too—because if the younger Tannehill had gotten a base knock against his brother, then he would have broken up Jesse's no-hitter. As things turned out, Jesse notched the no-no and enjoyed a much more productive career than his kid brother. Lee got a moment of his own, however—he won a championship and got a base hit in the 1906 World Series as a member of the White Sox.

230 Mo Vaughn hit (230) home runs for Boston. He is among the top 100 home run hitters in baseball history with 328 career bombs—and the 230 he hit for the Red Sox ranks him among the top ten in franchise history.

231 The batting average (.231) for Jason Giambi vs. Boston in the 2003 League Championship Series. Giambi was 0 for 5 in the series against Tim Wakefield, prompting the Yankees' slugger to say, "You're better off trying to hit Wakefield when you're in a drunken stupor." Giambi was 6 for 21 with three home runs against the rest of the Boston staff.

232 The number of starts (232) for pitcher Mel Parnell. He spent ten seasons with Boston from 1947-56, and he tossed 113 complete games. He also made 57 relief appearances, and he posted an overall record of 123-75. His victory total is the highest in franchise history for a lefty, and the fourth highest overall.

233 The number of hits (233) for outfielder Roy Carlyle as a member of the Memphis Chicks in 1924. That kind of production gets you off the farm and into the majors, and in 1925 Carlyle was roaming the outfield for the Red Sox. He only got a total of 157 hits, however, during an abbreviated two-year career—the highlight of which came on July 21 of his rookie campaign, when he hit for the cycle against the Chicago White Sox.

234 Frank Malzone hit (234) doubles for Boston from 1955-65. He led the club with a career high 34 doubles in 1959, four times he was among the top ten league leaders in doubles, and his career total with Boston is among the top 25 in franchise history.

235 The batting average (.235) for Mark McGwire in 1990. Oakland's feared slugger was second in the league with 39 home runs, despite the low average. His teammate Jose Canseco was third in the league with 37 home runs. Boston pitchers were tasked with shutting down the Bash Brothers when the two clubs met in the 1990 League Championship Series—and they did the job. McGwire hit just .154, Canseco only .182, and neither player hit a homer. That should have led to a good outcome, but unfortunately, the Oakland pitching staff limited the Red Sox offense to a single run in every game. It was an ugly sweep: 9-1, 4-1, 4-1, and 3-1.

236 The earned run average (2.36) for Rube Foster. He started 103 games and pitched in 138 total for Boston from 1913-17, and he posted a career record of 58-33. Foster was second in the league in ERA in 1914, and fifth in 1915, and his career mark—though it was a short career—ranks among the top ten in franchise history.

237 Jim Piersall hit (.237) in 1958. The All-Star outfielder struggled at the plate after putting together solid years offensively from 1955-57, but there was nothing wrong with the way he played defense. Piersall made 314 putouts and eight assists during 125 games in center field, and he became the first Red Sox outfielder to win a Gold Glove.

238 Kevin Youkilis played (238) consecutive games at first base without making an error—a major league record. The streak began in 2006 and lasted all of 2007, earning him a Gold Glove, before coming to an end in 2008. Oddly enough, once the streak ended, and after making only five errors ever in four seasons at first, Youkilis made four errors in a span of 49 games.

239 The number of strikeouts (239) for Pedro Martinez in 2002. It was the third time in a span of four seasons that Martinez led the league in strikeouts. He posted a 20-4 record and gave up only 144 hits during 199 innings of work, but he placed second in Cy Young Award balloting behind Barry Zito.

240 Wade Boggs set a franchise record when he got (240) hits in 1985. Boggs is among the top 30 in baseball history with 3,010 career hits, but 1985 was the only season he led the league in hits.

241 The number of strikeouts (241) for Roger Clemens in 1991. He posted an 18-10 record and led the league with one of the ten highest strikeout totals in franchise history. Clemens picked up his third career Cy Young Award for his performance that season.

242 The number of total bases (242) for Hall of Fame player-manager Jimmy Collins in 1903. His total was eighth highest in the league, but it was helped considerably by the fact Collins legged out 17 triples on the season—a total that is tied with Harry Hooper, Freddy Parent, and Russ Scarritt for the ninth highest in franchise history. Collins hit two more triples against the Pirates as he led Boston to victory during the 1903 World Series—the first in baseball history.

243 Bucky Dent hit only (.243) for the Yankees in 1978—and he hit just five home runs. He did a lot of damage on the field—and caused a lot of emotional pain—with his fifth and final home run of the season, however, as his wind-aided pop fly (*and did Mickey Rivers give Dent a corked bat after he fouled the 1-0 pitch off his foot?*) rallied the Yankees to victory in a one-game playoff for the division title after Boston and New York concluded regular season play with identical 99-63 records. Yankees' owner George Steinbrenner said after the game, "These are the two teams who should be playing for the World Series."

244 Dutch Leonard gave up (244) hits during 274 innings of work in 1916. The lefty was solid all season, but he got shellacked by the St. Louis Browns on August 29. He gave up two runs, two hits, a walk, he hit a batter, and he threw a wild pitch—and then he got the hook without even making it through the first inning. Skipper Bill Carrigan sent Leonard back to the mound the very next day against the same St. Louis lineup—and this time Leonard tossed a complete game no-hit shutout.

245 The batting average (.245) for George Scott in 1966. He was a 22-year-old rookie who quickly became a fan-favorite on a Red Sox team that had not placed higher than fifth in the pennant race since 1958. He struck out a lot, and his average was low, but he swung hard and could hit the ball a ton. Scott hit 27 big flies and was third in Rookie of the Year balloting—and though the 1966 team still struggled, Scott was a big part of the Impossible Dream that was 1967.

246 The number of strikeouts (246) for Jim Lonborg in 1967. His total led the league, and it remains one of the ten best in franchise history. Lonborg pitched seven seasons for Boston, but he never struck out more than 131 batters during any other year with the club.

247 The number of at bats (247) for Jose Tartabull in 1967. Tartabull was an afterthought on a deal that brought pitcher John Wyatt to the club in 1966. He saw limited duty in 1967 and hit only .223 with no home runs—but like every member of the Impossible Dream club that won the pennant by a single game, he made his contribution. Boston led the White Sox 4-3 in the ninth inning on August 27, and they had to win to stay tied for first, but Chicago got the tying run to third with one out. Duane Josephson hit a fly to right that looked to score the tying run—but Tartabull made the catch and then gunned down Ken Berry at the plate to end the game. Wyatt, oddly enough, was on the mound to get the save.

248 The earned run average (2.48) for Roger Clemens in 1986. It was the first of seven ERA titles during his career, four of which came for Boston. Clemens led the league with a 24-4 record and earned both the Cy Young Award and Most Valuable Player Award.

249 The team batting average (.249) in 1918. It was the sixth lowest average in the league, out of only eight teams, and yet, it was good enough to win the pennant. The club did even worse against the Cubs in the World Series, posting a .186 average during six games—and yet, it was good enough to win a world championship. No other team in the 20th century won the World Series with a lower batting average.

250 The batting average (.250) for George Whiteman in the 1918 World Series. He was an outfielder who spent parts of three seasons in the majors, but in a strange way and without much playing time. He played four games for Boston in 1907, and then did not play again until he took the field 11 times for New York in 1913, and then he dropped off the map again until resurfacing for 71 games with Boston in 1918. Whiteman got five hits in the 1918 World Series (only 70 hits in his career) and was recognized in several news accounts for being a key contributor to the Red Sox championship effort—and then he never played again.

251 The earned run average (2.51) for Ray Collins. He spent all seven years of his career in Boston, posting an 84-62 record and an ERA that remains among the top ten in franchise history. Collins, who played from 1909-15, also won two World Series titles with the club.

252 The number of total bases (252) for Harry Hooper in 1920. He led the club in hits, total bases, doubles, triples, home runs, average, and slugging. It was also his final season in Boston before being traded to the Chicago White Sox. He left town with 2,303 total bases over a dozen seasons for one of the ten best totals in franchise history.

253 The length in hours and minutes (2:53) of the 1999 All-Star Game at Fenway Park on July 13. Ted Williams made an appearance to the delight of fans and players alike—and then Boston ace Pedro Martinez put on a show, striking out four consecutive N.L. stars to start the game: Barry Larkin, Larry Walker, Sammy Sosa, and Mark McGwire. Martinez got the win in a 4-1 A.L. victory.

254 Manny Ramirez hit (254) home runs from 2001-07. He hit a league best 43 in 2004, and after only seven seasons in Boston he was among the top five leaders in franchise history. Manny hit 20 home runs for Boston in 2008, raising his total with the club to 274 before being traded to the Dodgers.

255 The number of extra-base hits (255) for Johnny Pesky during seven-plus seasons with Boston. He hit only 17 career home runs—and only 13 of those came for Boston. His extra-base hits total for the club, however, actually ranks among the top 50 in franchise history. In all fairness, he is tied with Ira Flagstead—an outfielder in the 1920s who also got 255 extra-base hits for Boston—but Pesky has his own pole.

256 Jesse Tannehill gave up (256) hits during 281 innings in 1904—but in nine innings of work against the White Sox on August 17, he did not give up a single hit. It was the second no-hitter of the season for Boston. The first was a perfect game for Cy Young back on May 5.

257 The number of strikeouts (257) for Roger Clemens in 1996. It was a strange season, as Clemens led the league in Ks but posted a losing 10-13 record. It was only his second losing record during his time in Boston, but it was the third time he led the league in strikeouts.

258 The number of strikeouts (258) for Joe Wood in 1912. Hall of Fame legend Walter Johnson once said, "No man alive can throw harder than Smoky Joe Wood." His fastball was considered the best in baseball that season—and he used it to lead the club to victory against the New York Giants during the 1912 World Series. His strikeout total during the regular season was second in the league, and it set a franchise record that lasted 76 years.

259 The earned run average (2.59) for 23-year-old rookie Justin Masterson through his first four major league starts. He made his debut for Boston on April 24, 2008, and he tossed six innings of two-hit ball against the Angels, but got a no-decision. Masterson then reeled off three straight wins in consecutive starts against Kansas City, Tampa, and Seattle, to become the third Red Sox pitcher in three years to begin his career 3-0 before turning 24. Jon Lester did it in 2006, and Clay Buchholz did it in 2007.

260 Luis Tiant was a workhorse who tossed (260) innings during 35 starts in 1975—but he only got better in the postseason. He pitched a complete game three-hitter to beat Oakland in Game 1 of the League Championship Series, and then he tossed a complete game five-hit shutout to beat Cincinnati in Game 1 of the World Series. Boston trailed the Reds two games to one when Tiant took the mound again in Game 4, and this time he tossed another complete game—on the road, 161 pitches—for a 5-4 victory that tied the series at two games apiece. Tiant came back in Game 6 to try and stave off elimination, and this time he got the team into the eighth inning before yielding to the bullpen for the first time the entire postseason. Boston won all four of his postseason starts as Tiant logged 34 innings of work—but like so many other big names, he was a part of the Red Sox generation that never won a ring.

261 The number of times (261) Tris Speaker got on base in 1913. His total was the fifth highest in the league, and once on base, he posted 46 steals—also the fifth highest total in the league. Speaker owns three of the five highest steals totals in franchise history: 52 (1912), 46 (1913), and 42 (1914).

262 The earned run average (2.62) for Roger Clemens in 1991. He led the league with 271 innings and 1,077 batters faced, but only 79 of those batters got on base and scored an earned run against him. It was the third time he led the league in ERA, and he won his third Cy Young Award.

263 The earned run average (2.63) for Hall of Fame legend Cy Young. He won a major league record 511 games and from 1891-1908 he was among the top ten league leaders in ERA 16 times. Young won 192 games for Boston, and his 2.00 ERA with the club is the second best in franchise history.

264 The batting average (.264) for opponents vs. Rick Helling during road starts in 1999. Helling was a starter for the Texas Rangers who actually pitched better on the road than he did at home—opponents hit .281 against him in Texas. That was important, because on May 5, Helling tossed six-plus strong innings at Fenway. He gave up only seven hits and two runs as Texas won 8-3. Boston only got eight hits in the game, and that snapped a streak of nine consecutive games where Boston had collected ten or more hits. Boston began a new streak the next day, collecting ten or more hits in 13 consecutive games, a feat only one other team had accomplished since 1961 (the 1997 Chicago White Sox). If not for Helling, Boston's streak could have been 23, or more.

265 The on-base percentage (.265) for Earl Wilson during 11 big league seasons. That might seem low until you realize that he was a pitcher. Wilson hit only .195 in his career, but he was respected at the plate because his slugging percentage was .369, thanks to the 35 home runs he hit. Wilson, who was the first African American player signed by the Red Sox, posted consecutive season totals of five, six, and seven home runs from 1964-66, and 20 of his career blasts came while pitching for Boston. In fact, he hit a very significant home run on June 26, 1962, in a game he also tossed a 2-0 no-hit shutout against the Angels.

266 The career batting average (.266) for Leon Culberson. He was never a household name, but rather, he was a part-time outfielder who saw limited duty in parts of five seasons in Boston. That being said, there are still three extraordinary things Boston fans should remember Culberson for. He made it to the show, in Boston no less, where he wore his uni with pride, and where he shared a locker room with Ted Williams; in his 1943 rookie season he hit only three home runs (and hit only 14 for his career), but on July 3, 1943, against the Cleveland Indians, he hit for the cycle; and, last of all, he got nine at bats during the 1946 World Series—and like every other Red Sox player of that era he did not get a ring—but in Game 5, with the Cardinals and Red Sox tied two games each, Culberson hit a sixth inning home run that gave Boston a 3-1 lead in a game they had to win.

267 Tris Speaker stole (267) bases for Boston. Speaker is among the top 60 in baseball history with 432 career steals. He never led the league in steals in any one season, but his career total for Boston is the second highest in franchise history.

268 Bill Lee walked (2.68) batters per nine innings from 1969-78. Lee was among the top ten league leaders for fewest walks per nine innings four times during his career—three of those seasons came during his tenure with Boston, and his career ratio with the club is among the 30 best in franchise history.

269 The batting average (.269) for Yankees DH Chili Davis in 1999. He hit 350 home runs in his career, the last 19 of which came in 1999—and one of those came against Boston ace Pedro Martinez on September 10. He hit the blast with two outs and the bases empty in the second inning to stake New York to a 1-0 lead, but in one of the most dominating performances ever by an opponent at Yankee Stadium, Pedro did not give up another hit. It was the third one-hitter of Pedro's career, and he also struck out 17 batters (including Davis twice) as Boston won the contest 3-1. New York outfielder Paul O'Neill said, "We didn't get beat by the Red Sox. We got beat by Pedro Martinez."

270 The earned run average (2.70) for Hall of Fame pitcher Lefty Grove in 1935. It was the sixth time the 35-year-old veteran led the league in ERA, but it was his first as a member of the Red Sox. Grove was not done yet either—he led the league in ERA four times from 1935-39.

271 The batting average (.271) for Bobby Doerr in 1946. He hit well below his lifetime .288 average during his first season back after serving a year in the Army, but he was also among the league leaders with 116 RBI and he placed third in league MVP balloting. Doerr got 158 hits that season, but in one stretch he was so hot that he got three or more hits five times in a span of eight games. Not many Boston players have done that trick since: Vern Stephens and Billy Goodman (1950), Pete Runnels (1961), Carlton Fisk (1974), Johnny Damon (2004), and Dustin Pedroia (2008).

272 The number of total bases (272) for Dom DiMaggio in 1942. His career high total was also the fourth best in the league, and it came on the strength of a career high 14 home runs. He was ninth in the league in home runs—the only time in his career he cracked the top ten in that category. DiMaggio legged out 2,363 total bases during his career for one of the ten highest totals in franchise history.

273 The batting average (.273) for Jack Wilson in 1940. Not bad, considering he was a pitcher. Wilson was 12-6 on the mound, and at the plate he was 18 for 66 with a .424 slugging percentage. Wilson hit two doubles, a triple, and two home runs that season—and he posted the best winning percentage (.667) on the staff.

274 Dutch Leonard pitched (274) innings in 1916 and posted a record of 18-12. His best work of the season came on August 30, against the St. Louis Browns. In that game he tossed nine scoreless innings in a 4-0 victory—and notched the second no-hitter of the season by a Red Sox hurler.

275 Mike Greenwell hit (275) doubles during his Red Sox career. He hit a career high 39 doubles in 1988, the same season he batted .325 with 119 RBI and placed second in MVP balloting behind Oakland's Jose Canseco. Greenwell—who remains ninth in franchise history for career doubles—was not shy about speaking his mind in the aftermath of the book *Juiced*. He said of Canseco, "He's an admitted steroid user—I was clean. If they are going to start putting asterisks by things, let's put one by the MVP. I do have a problem with losing the MVP to an admitted steroids user."

276 The batting average (.276) for Danny Cater from 1964-75. Not bad—but then again, he hit only .237 in 1972 after the Red Sox traded 27-year-old lefty Sparky Lyle to get Cater from the Yankees. Cater hit right handed and was a 32-year-old utility player. "Good move" on the part of Boston GM Dick O'Connell, who got Cater because the Red Sox "were in need of a first baseman." Cater hit nine home runs in three seasons, and then was traded to the Cardinals for Danny Godby (who never played a game for Boston). Lyle, on the other hand, became one of the premier relievers in the game the next six seasons, winning a Cy Young Award and three pennants with New York.

277 The earned run average (2.77) for Mel Parnell in 1949. He is often credited for naming Pesky's Pole, after the light-hitting Johnny Pesky hit a game-winning home run that curled just fair around the pole in right field at Fenway in a game that Parnell won. Parnell won a lot on his own though in 1949—he posted a league best 25-7 record and his ERA was second best in the league.

278 The batting average (.278) for the St. Louis Cardinals in 2004. The Cardinals led the N.L. in batting, runs (855), and victories (105) that season—but as a team they hit only .190 against Red Sox pitching during the 2004 World Series. Curt Schilling, Pedro Martinez, and Derek Lowe started and got the wins in the final three games of the series—and none of them gave up an earned run. St. Louis scored only 12 runs the entire series, but they scored nine of those runs in the first game.

279 Nomar Garciaparra hit (279) doubles during his Red Sox career. He led the league with 56 in 2002, and was among the top four league leaders four times from 1997-2002. He was also the team leader three times during that period—and his career total in Boston is one of the ten best in franchise history.

280 The batting average (.280) for Bob Johnson in 1945. He was sometimes referred to as Indian Bob because he was part Cherokee—but opposing pitchers simply referred to him as a hitter deserving of their respect. Johnson hit 288 home runs in a career that did not begin until he was approaching 30 years of age. He hit .324 for Boston in 1944, after the club bought him from the Senators, but by 1945 Johnson was starting to slow down and the club released him at the end of the season. He never made it back to the majors again, but he kept right on playing ball until the early 1950s, in the minors, in Mexico, anywhere, just to play the game.

281 The earned run average (2.81) for Lefty Grove in 1936. Teams combined to score more than 7,000 runs in the A.L. that season for the first time since play began in 1901—an average of 5.67 runs per game. Grove did just a touch better than your normal A.L. pitcher that season, giving up fewer than half that number in earned runs on his way to posting the best ERA in the league.

282 The batting average (.282) for Scott Cooper in 1994. The third baseman was given the unenviable task of replacing Wade Boggs, who left Boston for the Bronx prior to the 1993 season. Cooper hit from the left side, as did Boggs, and he made the All-Star team in both 1993 and 1994—but he never came close to replicating the numbers Boggs routinely posted. Cooper's .282 average in 1994 was a career high, although he did have one very spectacular game that season. On April 12, against the Royals, Cooper hit for the cycle—going 5 for 6 at the plate, with a home run, triple, two doubles, a single, two runs, and five RBI.

283 The number of putouts (283) for Carl Yastrzemski in 1963. He set a career high with 18 outfield assists and earned his first Gold Glove. Yaz won his final Gold Glove in 1977, bringing his career total to seven.

284 The number of strikeouts (284) for Pedro Martinez in 2000. He led the league with one of the five highest totals in franchise history. Martinez gave up only 128 hits during 217 innings, becoming the first starting pitcher in baseball history to strike out more than twice as many batters as he gave up hits. Randy Johnson became the second player to accomplish the feat when he did it for the Arizona Diamondbacks in 2001.

285 Joe Cronin hit (.285) in 1940. His average was well below his lifetime mark of .301, but he established a career high that same season when he blasted 24 home runs. The Hall of Fame infielder was among the top ten league leaders with 65 extra-base hits—a feat the Detroit Tigers were painfully aware of, as Cronin hit for the cycle against the Tigers on August 2, 1940.

286 Billy Werber batted (.286) during four games with the Yankees in 1930. Werber was the first All-American basketball player in the history of Duke University—but he secretly signed with the Yankees after his freshman year of college, and he began to play both sports. He made his big league debut in 1930, but was sold to Boston in 1931, where he put up some of his best numbers. Werber is best known for accomplishments outside of Boston, however, because as a member of the Cincinnati Reds he became the first player in baseball history to bat on live TV on August 26, 1939. He also hit .370 as he led the Reds to victory in the 1940 World Series.

287 The minor league batting average (.287) for Jed Lowrie from 2005-08. The infielder made his big league debut in 2008, filling in for an injured Julio Lugo. Lowrie hit .258 as a rookie, but he played his way onto the postseason roster where he hit .364 vs. Anaheim in the Division Series—including a walk-off single in Game 4 that won the series. He said afterwards, "That's what this team is about, especially the last few years. It's October, they've won a lot of games, and to be a part of that is awesome."

288 The number of times (288) on base for Dom DiMaggio in 1948 and Mike Greenwell in 1988. DiMaggio was third in the league in 1948, just one of seven seasons in which he was among the top ten league leaders. Greenwell was second in the league in 1988, and cracked the top ten again in 1990. They share a total that ranks among the top 30 season efforts in franchise history.

289 The batting average (.289) for Orlando Cepeda in 1973. It was the only year in Boston for the Hall of Fame slugger, and the only reason he was there is because the league was using the DH rule for the first time. Cepeda, who was on the Cardinals squad that beat Boston in the 1967 World Series, was slowed by knee troubles and could no longer play in the field—but he could still hit. He officially became the first DH in franchise history when he batted against Mel

Stottlemyre and the Yankees on April 6. Cepeda hit 20 home runs on the season, but in his debut as DH he was 0 for 6 and he struck out twice, although the club won the game 15-5.

290 Hobe Ferris hit (.290) during the 1903 World Series. He booted a ball during the first inning of Game 1 for the first error in World Series history, and that error led to four runs in a 7-3 loss to the Pirates. Ferris redeemed himself nicely though. In addition to his .290 average, he drove home seven runs—including all three runs in the deciding eighth game that clenched the series for Boston.

291 The number of strikeouts (291) for Roger Clemens in 1988. It was the first time he led the league in strikeouts, and he did so in record-breaking fashion. Clemens surpassed the 258 strikeouts for Joe Wood in 1912 for the highest total in franchise history—but his record only lasted until 1999, when Pedro Martinez shattered it with 313 strikeouts.

292 The earned run average (2.92) for Carl Mays. He was 207-126 from 1915-29, playing for Boston, the Yankees, Reds, and Giants. Mays never posted anything higher than a 2.60 ERA during four-plus seasons in Boston—so owner Harry Frazee sold him to the Yankees for a couple of nobody's and $40,000 in cash in 1919. Mays won 26 games for New York in 1920 and 27 games in 1921. He might have left Boston too soon, but the 2.21 ERA he posted during his tenure with the club remains the sixth best in franchise history.

293 Hall of Fame catcher Carlton Fisk hit (.293) in 1972. He was a 24-year-old rookie who also hit 22 home runs and tied for the league lead with nine triples. His strong play earned him a fourth place finish in league MVP balloting, and he became the first player in league history to unanimously win the Rookie of the Year Award.

294 The earned run average (2.94) for Tex Hughson. He played eight years from 1941-49, every one of them in Boston. Hughson twice was a 20-game winner and four times he was among the top ten league leaders in ERA. He posted a 96-54 career record for a .640 winning percentage that remains one of the top ten in franchise history.

295 The number of at bats (295) for Mike Greenwell in 1996—his final season. He missed two months with a broken finger and played just 77 games, driving home 44 runs. He got nine of those RBI in one game though—on September 2, when he rallied Boston past Seattle with a two-run home run in the fifth, a grand slam in the seventh, a two-run double in the eighth—and for good measure, a game-winning single in the tenth. The AP story said, "No one in baseball worked harder on Labor Day than Mike Greenwell." Boston trailed 5-0 in the fifth, but won 9-8, and Greenwell's RBI total set a record for the most in a game that also accounted for all of his team's runs.

296 John Valentin hit (.296) in 1996. His average got a boost on June 6, at the expense of White Sox starter Joe Magrane. Valentin hit a home run in the first inning, a triple in the third, a single in the fourth, and then capped off a perfect 4 for 4 performance against Magrane by hitting for the cycle with a double in the sixth inning. Valentin was the last player for the Red Sox to hit for the cycle during the 20th century.

297 The number of times (297) on base for David Ortiz in 2007. He led the club and was second in the league behind the 299 times on base for the Yankees' Alex Rodriguez. Ortiz was among the top three league leaders in times on base four consecutive seasons from 2004-07.

298 Dom DiMaggio posted a (.298) batting average during a decade of playing ball at Fenway. His high average led to a lot of runs—and the 1,046 times he crossed the plate gives him one of the top ten totals in franchise history.

299 The batting average (.299) for rookie infielder Jed Lowrie after Boston beat the Toronto Blue Jays 6-5 on August 24, 2008. Lowrie was 1 for 5, but that one hit was an extra-inning home run that gave the Red Sox a much-needed victory as they sought to keep pace with the surging Tampa Bay Rays in the race for the division title. It was only his second homer of the season—both of which broke late-inning ties and proved to be game-winning shots—but his blast against the Blue Jays also snapped a streak during which Boston had lost 16 consecutive one-run games on the road. Lowrie was filling in at third for an injured Mike Lowell.

300 Harry Hooper stole a franchise record (300) bases for Boston during his Hall of Fame career. His total includes two seasons that rank among the top ten in franchise history: 40 steals in 1910 and 38 steals in 1911.

Wade Boggs—five time batting champion.
(Courtesy National Baseball Hall of Fame Library, Cooperstown, NY)

"I used to tell my pitchers I could get them two strikes on Boggs easy, but from then on they were on their own. There's no doubt in my mind that he is the best two-strike hitter in history."
— Rene Lachemann, former Major League manager

Chapter 4

The Batting Champions

TED WILLIAMS OWNS the most batting titles in franchise history—that's an easy one—but who won the first batting title for the Boston Red Sox? Tris Speaker is a good guess. Spoke owns one of the top ten averages in baseball history after all—and he hit .383 for Boston in 1912, and .363 in 1913. Only problem is he placed third both of those seasons behind the same two guys: Ty Cobb and Joe Jackson. Did the Hall of Famer with a .345 career average ever win a batting title?

You bet—in 1916, his first year after being traded to Cleveland.

Buck Freeman (.339), Patsy Dougherty (.342), Jimmy Collins (.332), Earl Webb (.333), and Joe Harris (.335) all cracked the league's top ten on at least one occasion—a couple even made the top five—but nobody won a batting title for Boston until 1932.

Dale Alexander hit .343 with 25 home runs and 137 RBI for the Detroit Tigers in 1929, and he was a rookie. Detroit expected big things from the powerful slugger they called Moose, and he delivered again his sophomore season, batting .326 with 20 homers and 135 RBI. His production fell in 1931, however, and he hit only three home runs in 517 at bats.

Earl Webb hit a franchise record 67 doubles for Boston in 1931, after nearly winning the 1930 batting title, but in 1932 he got off to a slow start—hitting only nine doubles in 52 games. Alexander was off to another slow start for Detroit—hitting only .250 with no home runs—so on June 12, 1932, Boston traded Webb for Alexander.

And it was Dale Alexander who became the first batting champion in franchise history, despite his slow start in Detroit.

Alexander caught fire, batting .372 while collecting 140 hits in 101 games. He raised his overall average to .367 for the season, narrowly beating out Jimmie Foxx (.364) of the Philadelphia Athletics—which is a bit ironic, because Foxx is the guy who won the second batting title in Boston history when he hit .349 for the club in 1938.

Ted Williams won his first batting title in 1941, which obviously makes his .406 average the highest in franchise history to win a title. The highest average in franchise history to *not* win a batting title is Tris Speaker's .383 in 1912. Who holds the record for the lowest average in history to *win* a league batting title?

The answer is in chapter four.

Also in this chapter: Wade Boggs was not the first third baseman to win a batting title for Boston, so who was? And who won their only career batting title as a utility player filling in for an injured Ted Williams?

The answers to those questions are also in chapter four—along with titles for Manny, Nomar, Fred Lynn, Bill Mueller, and Wade Boggs, a startling realization about Ted Williams' sixth crown, a revealing statement from Yaz, and some great individual performances at the plate: J.D. Drew's All-Star bash, Trot Nixon's postseason heroics, Dustin Pedroia's rookie effort, Tony Conigliaro's first game back, Jacoby Ellsbury's postseason coming out party, Jim Rice terrorizing the league in 1978, and Mike Lowell taking top honors in the Fall Classic.

In the clean-up spot...

301 Hall of Fame legend Carl Yastrzemski hit (.301) in 1968. It was a good year to be a pitcher, as hits and runs were tough to come by in both leagues. Seven different pitchers posted a 1.99 earned run average or better, and Denny McLain won 31 games. The pitching was so good that Yaz was the only player in the league to bat above .300—setting a record for the lowest average in history to win a batting title.

302 The batting average (.302) for J.D. Drew prior to the 2008 All-Star break. His average was hovering around .280 when May ended, but in June he began swinging a hot bat. He hit 12 home runs that month and saw his average climb all the way to .327 at one point. That success earned him player of the month honors in June and a berth in the mid-Summer Classic for the first time in his career. In his first at bat in the All-Star Game he hit a two-run home run that tied the game in the seventh inning—and when the A.L. prevailed in extra-innings, Drew earned MVP honors for the game.

303 The number of total bases (303) for Carl Yastrzemski in 1962. It was only his second season but his total led the club and placed fourth among league leaders. Yaz went on to lead the league in total bases twice (1967, 1970) and he was among the top ten leaders seven times. In his career he posted 5,539 total bases—the eighth highest total in baseball history, and a franchise record.

304 The number of total bases (304) for Bobby Doerr in 1950. It was a career high for the 32-year-old veteran, who also tied a career high with 27 home runs. Doerr was among the league's top ten leaders in total bases for the seventh time that season, and his 3,270 career total bases ranks among the ten highest in franchise history.

305 The earned run average (3.05) for Hugh Bedient from 1912-14. He won 20 games as a 22-year-old rookie in 1912, and he also worked 18 innings during the 1912 World Series, giving up just one earned run while picking up a victory in Game 5. He won only 23 games total the next two seasons, but his career ERA with Boston remains among the top 25 in franchise history.

306 The batting average (.306) for Trot Nixon in 2003. He also hit 28 home runs, setting career highs for both average and the long ball—and he was just getting started. Boston fell behind two games to none in the best-of-five Divisional Series against Oakland, and the club faced elimination at home in Game 3. Tied 1-1 in the eleventh, Nixon hit a walk-off home run against Rich Harden to keep Boston's hopes alive. The team rallied to win the series, and then Nixon hit three more home runs against New York in the League Championship Series.

307 The number of total bases (307) for Ted Williams in 1957. He was a 38-year-old veteran who hit 38 home runs for his highest total in nearly a decade. He was second in the league in home runs and third in total bases. It was the fourth and final time that he placed second in MVP balloting. In his career he compiled 4,884 total bases—the second highest total in franchise history.

308 The earned run average (3.08) for Lefty Grove in 1938. It was his highest ERA in four seasons, but teams were scoring so many runs in 1938 that it was still the lowest number in the league. Grove posted a 14-4 record and also led the league with a .778 winning percentage.

309 The length in hours and minutes (3:09) of the Boston vs. New York match-up on April 13, 2002, at Fenway Park. It was early season baseball, but it was a statement game as third baseman Shea Hillenbrand hit a two-out home run in the last of the eighth against Yankees' closer Mariano Rivera to cap a four-run rally and give Boston a 7-6 lead. Alfonso Soriano pinch-ran for Jorge Posada as the potential tying run in the ninth, but he was gunned down trying to steal second by catcher Jason Varitek to end the game. Boston spent 62 days in first that season, but finally succumbed to the Yankees in late June.

310 The number of times (310) Tris Speaker got on base in 1912. His total led the league, and once on base, Speaker posted a career high 52 steals. His steals total was a club record that lasted 61 years, and it remains the second best in franchise history.

311 The on-base percentage (.311) for Boston in 1922. The club was dead last among eight teams in the league. No surprise there—most of Boston's best players were in the Bronx by that time and the club scored the fewest runs in the league, and won the fewest games in the league as a result. You won't hear us criticizing the current owners for spending top money to get quality players. In this game, you want to be a buyer—not a seller.

312 The earned run average (3.12) for Don Aase in 1977. He was a rookie who got off to a good start. Aase tossed a complete game against the Milwaukee Brewers in his major league debut on July 26, 1977, as Boston won 4-3. He was 6-2 on the season, but Red Sox fans might remember him better as the guy who was traded for Jerry Remy. His debut was actually a pretty rare feat, as the next time a rookie tossed a complete game one-run victory in their major league debut was 1992—when a guy named Tim Wakefield did it for the Pittsburgh Pirates.

313 The number of strikeouts (313) for Pedro Martinez in 1999. His total led the league and set a franchise record—and he did it in only 213 innings, striking out a mind-boggling 13.20 batters per nine innings of work for a major league record (surpassed by Randy Johnson in 2001).

314 The length in hours and minutes (3:14) of Game 4 of the 2004 World Series. On October 27, 2004, at 10:40 p.m. EST, Edgar Renteria hit a comebacker to closer Keith Foulke to end 86 years of frustration for Red Sox fans. On April 11, 2005, Boston raised the World Series championship flag at Fenway Park and then celebrated again by beating the Yankees 8-1.

315 The number of total bases (315) for All-Star shortstop Rico Petrocelli in 1969. His total led the club and was the fifth highest in the league. Petrocelli also set a career high with 40 home runs to tie teammate Carl Yastrzemski for the team lead. It was the only time Petrocelli surpassed 300 total bases in a season, but he ranks among Boston's all-time top ten with 2,263 career total bases.

316 Johnny Damon hit (.316) during the 2003 Division Series vs. Oakland—but he was involved in one of the scariest moments in Red Sox postseason play during the deciding Game 5. In the sixth inning, Damon and second baseman Damian Jackson were involved in a head-to-head collision in pursuit of a shallow fly ball off the bat of Jermaine Dye. The game was delayed for more than ten minutes as Damon lay unconscious on the outfield grass, before finally being lifted on a stretcher into a waiting ambulance that carried him off the field. Boston held on to win the game 4-3, but Damon was not able to play again until Game 3 of the League Championship Series. In his return, he went 3 for 4 and scored a run—but the Yankees won that game, and the series.

317 Dustin Pedroia hit (.317) in 2007. The 23-year-old rookie second baseman scored 86 runs and was tenth in the league in batting. Pedroia also hit a pair of postseason home runs—including one in the World Series—won a ring, and picked up Rookie of the Year honors.

318 The batting average (.318) for Boston vs. Cleveland during the 1999 Division Series. Boston hit only .252 during the 1998 Division Series vs. Cleveland, losing that series in four games. It was a different story in 1999, as Boston erupted for 24 hits in a 23-7 victory in Game 4. John Valentin drove home seven runs in that contest—and Boston won the series the next day.

319 The number of times (319) on base for Wade Boggs in 1989. He was second in the league with 205 hits and third in the league with 107 walks—but it was the seventh consecutive season he led the league in times on base. His total from 1989 remains among the top ten in franchise history, and it was so good that the next season he reached base 44 fewer times—and still led the league an eighth straight season.

320 Jimmie Foxx hit (.320) during his tenure in Boston. He won two career batting titles and his .325 average is among the top 50 in baseball history. Foxx was an All-Star during six consecutive seasons with Boston from 1936-41, and his average for the Red Sox is the fifth highest in franchise history.

321 Carl Yastrzemski hit (.321) in 1963. He was a 23-year-old outfielder in his third big league season when he won the first batting title of his career. Yaz once replied to a reporter's question by saying, "Well, sometimes the pitcher does get you out." The implication was clear—the rest of the time the pitcher got lucky. Yaz won three batting titles and five times he led the league in on-base percentage.

322 The number of total bases (322) for Manny Ramirez in 2001. He hit 41 home runs with 125 RBI during 142 games. It was his first season in Boston, and his 322 total bases led the club and ranked sixth among league leaders.

323 Nomar Garciaparra hit (.323) as a member of the Red Sox—the fourth highest average in franchise history. Nomar broke into the majors in a big way in 1997 as he batted .306 and led the league with 209 hits. He later won consecutive batting titles in 1999 and 2000.

324 Mike Lowell hit (.324) in 2007. The third baseman led the club with 191 hits and 120 RBI, and earned the Thomas A. Yawkey Award for being the Red Sox Most Valuable Player. The club rewarded his performance by signing him to a new three-year contract worth $12 million per season. Lowell reportedly said, "I can't say that I'm upset with the situation."

325 The slugging percentage (.325) for Kevin Romine. The outfielder spent parts of seven seasons playing at Fenway. He hit just .251 with five career home runs, and only 36 of his 158 career hits went for extra-bases. Romine hit some spectacular shots, however, as his first big league homer was a walk-off shot against Steve Farr and the Royals; and then two years later, his third big league homer was another walk-off shot, this time against Kenny Rogers and the Rangers.

326 Bill Mueller hit (.326) in 2003. The third baseman edged out teammate Manny Ramirez (.325) and Yankees shortstop Derek Jeter (.324) to win the league batting title during his first season in Boston.

327 The slugging percentage (.327) for Harry Hooper in 1915. He hit only two home runs and just 35 extra-base hits during 566 at bats in the regular season—but he hit two home runs in the deciding Game 5 of the 1915 World Series against the Philadelphia Phillies. Hooper posted a .650 slugging percentage for the series, and his second home run came in the top of the ninth and proved to be the series-winning hit in a 5-4 victory.

328 Ted Williams hit (.328) in 1958 to win the sixth and final batting title of his career. He won the title with an average significantly lower than his .344 career mark, which speaks volumes about the caliber of his play throughout his career.

329 Carl Yastrzemski hit (.329) in 1970—and he hit 40 home runs for the second year in a row. Yaz also made his sixth consecutive All-Star team, and though he went on to make 15 consecutive trips to the mid-Summer Classic, none of them matched what he did in 1970—he batted 4 for 6 with a double, a run scored, and an RBI, and he earned MVP honors for the game.

330 The on-base percentage (.330) for Dave Roberts during 45 games with Boston in 2004. Boston got Roberts on the July 31, trade deadline—exchanging prospect Henri Stanley for the fleet-footed outfielder. Roberts fittingly got 86 at bats for Boston, but it was his speed on the bases that the Red Sox sought—and it was his speed that brought to an end 86 years of frustration for the Fenway Faithful. Roberts later said, "Maury Wills once told me that there will come a point in my career when everyone in the ballpark will know that I have to steal a base—and I will steal that base. When I got out there, I knew that was what he was talking about." Roberts pinch-ran for Kevin Millar in the ninth inning of Game 4 of the 2004 League Championship Series, stole second, scored the tying run on a Bill Mueller single—and the rest is, well, history.

331 Fred Lynn hit (.331) in 1975. He was second in the batting title race, but as a 23-year-old rookie who did lead the league in runs, doubles, slugging, and OPS, Lynn became the first player in league history to simultaneously earn Rookie of the Year and Most Valuable Player honors.

332 The earned run average (3.32) as a member of the Red Sox for Denny Galehouse in 1947. He posted a 6.12 ERA in Cleveland that season, but he improved greatly once he was traded to Boston. His most memorable game came against New York on August 17. In that game, Ted Williams robbed Joe DiMaggio of extra-bases when he snared a 400 foot drive—and then DiMaggio returned the favor by gunning down Williams at the plate in the tenth inning. Dom DiMaggio said of his brother, Joe, "That's the best throw I've seen him make in a long time." In the end, Boston won 3-0 in 11 innings, with Galehouse tossing a six-hit complete game shutout at Yankee Stadium.

333 Fred Lynn hit (.333) in 1979. He posted the biggest numbers of his career—setting highs in on-base and slugging percentage, batting, doubles, home runs, runs, and RBI. Lynn only placed fourth in MVP balloting, but he made his fifth consecutive All-Star team and won his only career batting title.

334 The earned run average (3.34) for Lefty Grove during 214 games for Boston. The Hall of Fame lefty made 190 starts for the Red Sox, completed 119 of them, and notched 15 shutouts. He closed out his tenure with the club at 105-62, ranking him among Boston's top ten for career wins.

335 Johnny Pesky hit (.335) in 1946. He was third in the league in batting during his first season after serving three years in the Navy during the war. Pesky, who is one of the most popular players in franchise history, batted .320 during seven-plus seasons with the Red Sox—an average that places him among the top ten in franchise history.

336 Carney Lansford hit (.336) in 1981. The All-Star third baseman came to the club prior to the season in a trade that sent fan-favorites Rick Burleson and Butch Hobson to the West Coast—so it was crucial that Lansford validate the front office move. He did a pretty good job of it, seeing as he won the league batting title and earned the Silver Slugger Award.

337 Tris Speaker hit (.337) during his tenure in Boston—the third highest average in franchise history. Speaker got 1,327 hits for the club from 1907-15. He went on to collect 3,514 hits and a .345 average for his career, numbers that rank among the top ten in baseball history.

338 Wade Boggs hit (.338) during his tenure in Boston. The Hall of Famer won five batting titles, including four consecutive titles from 1985-88. Boggs is among the top 40 in baseball history with a .328 career average, and his .338 mark for the Red Sox is the second highest in franchise history.

339 Jim Rice scored (339) runs from 1977-79. He surpassed the century mark all three seasons—the only times in his career that he did so—and each time he was among the top four league leaders. Rice scored a career high 121 runs in 1978, and his total of 1,249 career runs is the fourth highest in franchise history.

340 The number of times (340) on base for Wade Boggs in 1985. He led the league in this category every season from 1983-90, and his total from 1985 is one of the five best in franchise history.

341 The length in hours and minutes (3:41) of the Boston vs. Baltimore game on opening day, April 8, 1969. This is an important date in Red Sox history because it was the first game back for Tony Conigliaro after being struck in the face by a pitch on August 18, 1967. The only thing that could have made the day any better is if the game had been played at Fenway instead of on the road. Conigliaro hit a two-run home run in the tenth inning, and after the bullpen failed to hold the lead, he reached on a walk in the twelfth and scored the winning run in a 5-4 decision.

342 The number of times (342) on base for Wade Boggs in 1988. He was second in the league with 214 hits, was hit by a pitch three times, and he led the league with 125 walks. The result was a career high and league best .476 on-base percentage as he led the league in times on base for the sixth straight season.

343 Ted Williams hit (.343) in 1947. In his second season after returning from active duty during World War II, Williams won his third batting title and his second career Triple Crown. He also earned Major League Player of the Year honors for the third time, but he was second in league MVP balloting behind Joe DiMaggio.

344 The batting average (.344) for Hall of Fame legend Ted Williams. His career average is a franchise record that also ranks among the top ten in baseball history. Williams won six batting titles and was among the top ten league leaders 13 times during his career.

345 The number of times (345) on base for Ted Williams in 1947. It was just one of the eight seasons that Williams led the league in this category—one shy of the major league record nine seasons that Pete Rose led the N.L. in times on base. One interesting footnote, in seven out of the eight seasons that Williams led the A.L., he did so with a number that surpassed the career high 311 times on base for Pete Rose.

346 The earned run average (3.46) for Bill Dinneen in 1909. Pitching his final big league season and no longer a member of the Red Sox, Big Bill was 6-7 for the St. Louis Browns. He was only 33, however, and the hero of the 1903 World Series was not yet ready to walk away from the game—so he became an umpire. He clinched a world championship and threw a no-hitter as a player, and then as an umpire from 1909-37 Dinneen took the field for five additional no-hitters, eight World Series, and the inaugural All-Star Game.

347 The earned run average (3.47) for Frank Sullivan from 1953-60. He won 13 or more games five consecutive seasons from 1954-58, he led the league with 18 wins in 1955, and twice he was an All-Star during that stretch. Sullivan was among the top ten league leaders in ERA three times, and his career mark with the club is among the top 35 in franchise history.

348 Jon Lester posted a (3.48) earned run average during his first 19 starts of 2008, a number helped by his no-hit shutout against the Royals. On July 3, however, he reduced that number to 3.21 with a start that was just as impressive as his no-no. Lester shutout the Yankees in his first career start in the Bronx, becoming the first player for Boston to toss a complete game shutout against New York since Pedro Martinez did it in 2000. Lester said afterwards, "It was cool." Yankees starter Andy Pettitte, who gave up nine hits and six runs in four innings of work, had a slightly different opinion, saying, "Absolute, horrible game."

349 Manny Ramirez hit (.349) in 2002. The playing time for the future Hall of Fame outfielder was limited by injuries that season—he only appeared in 120 games—but as is usually the case with Manny, when his bat was in the lineup he was productive. He led the league with a .450 on-base percentage, and won the league batting title.

350 The winning percentage (.350) for player-manager Chick Stahl in 1906. Jimmy Collins began the season at the helm, but guided the club to an abhorrent 35-79 record before Stahl took over. Stahl was only marginally better—posting a 14-26 record during the final 40 games. It was Stahl's only season as skipper, and his final as a player. His best numbers for Boston came on the base paths, where he swiped 105 bases during six seasons—a career total that remains among the ten best in franchise history.

351 The on-base percentage (.351) for Tommy Harper in 1973. He got on base 221 times, and then he was off—leading the league and breaking a franchise record after stealing 54 bases.

352 The number of RBI (352) for Tony Armas from 1983-86. Armas came from Oakland in exchange for third baseman and batting champion Carney Lansford—a guy named Boggs made this deal possible. Armas put a hurt on opposing pitchers, which is why the club went out and got him. He hit 113 home runs with 352 RBI during four seasons in Boston—and in 1984 he was the league leader in total bases, home runs, and RBI.

353 Jacoby Ellsbury hit (.353) in 2007. He was a 23-year-old rookie who got 41 hits in 33 games. Ellsbury was named the Red Sox Minor League Player of the Year in 2006, and again in 2007—the second time sharing the honor with teammate Clay Buchholz—but it was his play down the stretch and into October for the big club that earned the respect of Red Sox Nation everywhere. Ellsbury hit .360 and scored eight runs during the postseason as Boston beat Anaheim, Cleveland, and Colorado to win the World Series.

354 Billy Goodman hit (.354) in 1950. He was referred to as "the best one-man bench in baseball" by an article in the September 18, 1950 issue of *Time* magazine. That same article quoted Red Sox manager Steve O'Neill calling Goodman "the best utility player I ever saw." He was exactly that—a utility man who played first, second, third, short, and outfield—at least until Ted Williams shattered his elbow during the 1950 All-Star Game. Then Goodman was forced to take over duty in left field for the Hall of Fame legend, and all he did was go out and win the league batting title.

355 The on-base percentage (.355) for Jimmy Sebring during the 1903 World Series. He was the starting right fielder for Pittsburgh, and his bat gave the Red Sox a scare in more than one way. He hit .333 with a home run in the series, but he also hit a screaming line drive in the third inning of the decisive Game 8 that split open a finger on Boston starter Bill Dinneen's pitching hand. This was 101 years before Curt Schilling's bloody sock, and his finger was described by the *Boston Post* as having "bled freely throughout the contest, each pitch causing him intense pain." Dinneen stayed on the mound and clinched the title in fine fashion—a four-hit shutout.

356 Ted Williams hit (.356) in 1942. The previous season he won the batting title with a .406 average but placed second in MVP balloting behind Joe DiMaggio. Williams not only defended his batting title in 1942, he also won the Triple Crown—but again, he placed second in MVP balloting behind a Yankee. This time it was Joe Gordon, a second baseman who hit .322 with 18 home runs (Williams hit 36 home runs).

357 Nomar Garciaparra hit (.357) in 1999. He was among the top ten league leaders for both hits and extra-base hits—and after battling Yankee shortstop Derek Jeter (.349) down the stretch, he came out on top and won his first career batting title.

358 The number of times (358) on base for Ted Williams in 1949. His total is a franchise record and the third highest in baseball history. He set career highs with 194 hits and 162 walks—and he got plunked by a pitch twice—on his way to winning his second career Most Valuable Player Award.

359 The earned run average (3.59) for Jose Santiago in 1967. Only 11 of his 50 games were starts, and his ERA was the second highest among eight pitchers on the staff with at least 20 games—but on September 30, he got the nod vs. Minnesota with Boston trailing the Twins by a single game in the standings, and two left to play. He gave up only two runs in seven innings, and he got the biggest decision of his career in a 6-4 Boston victory.

360 The number of total bases (360) for Carl Yastrzemski in 1967. His career high total was only one of several categories that he led the league in that season. Yaz also led the league in batting, home runs, and RBI—giving him the Triple Crown and earning him the Most Valuable Player Award.

361 Wade Boggs hit (.361) in 1983. He batted .349 as a rookie in 1982 but only placed third in Rookie of the Year balloting—and then in 1983 he was second in the league in hits and he won his first career batting title, but he only placed 12th in league MVP balloting.

362 The on-base percentage (.362) for Johnny Damon from 2002-05. Twice during that stretch he was among the league's top ten leaders for times on base, but all four seasons he was among the top ten scorers. Damon scored 461 runs for Boston—plus 18 more in the postseason.

363 Wade Boggs hit (.363) in 1987. He won his third consecutive batting title and fourth overall in five seasons, and he also led the league in OPS after hitting a career high 24 home runs—and yet somehow, Boggs placed only ninth in league MVP balloting.

364 The on-base percentage (.364) for infielder Billy Werber. Born in 1908, Werber was a teammate and hunting buddy of Ted Williams, and in 2008, at 100 years of age, he was the oldest living MLB player and the last surviving teammate of Babe Ruth. Werber got on base a lot during his four seasons in Boston—and once on base he made good use of his speed. He stole 40 bases in 1934, and his 107 career steals for Boston is among the ten best totals in franchise history.

365 The number of total bases (365) for Nomar Garciaparra in 1997. He led the club and was second in the league in both total bases and extra-base hits. Garciaparra hit 44 doubles, 11 triples, and 30 home runs, and his 365 total bases is one of the ten best season efforts in franchise history.

366 Wade Boggs hit (.366) in 1988. It was his fourth consecutive batting title—and the overall fifth and final of his Hall of Fame career.

367 Dale Alexander hit (.367) in 1932. He batted .343 and led the league with 215 hits as a rookie for the Tigers in 1929—and he won the 1932 league batting title after coming to the Red Sox in a trade with Detroit. Alexander was on his way to stardom when a leg injury ended his major league career. He played only 94 games in 1933, and though he spent another decade playing ball with various minor league teams across the country he never played again in the majors.

368 Wade Boggs hit (.368) in 1985. He set a career high and won the league batting title with an average that ranks among the ten best in franchise history.

369 Ted Williams hit (.369) in 1948. It was his fourth career batting title—but only the third highest average of his career.

370 The on-base percentage (.370) for Jim Rice in 1978. He got on base a lot, and he did so with a lot of power as well. Rice set a franchise record with 406 total bases.

371 The ratio (3.71) of strikeouts per walk for Roger Clemens in 1991. Clemens led the league in this category four times while pitching for Boston, but his ratio in 1991 was only the third best in the league, although it remains among the top 20 in franchise history.

372 Nomar Garciaparra hit (.372) in 2000. It was his third major title in four years—he won Rookie of the Year in 1997, and he earned back-to-back batting titles in 1999 and 2000. Garciaparra also tied Dale Alexander for the fourth highest average in franchise history. Alexander hit .372 in 101 games for Boston in 1932, but he actually hit only .367 for the season—he hit .250 for the Tigers in 23 games prior to being traded to Boston.

373 Jim Rice hit (373) career doubles. The slugger, who was never exactly fleet of foot, actually led the league in triples with 15 in 1978, but he never led the league in doubles his entire career. Rice was among the top ten league leaders in triples four times, but he managed to rank that high in doubles only three times—but no matter, his career total is among the ten best in franchise history.

374 The on-base percentage (.374) for Ira Flagstead while playing for Boston from 1923-29. He was one of the few players that Boston actually bought from another club during the 1920s, the era in which Boston notoriously sold a great many players. Flagstead proved to be a good deal for the club—in 789 games he collected 867 hits and scored 466 runs, and all three of those totals rank among the top 50 in franchise history.

375 The winning percentage (.375) for Jim Lonborg in 1968. He was the reigning Cy Young winner who clinched the 1967 pennant for Boston on the final day of the season, tossed a one-hit shutout in Game 2 of the 1967 World Series, and then tossed a complete game three-hitter to keep the Red Sox alive in Game 5. Then in 1968, Lonborg fell to just 6-10 on the mound, and literally, it was all because of a very real fall he experienced in the off-season. He was involved in a treacherous skiing accident that did significant damage to his knee, and he never regained his Cy Young form.

376 The number of at bats (376) for rookie catcher Jim Pagliaroni in 1961. He hit only .242 on the season, but 11 of those at bats came on one very memorable day. In the first game of a doubleheader against the Washington Senators on June 18, the Red Sox trailed by seven runs with two outs in the last of the ninth. They rallied for three and loaded the bases for Pagliaroni, who hit a grand slam to tie the game. Boston scored again to win, 13-12. In the second game, Pagliaroni came to bat in the last of the thirteenth with the score tied 5-5. He hit a walk-off home run. The two home runs were his only hits of the day, as pointed out by a reporter who observed, "You had a rough day at the plate today. You were only 2 for 11."

377 The slugging percentage (.377) for Larry Gardner during ten seasons with the club from 1908-17. He hit only 16 career home runs for Boston during the regular season, playing most of his games in the dead ball era. Gardner did, however, hit a much livelier ball come postseason time—he hit three World Series home runs for Boston, and seven of his 12 postseason hits for the club went for extra-bases.

378 The earned run average (3.78) for Oil Can Boyd in 1986. He was 16-10 for the pennant-winning Red Sox with a better than respectable ERA that was nearly half a point beneath the league average. He also benefitted from some generous run support while visiting Cleveland, where he won two starts by scores of 13-7 and 24-5. It was also in Cleveland where Boyd, after a game was postponed due to fog off Lake Erie, famously said, "That's what you get when you build a stadium by the ocean."

379 Dwight Evans hit (379) home runs for Boston. He hit 20 or more home runs 11 times, including a career high 34 home runs in 1987. His only home run title was during the strike-shortened 1981 season, when he hit 22 in only 108 games. Evans is one of the top 60 home run hitters in baseball history, and his total for Boston is the fourth highest in franchise history.

380 The number of innings (380) for Cy Young in 1904. He led the club with the fifth highest total in the league, but of greater significance is what he did during nine of those innings on May 5, against the Philadelphia Athletics—he pitched the first perfect game of baseball's modern era.

381 Bobby Doerr hit (381) career doubles. He never led the league and was only among the top ten leaders four times—but the Hall of Fame second baseman closed out his career with a total that is among the ten best in franchise history.

382 Jim Rice hit (382) career home runs—the third highest total in franchise history. Rice hit a career high 46 home runs in 1978, and he hit 25 or more home runs seven times. He also won three home run titles, and he ranks among the top 60 home run hitters in baseball history.

383 Tris Speaker hit (.383) in 1912. It was the highest average during seven full seasons in Boston for the Hall of Fame legend, and it remains the third highest average in team history—but it was only the third best in the league that season. Speaker did lead the league with a .464 on-base percentage. He also earned league MVP honors and Boston won the World Series.

384 The slugging percentage (.384) for Doc Cramer in 1940. He led the league with 200 hits, but only 40 went for extra-bases—and only one of those left the yard—as the All-Star outfielder also led the league with 160 singles. His singles total tied a franchise record set by Patsy Dougherty in 1903, and it remains among the top ten totals in franchise history.

385 The winning percentage (.385) for Boston vs. Toronto in 1989. Toronto won the division title by six games over the third place Red Sox, but it was a series in June that changed the course of the season for both clubs. Boston and Toronto met on June 2, with the Red Sox only 2.5 games back of Baltimore and in second place—while the Blue Jays were eight games back and in dead last. Toronto won that day 7-2, won again the next day 10-2, but in the final game of the series at Fenway, Boston took a 10-0 lead after six innings—only to give up two in the seventh, four in the eighth, and five in the ninth. Boston had to rally for a run in the ninth to send the game into extra-innings, but Toronto won 13-11. Boston was 5-8 against Toronto on the season, and though the Red Sox made one last surge in mid-August, it was the Blue Jays who fought their way to the division title.

386 The earned run average (3.86) for Rick Wise in 1974. Wise, Luis Tiant, and Bill Lee were set to anchor the rotation that year as Boston expected to make a strong run for the division title. Wise was effective when he was on the mound—only 47 hits in 49 innings of work—but the problem was he only made nine starts. He was out due to an injured shoulder early in the year, and then just as he was getting things going again his wife accidentally slammed a door on his hand, breaking a finger. His battery mate Carlton Fisk was lost for the season due to injury as well, which just added to the frustration when the team blew a seven-game lead and lost the division.

387 David Ortiz hit (.387) in the 2004 American League Championship Series. He batted 12 for 31, including three home runs. Ortiz hit a walk-off home run to win Game 4 in the twelfth inning, and then he hit a walk-off single to win Game 5 in the fourteenth inning. He hit his third home run of the series in the deciding Game 7—and when Boston became the first team in history to overcome a 3-0 deficit in a best-of-seven series, it was Ortiz who won the series Most Valuable Player Award.

388 Ted Williams hit (.388) in 1957. He won his fifth batting title and earned Major League Player of the Year honors for the fifth time as well—and his average remains the second highest in franchise history.

389 Boston gave up (389) earned runs in 1916. The club gave up just 480 runs total, while scoring 550, and won both the pennant and the 1916 World Series on the strength of pitching. The team leader in wins that season was Babe Ruth. He won 23 games, and he also gave up just 6.40 hits per nine innings he pitched—a ratio that remains one of the ten best in franchise history.

390 The center field fence at Fenway Park is (390) feet from home plate—but that is not the deepest part of the ballpark, because the *deep* center field fence is 420 feet from the plate. Fenway is a unique and beloved structure, and the park itself has contributed much to the storied history of the franchise. It is 310 feet from the home plate that Carlton Fisk first crouched behind to begin his Hall of Fame career to the foul pole alongside the Green Monster in left where his historic home run curled around and into postseason lore—the same pole that the Faithful now call Fisk Pole. The Monster is 37 feet high, but it is only 302 feet from home plate to the foul pole in right that is affectionately dubbed Pesky's Pole—and there the fence is only three feet high. Johnny Pesky only hit six career home runs at Fenway, but one of them was a game-winner that wrapped around that pole, and the rest, as they say, is history.

391 The earned run average (3.91) for Roger Clemens during home starts in 1988. He was only 6-8 at Fenway, but 12-4 with a 2.09 ERA on the road. Clemens did toss three complete game shutouts at Fenway that year, after notching four complete game shutouts at home the previous season. To put into perspective the magnitude of that accomplishment, the next time a pitcher recorded back-to-back seasons with three or more home shutouts was Chris Carpenter, who did it for the Cardinals in 2005-06.

392 The earned run average (3.92) for Dennis Eckersley as a member of the Red Sox. He won 20 games and placed fourth in Cy Young balloting during his first season with the club in 1978, and twice during his tenure in Boston he was among the top seven league leaders in ERA.

393 The on-base percentage (.393) for Dom DiMaggio in 1946. It was not his career high, not by a long shot, but it did place him among the top five league leaders and it contributed to his ninth place finish in league MVP balloting. It was also the only time during his ten full seasons that he received more votes for MVP than did his Hall of Fame brother Joe, who won the award three times for the Yankees, but did not place among the top ten during 1946.

394 The on-base percentage (.394) as members of the Red Sox for Joe Cronin, Rick Ferrell, and Mo Vaughn. Cronin and Ferrell are members of the Baseball Hall of Fame, and Vaughn was one of the most feared sluggers in the game during his tenure with the Red Sox—and all three share an OBP that ranks among the top ten in franchise history.

395 The slugging percentage (.395) for Jim Piersall in 1954. He hit only eight home runs but he made his first All-Star team that season. Piersall is the Red Sox player who suffered from severe psychological issues that were the result of being driven to succeed in baseball—so much so that he was eventually hospitalized for treatment. Piersall wrote a best-selling book titled *Fear Strikes Out* in which he candidly discusses his mental problems—and it was also made into a very successful movie starring Anthony Perkins.

396 The on-base percentage (.396) for Trot Nixon in 2003. That number was seventh best in the league—but only third best on the team. Manny Ramirez and Bill Mueller were one-two for Boston, and first and sixth respectively in the league.

397 The earned run average (3.97) for Curt Schilling in 2006. Schilling led the club in ERA thanks in part to his league best 1.24 walks per nine innings ratio. He gave up just 28 free passes during 204 innings of work, and he posted a 15-7 record.

398 The number of total bases (398) for Hall of Fame legend Jimmie Foxx in 1938. His total set a franchise record that lasted 40 years—and it was also the third and final time he led the league in total bases. Foxx ranks among the top 20 in baseball history with 4,956 career total bases.

399 The number of strikeouts (399) for Carl Mays while pitching for Boston from 1915-19. He was 72-51 prior to becoming a Yankee, including 14 complete game shutouts. His strikeout total was not particularly impressive, but then he didn't give up very many hits either—only 918 in 1,105 innings.

400 Mike Lowell hit (.400) in the 2007 World Series. The All-Star third baseman batted 6 for 15, including three doubles and a home run against the Rockies. He also scored six runs, and when Boston swept the series it was Lowell who got the hardware for series Most Valuable Player.

Boston Red Sox 2004 World Series Roster

- *Terry Francona, Manager*
- *Bronson Arroyo*
- *Alan Embree*
- *Keith Foulke*
- *Curtis Leskanic*
- *Derek Lowe*
- *Pedro Martinez*
- *Mike Myers*
- *Curt Schilling*
- *Mike Timlin*
- *Tim Wakefield*
- *Doug Mirabelli*
- *Jason Varitek*
- *Mark Bellhorn*
- *Orlando Cabrera*
- *Doug Mientkiewicz*
- *Bill Mueller*
- *David Ortiz*
- *Pokey Reese*
- *Kevin Youkilis*
- *Johnny Damon*
- *Gabe Kapler*
- *Kevin Millar*
- *Trot Nixon*
- *Manny Ramirez, World Series MVP*
- *Dave Roberts*

"It's so exciting to be part of one. Each one is so different. Just let him enjoy the moment—it was his moment."
— *Jason Varitek, after catching Jon Lester's no-hitter on May 19, 2008*

Chapter 5

Defining Moments

IN BASEBALL, OFTEN a single moment can define an entire career: think Bobby Thomson, Don Larsen, Bill Mazeroski, or Joe Carter. Boston's own history, of course, is full of similar moments: think Carlton Fisk, Bucky Dent, Bill Buckner, or Aaron Boone. This chapter is all about defining moments—events that change the player, team, and fans . . . forever.

Boston did the unthinkable in the 2004 postseason.

Yes, they rallied past the Yankees.

Yes, they won the World Series.

And yes, they exorcised 86 years of demons—but as noted author and Boston fan Stephen King wrote of his experiences following the Red Sox that season, "This is not a dream."

It was real!

Boston fans dreamed of such a triumph for generations, but they never dared to imagine such a dream could become reality. Johnny Pesky said, "We got 'em now." When did he say that? Right before the ball went through Buckner's legs in 1986. Rich Gedman was the catcher for Boston during the 1986 World Series. His wife could be seen on TV, sitting in the stands at Shea during Game 6 with Boston one out from victory—but she could not bear to look because, after all, this is Boston we're talking about.

Well, the 2004 Boston Red Sox changed everything—and what a moment it was.

Sports Illustrated managing editor Terry McDonell said, "We are naming the Red Sox the Sportsmen of the Year because of the way they underline the connection between a team, a franchise, a town, and the fans. Every Sox fan everywhere shares in this with the team."

Bronson Arroyo was a part of the 2004 team. He is in chapter five for a defining moment that many believe is responsible for reshaping the attitude of the club into something that could compete in the postseason. What was it?

A single pitch is all.

One that plunked Yankees' third baseman Alex Rodriguez, setting off a brawl between A-Rod and Red Sox catcher Jason Varitek—one that fired up the club, and led to a sizzling record in the Dog Days of August.

Ted Williams is also in this chapter for his performance on the season's final day in 1941. You already know he went 6 for 8 in a doubleheader to bat .406, but in this chapter you will find out what he "really hit" that season.

Tim Wakefield is here. He won 16 games in 2005, including a milestone win on August 2—and to find out what that milestone was, keep reading.

On September 18, 1996, only 8,997 fans were in Detroit to see the Tigers take on the Red Sox. Roger Clemens struck out 20 batters that night, tying the major league record he set a decade earlier. It was a defining moment for his career to be sure, but it was also a defining moment for GM Dan Duquette, who thought Clemens' career was over and did not resign him in the off-season. That victory was the last of his Red Sox career, and it was also number 192, tying him with Cy Young for the franchise record. Duquette was wrong about him, of course, seeing as Clemens won four additional Cy Young Awards after leaving Boston.

Dave Henderson was a teammate of the Rocket back in 1986, and with one swing of the bat in the postseason he defined his career and saved the team long enough for Bill Buckner to have his career defining moment... polar opposite moments, of course.

Tek is also here.

Boston's leader, he called his fourth career no-hitter in 2008. Can you name the four pitchers who threw them?

And the fans are here too.

What prompted "Thank You Fans" to be flashed on the center field scoreboard as Red Sox owners, management, and players greeted fans entering Fenway Park?

It's all here in the fifth...

401 The on-base percentage (.401) for infielder Pete Runnels in 1960. He led the club with the third highest on-base percentage in the league, and he won his first career batting title after hitting .320 on the season. Runnels also led the club with 169 hits—nine of which came on August 30, when he tied a major league record for most hits during a doubleheader. He got six hits in the first game, and three in the second.

402 The number of extra-base hits (402) for Carlton Fisk from 1971-79. His most famous extra-base hit, of course, came in the postseason—but Pudge cracked the top ten league leaders twice while playing for Boston, and his career total of 844 extra-base hits ranks among the top 100 in baseball history. His total with Boston is among the top 25 in franchise history.

403 The earned run average (4.03) for Bronson Arroyo in 2004. He was 10-9, but in four starts vs. New York he got knocked around pretty good—posting a 5.25 ERA, though escaping with four no-decisions. It was a pitch Arroyo made against Yankees' superstar Alex Rodriguez, however, that many believe turned Boston's season around. On July 24, he gave up ten hits and eight runs in five-plus innings of work against New York, but he also drilled Rodriguez with a pitch in the third inning that set off a brawl between catcher Jason Varitek and Rodriguez. That brawl fired up the club, and in the ninth Bill Mueller hit a walk-off home run against Mariano Rivera to cap a three-run rally—and Boston stayed fired up, winning 21 games in August to get back into the hunt for October.

404 The number of extra-base hits (404) for John Valentin from 1992-2001. The Red Sox infielder from Seton Hall cracked the top ten league leaders in doubles four times, and led the league with 47 doubles in 1997. He was among the top ten league leaders in extra-base hits twice, and his career total is among the top 25 in franchise history.

405 The ratio (4.05) of strikeouts per walk for Cy Young in 1908. It was the last season in Boston for the Hall of Fame legend, and he struck out 150 batters while giving up just 37 free passes. Young led the league in this category 11 times previously, but his ratio in 1908 was only the third best, although it remains among the top 20 in franchise history. Incidentally, it is the lowest of the *six* ratios Young holds that are among Boston's top 20.

406 Ted Williams hit (.406) in 1941 to win his first batting title and set a franchise record—but the way he went about hitting .406 is part of what makes him such an iconic legend. He began play on the final day of the season with a .39955 average. He could easily have sat out a doubleheader against Philadelphia, but Williams never took the easy way out of anything. He played both games and batted 6 for 8 with a home run to become the last player of the 20th century to hit .400 for an entire season. Al Hirshberg of the *Boston Post* wrote, "Give credit to the Kid, he did it the hard way."

407 The number of runs (407) Pete Runnels scored during five seasons from 1958-62. He was a two-time batting champion with the club, and twice he was among the league's top ten leaders in runs. Runnels led the team with 103 runs in 1958, and his career total with the club ranks among the top 50 in franchise history.

408 The on-base percentage (.408) as a member of the Red Sox for Pete Runnels. He was a three-time All-Star during five seasons in Boston, during which time he also placed among the top five league leaders in OBP four times, and he posted one of the ten best marks in franchise history.

409 The batting average (.409) for Julio Lugo with the bases loaded in 2007. He was 9 for 22 and hit one grand slam—but his biggest bases juiced hit was just a routine single in appearance, but it was monumental in terms of its impact. Lugo and the Red Sox trailed Baltimore 5-0 in the bottom of the ninth on May 13. Lugo hit a weak groundout to start the inning, but an error, double, single, walk, walk, double, walk, and groundout later, Lugo was back up with the bases full, two outs, and the Red Sox down 5-4. He delivered a two-run walk-off single that kept the Red Sox rolling early in the season. That entire inning was a rare feat, as Boston had last won a game in which they trailed by at least 5-0 as late as the seventh inning back in 1984.

410 Boston gave up on average (4.10) runs per game in 2002. Pedro Martinez, Derek Lowe, and Tim Wakefield were directly responsible for that average, which was the third lowest in the league, as the big three Boston hurlers placed first, second, and fourth respectively among league leaders in earned run average.

411 Ted Williams actually batted (.411) in 1941. That season a new rule counted sacrifice flies as official at bats—and Williams hit six sacrifice flies that year, which brought his average down .005 points. He is the only .400 hitter in history who was forced to play under that rule, prompting his manager Joe Cronin to say, "If there's ever a ballplayer who deserved to hit .400, it's Ted . . . He wouldn't think of getting out of the lineup to keep his average intact. Moreover, most of the other stars who have bettered the mark before were helped by no foul strike rules or sacrifice fly regulations."

412 The number of at bats (412) for Dwight Evans in 1981. He got three hits during five at bats on the last day of the season—and two of them left the yard, including one in his final at bat. The pair of home runs gave him 22 during the strike-shortened season and a share of the league home run title with three other players: Tony Armas, Bobby Grich, and Eddie Murray. Murray also hit a home run on the last day of the season.

413 Freddy Parent played in the first (413) games in franchise history. He was the starting shortstop when the club opened play as the Boston Americans on April 26, 1901, and he played every game until September 25, 1903. He also was the starting shortstop when Boston won the first ever World Series in 1903. Parent was the last surviving player from the 1903 World Series at the time of his death on November 2, 1972.

414 The on-base percentage (.414) as a member of the Red Sox for Tris Speaker. He is among the top 15 in baseball history for career on-base percentage, but the Hall of Fame legend is among the top five in franchise history for the number he posted during his tenure with the club.

415 The earned run average (4.15) for Tim Wakefield in 2005. That number led the club, as did his 16 victories—one of which was a milestone for him on August 2. He beat the Royals 6-4 to pass Mel Parnell for third place in the franchise record book with career win number 124. Wakefield said afterwards, "I'm truly honored and blessed to be mentioned with Cy and Roger and Mel Parnell and Luis Tiant and those guys. I owe it to all of my teammates, not only the guys I'm playing with this year but to the 350-plus guys I played with my whole career here."

416 The on-base percentage (.416) for Mike Greenwell in 1988. He was third in the batting title race with a .325 average—but he was only second on the club, because his teammate Wade Boggs won that race with a .366 average. Greenwell was second in the league in OBP, but again, he did not even lead the team because it was Boggs who beat him with a .476 OBP.

417 The on-base percentage (.417) for Dwight Evans in 1987. Dewey hit .305, and his OBP was a career high and the third highest in the league.

418 The on-base percentage (.418) for Nomar Garciaparra in 1999. That led the club and placed Nomar among the top ten league leaders as well—but despite winning the batting title, slugging 27 home runs, and picking up 104 RBI, Nomar placed only seventh in MVP balloting.

419 Fred Lynn hit (.419) in 1974. He was a 22-year-old outfielder who got a cup of coffee with the big club—15 games, 43 at bats—and he used it exceptionally well. Six of his 18 hits went for extra-bases, and he gave the Fenway Faithful a glimpse of the immediate future. Lynn hit .300 or better four times in six seasons with Boston—and he ranks among the top 15 in franchise history with a .308 career average with the club.

420 Mo Vaughn posted a career high (.420) on-base percentage in 1996. He did it on the strength of 207 hits—a total that ties him with Johnny Pesky (1947) and Wade Boggs (1986) for one of the ten highest in franchise history. Vaughn also hit 44 home runs. Only eight of the 207 hits for Boggs left the yard in 1986—and Pesky, who hit only 17 career home runs, did not have any in 1947.

421 The earned run average (4.21) for Willard Nixon in 1956. Boston placed a distant fourth behind the pennant-winning Yankees, and New York was also the highest scoring team in the league by a large margin—but none of that mattered to Nixon on August 7, 1956. He was only 9-8 (though with a respectable ERA), but on that particular day he was brilliant as he tossed 11 innings at Fenway Park for a complete game 1-0 shutout against the high-powered Yankees.

422 Wade Boggs hit (422) doubles for Boston. He used the Green Monster with the efficiency of a finely tuned machine, which many would argue is exactly what Boggs was when he put on his spikes. He led the league in doubles twice and was among the top four leaders eight times as a member of the Red Sox. His 578 career doubles ranks among the top 20 totals in baseball history, and the 422 he hit for Boston ranks among the top five in franchise history.

423 The number of at bats (42.3) per strikeout for Stuffy McInnis in 1918. McInnis struck out only ten times in 423 at bats, breaking the franchise record ratio of 39.1 at bats per strikeout set by Tris Speaker in 1915. McInnis' ratio from 1918 is now the fifth best in franchise history—but he still owns the top spot after setting a new record in 1921.

424 The on-base percentage (.424) for Hall of Fame legend Eddie Collins. His career mark is among the top 15 in baseball history—and he was among the top ten league leaders every season from 1909-26. Collins picked up 3,315 career hits, won six pennants, and four World Series titles. He never played for Boston—but he was both a winner and a respected baseball man, so when Tom Yawkey bought the struggling Red Sox franchise in 1933 his first move was to hire Collins to be his Vice President and General Manager. Boston fans were encouraged for the first time in years when Yawkey said, "I don't intend to mess around with a loser."

425 The number of earned runs (425) Ray Culp gave up while pitching for Boston from 1968-73. Boston got him from the Cubs at the perfect time—that, or joining the club made him better. The most productive stretch of his career began in 1968, when he posted a 16-6 record for the second best winning percentage in the league. Culp won 17, 17, and 14 games the next three seasons. In six seasons total he posted a 71-58 record and a 3.50 earned run average, while pitching nearly 1,100 innings.

426 The slugging percentage (.426) for Bobby Doerr in 1947. It was his lowest slugging percentage in a decade, but it was still good enough for the tenth highest number in the league—and his 50 extra-base hits were also among the top ten league leaders. There were some teams that thought his bat speed might be slowing down—but the White Sox probably disagreed. On May 13, Doerr lit up Chicago as he hit for the cycle for the second time in his career, and led the Red Sox to a 19-6 victory.

427 The on-base percentage (.427) for Manny Ramirez in 2003. The slugger led the club with 37 home runs, but he also hit .325 and led the club in OBP. Manny got on base 290 times, the second highest total in the league behind Carlos Delgado of the Toronto Blue Jays.

428 The on-base percentage (.428) as a member of the Red Sox for Wade Boggs. His career on-base percentage is among the top 30 in baseball history—but during his tenure with the Red Sox he led the league six times and posted the third highest number in franchise history.

429 The on-base percentage (.429) as a member of the Red Sox for Jimmie Foxx. His career on-base percentage is among the top 15 in baseball history—but the Hall of Fame slugger posted the second highest on-base percentage in franchise history. Foxx led the league in on-base percentage three times during his career, two of which were for the Red Sox.

430 Boston gave up (430) walks in 2002—the second lowest total among 14 teams in the league. Boston also gave up 1,339 hits for a total that was the lowest in the league. With a staff that good, seeing Red Sox hurlers on top of the league leader boards at the end of the season was not a surprise—but seeing three of them take the top three spots for one category was a pretty rare feat. The top three league leaders in walks plus hits per innings pitched (WHIP) from

2002: Pedro Martinez (.923), Derek Lowe (.974), and Tim Wakefield (1.053).

431 The earned run average (4.31) for David Cone in 2001. He was just 9-7 during his one season in Boston. Cone, who once tossed a perfect game for New York, gave his best performance for Boston during a game in which the man who replaced him in the Bronx was nearly perfect at Fenway. On September 2, 2001, Boston was riding a seven-game losing streak that took them out of contention for the division title when Cone and Mike Mussina took to the mound. Cone pitched scoreless ball into the ninth before giving up an unearned run. Mussina was perfect with two outs in the ninth, 13 strikeouts in the book, and two strikes on pinch-hitter Carl Everett—who lined a single to left. Boston still suffered their longest losing streak of the season at the worst possible time—nine games from August 25, through September 4—and finished the season a distant 13.5 games back of New York.

432 The number of pages (432) in *Faithful*. Best-selling authors and self-proclaimed die-hard Red Sox fans Stephen King and Stewart O'Nan collaborated to document the 2004 season—and by sheer coincidence they picked the perfect year to do so. King penned these words in conclusion, "This is not a dream. We are living real life."

433 The slugging percentage (.433) for Marty Barrett during the 1986 American League Championship Series. He hit .367 in the series, picking up 11 hits and scoring four runs. Barrett and the Red Sox rallied from a three games to one deficit vs. California to win the pennant, and it was Barrett who won series MVP honors.

434 On August 19, 2008, Jason Varitek hit a home run in a 7-2 victory vs. Baltimore for career extra-base hit number (434)—a blast that moved him ahead of Joe Cronin and into the top 15 in the franchise record book. The night before Varitek had hit a home run in a 6-3 victory vs. Baltimore to tie Cronin with 433 extra-base hits.

435 The winning percentage (.435) for Roger Clemens in 1996. On September 18, as his tenure in Boston was coming to an end, Clemens took the mound against the Tigers in Detroit with just 8,997 fans in attendance—but boy did they get a show. Clemens tossed a five-hit shutout and notched 20 strikeouts for the second time in his career. Clemens later said, "I knew I had it in the upper teens. I didn't know I was approaching 20." He was only 10-13 on the season, however, prompting GM Dan Duquette to infamously predict that Clemens was in the "twilight of his career." Boston did not resign Clemens, and the

Rocket went on to win four more Cy Young Awards and two World Series titles.

436 The slugging percentage (.436) for Boston in 1980. That was the second highest among 14 clubs. Tony Perez led the team with 25 home runs, Jim Rice hit 24, and the team total of 162 was the third highest in the league. That was the good news—but the bad news was the club couldn't pitch. The staff earned run average was 11th highest in the league—a stat that cost skipper Don Zimmer his job before the season was over.

437 The on-base percentage (.437) for Johnny Pesky in 1950. His career high number was also the third best in the league—and the .401 OBP that he posted during seven-plus seasons with the club is among the ten best in franchise history.

438 Jacoby Ellsbury hit (.438) in the 2007 World Series. He was a 23-year-old rookie with only 33 games under his belt at the major league level—but he batted 7 for 16 against the Rockies, picked up four doubles, scored four runs, and got a ring.

439 Dustin Pedroia hit (.439) during a stretch of 26 games beginning June 14, 2008. He got 50 hits in those games, becoming just the fourth Red Sox player since 1940 to get that many hits over a span of 26 games or less: Lou Finney (1940), Dom DiMaggio (1951), and Wade Boggs (1985) were the others.

440 The number of RBI (440) for Vern Stephens from 1948-50. It was easily the most prolific stretch of seasons for Stephens, a shortstop who spent five years in Boston. He was second in the league with 137 RBI in 1948, but in 1949 he led the league with 159 RBI, and in 1950 he led the league with 144 RBI. The intriguing part is that both of his league leading totals are among the ten best in franchise history—but in both cases he was matched equally by one of his teammates in those same seasons: Ted Williams (159 RBI in 1949), and Walt Dropo (144 RBI in 1950).

441 The number of runs (441) Tony Conigliaro scored for Boston. Conigliaro's total with the club still ranks among the top 50 in franchise history. His seven seasons spanned 1964-75, and 162 times he drove himself home with the long ball.

442 Johnny Damon hit a home run every (44.2) at bats for Boston from 2002-05. He posted season totals of 14, 12, 20, and ten—plus he added four more in the postseason—and despite being a leadoff guy his at bats per home run ratio is among the top 50 in franchise history.

443 The number of extra-base hits (443) for Mike Greenwell. He made his debut in 1985, but did not play fulltime until 1987, and he only played seven seasons of at least 100 games. He could flat hit, however, and when he was on the field he was a game-changing kind of player. Three times he was among the top ten league leaders in doubles, once for extra-base hits, and once for total bases—but his extra-base hits total ranks among the top 15 in franchise history.

444 The slugging percentage (.444) for Dave Henderson during the 1986 American League Championship Series. He hit only .111 in the series, but that lone hit came in the ninth inning of Game 5, and it was a dramatic two-out, two-strike, two-run home run against Angels' reliever Donnie Moore that kept the Red Sox pennant hopes alive. Michael Madden wrote in the *Boston Globe*, "It was a game for the Valium pouch and psychiatrist's couch." Dan Shaughnessy added, "The Red Sox didn't need a plane to fly home last night."

445 The on-base percentage (.445) for David Ortiz in 2007. The Boston slugger continued his dominance over opposing pitchers by posting the highest on-base percentage in the league.

446 The number of runs (446) Ellis Burks scored for Boston. Burks was a first-round draft choice of the Red Sox in 1983. He scored 94 runs as a rookie in only 133 games in 1987, but never reached that total again for Boston. After leaving the club as a free agent Burks became a star in Colorado where he led the N.L. with 142 runs in 1996.

447 Jon Lester, Clay Buchholz, Derek Lowe, and Hideo Nomo combined to throw (447) pitches to catcher Jason Varitek during their no-hit games. Nomo (105 pitches) was the first no-hit game caught by Varitek, Lowe (97) the second, Buchholz (115) the third, and Lester (130), on May 19, 2008, was the fourth—making Tek the first catcher in history to call four no-hitters.

448 The number of extra-base hits (448) for Jimmie Foxx during six-plus seasons with Boston from 1936-42. He cracked the top ten league leaders in extra-base hits five times during that stretch, and his total with the club is among the top 15 in franchise history. Foxx abused major league pitchers for 1,117 extra-base hits during his career—a total that is among the top 15 in baseball history.

449 The slugging percentage (.449) for third baseman Larry Gardner in 1912. Only 45 of his 163 hits went for extra-bases that season—but of those, a team high 18 went for three bases. Gardner, who was a native of Vermont, also won three World Series titles for Boston, and a fourth while playing for Cleveland—earning him the distinction of having more championships than any player in history who hails from the Green Mountain State.

450 The earned run average (4.50) for Joe Wood during the 1912 World Series. Hall of Fame legend Christy Mathewson posted a 0.94 ERA for the Giants, giving up just three earned runs in 28-plus innings of work against Boston. Wood gave up 11 earned runs in 22 innings of work against New York—but it was Wood who posted a 3-1 record for the world champion Red Sox, and Mathewson was 0-2 for the Giants.

451 The winning percentage (.451) for Boston in 1992. The club never led the division and never won more than four games in a row all season. Boston scored the second lowest run total in the league and was shutout 13 times, came in 18 games below .500, and placed 23 games back of the Blue Jays at season's end. Fans knew they were in for a long year when Matt Young tossed a no-hitter vs. Cleveland during the fourth game of the season—but lost the decision by a score of 2-1. Young later said, "No-hitters are supposed to be when you strikeout the last guy and your catcher comes out and you jump around—this is like being in purgatory."

452 Carl Yastrzemski hit (452) career home runs. Yaz hit 20 or more home runs only eight times, but he is one of the top 40 home run hitters in baseball history, with a career total that is the second highest in franchise history.

453 The on-base percentage (.453) for Wade Boggs in 1986. It was the second consecutive season he led the league OBP, and he would go on to post the best mark in the league for five consecutive seasons from 1985-89. Boggs also batted .357 in 1986 as the Red Sox won the pennant and he took home his third career batting title.

454 The number of times (454) Trot Nixon walked from 1996-2006. That total is among the top 25 in franchise history, and it contributed to his career .366 on-base percentage that also ranks among Boston's top 25.

455 The slugging percentage (.455) for Ellis Burks during parts of seven seasons with Boston from 1987-2004. His first six seasons were in Boston, during which time he hit 93 of his 352 career home runs. Burks came back home for 11 games in 2004—and hit the final home run of his career as a member of the Red Sox. His career slugging percentage for Boston ranks among the top 30 in franchise history.

456 Boston celebrated (456) consecutive sellouts at Fenway Park on September 8, 2008. Boston's streak eclipsed the mark set by the Cleveland Indians at Jacobs Field on April 2, 2001, and set a new major league record. To commemorate the event Red Sox owners John Henry and Tom Werner, team president Larry Lucchino, former player Johnny Pesky, and current players Tim Wakefield and Mike Timlin greeted fans as they entered the ballpark. Three fans also were selected to throw out ceremonial first pitches, with Wakefield, Timlin, and David Ortiz catching them. "Thank You Fans" was flashed on the center field scoreboard when Boston took the field in the top of the first, and the home team gave the Fenway Faithful a 3-0 victory over the Tampa Bay Rays to cap off the evening.

457 The number of career at bats (457) for Marv Olson. He was a middle infielder of slight stature who made it to the big leagues for parts of three seasons from 1931-33, all of them for Boston. He got to play, and though he hit just .241 in those at bats—and never hit a home run—he is a part of franchise history because he took the field wearing a Red Sox uni. Olson never achieved stardom as a player, but when baseball is in your blood you stay with the game. He later became a highly successful minor league manager, and eventually scouted for the Minnesota Twins for more than two decades.

458 The earned run average (4.58) for Bill Monbouquette after 22 starts during the 1962 season. The three-time All-Star, who is also a member of the Red Sox Hall of Fame, was only 8-10 when he took the mound against the White Sox on August 1, 1962, in his 23rd start of the season—but he got hot in a hurry. He tossed a no-hitter, missing a perfect game by a single walk, and led Boston to a 1-0 victory. His ERA improved to 4.29 after the game, but only got better from there. His hot-hand continued, and he closed out the season with a 15-13 record and a 3.33 ERA.

459 The slugging percentage (.459) for Troy O'Leary from 1995-2001. His best season was 1999, when he posted a career high .495 slugging percentage on the strength of 28 home runs. O'Leary was a solid player who contributed a great deal to Boston's resurgence as both a postseason mainstay and a force to be reckoned with in October—but unfortunately he was not there to get a ring. His career slugging percentage with the club remains among the top 30 in franchise history.

460 The minor league slugging percentage (.460) for outfielder Brandon Moss from 2002-08. Moss began 2008 with the big club in Tokyo, and he made a big impact on opening day. He was 2 for 5, including a game-tying home run that was the first of his career in the ninth inning against Oakland closer Huston Street. Boston won the game in extra-innings when Manny Ramirez hit a two-run double. Moss became just the second rookie in baseball history to hit an opening day home run for a team that was the defending World Series champion—the other was Carlos Delgado, for the Blue Jays in 1994—but neither Moss nor Manny were with Boston when the season ended. Moss went to Pittsburgh in the deal that shipped Manny to LA and Jason Bay to Boston.

461 Otis Nixon made (461) plate appearances for Boston in 1994—his only season with the club. The speedster, who was a first-round draft pick by the Yankees in 1979, played only 103 games for the Red Sox, but he led the club and was second in the league with 42 steals. That total is tied with Tris Speaker for one of the top five in franchise history.

462 Bill Dinneen posted a (.462) winning percentage after struggling to a 12-14 record in 1905. It was a disappointing year, especially considering he won 20 or more games four times in the previous five seasons. Dinneen did not disappoint in his start against the White Sox on September 27, however, as he tossed a complete game no-hit shutout. His gem came in the first game of a doubleheader, and in the second game the White Sox erupted for 15 runs—against Cy Young, no less. Chicago outscored Boston that day 15-3, but had to settle for a split of the two games.

463 The number of at bats (463) for Dwight Evans in 1974. He used them to hit a career high eight triples, a number he needed 630 at bats to equal in 1984. Dewey hit 73 triples during his career—all but one of them for the Red Sox—and his total with the club is among the ten best in franchise history.

464 The winning percentage (.464) for Cleveland pitcher Rick Waits in 1978. He was 13-15 on the season, but the Red Sox were especially grateful that Waits earned victory number 13—as it came vs. New York on the final day of the season. That loss for New York, combined with Boston's win over Toronto, gave the Red Sox new life as it forced a one-game playoff for the division title. On the Fenway scoreboard that day, these words: "Thank You, Rick Waits."

465 The winning percentage (.465) for Boston during one-run games in 2000. Boston was only 20-23 during games decided by a single run—which hurt, because at season's end they were 2.5 back of New York for the A.L. East title.

466 The slugging percentage (.466) for Tony Perez in 1975. He was the powerful first baseman on the Big Red Machine who hit three home runs against Boston during the 1975 World Series. Boston pitcher Bill Lee held a 3-0 lead in the sixth inning of Game 7 when Perez hit a two-run blast to get the Reds' offense going. Lee later wrote, "I had been having good success with Tony, throwing him my slow, arching curveball, so I thought it would be a good idea to throw it to him again. Unfortunately, so did Tony, who timed it beautifully. He counted the seams of the ball as it floated up to the plate, checked to see if Lee MacPhail's signature was on it, signed his own name to it, and then jumped all over it."

467 Josh Beckett's earned run average climbed to (4.67) after he gave up six earned runs at home vs. Milwaukee on May 18, 2008. He also gave up four home runs in the game, but Boston also hit four home runs and Beckett still got the win, 11-7, improving his season record to 5-3. It was the sixth time in Fenway history that both teams hit at least four home runs—but it was the first time since Jose Santiago on May 14, 1967, that a Red Sox starter gave up four home runs at home and still won the game.

468 The number of games (468) for speedster Darren Lewis for Boston from 1998-2001. He hit just .256 for the club, but in his first season in Boston he led the team with 29 steals and scored 95 runs. His play declined over his next three seasons, but after only four years and 468 games he amassed enough steals to rank among the top 35 in franchise history.

469 The number of extra-base hits (469) for Rico Petrocelli. He cracked the top ten league leaders in extra-base hits only three times, but his career total is among Boston's ten best.

470 The number of times (470) Wade Boggs struck out for Boston. To give you an idea of how tough it was to strikeout Boggs, he is seventh in franchise history for career at bats—but only 22nd for strikeouts. Boggs was among the ten toughest strikeouts in the league eight times from 1982-92, and he never struck out more times in a season than he walked while playing for Boston.

471 The winning percentage (.471) for Boston in 1920. On January 9, 1920, Yankees' owner Jacob Ruppert held a press conference in New York where he announced, "Gentlemen, we have just bought Babe Ruth from Harry Frazee of the Boston Red Sox." Frazee, who was not really a baseball man and was terribly unpopular with Red Sox fans already, lamely suggested to the Boston media that Ruth's home run record in 1919 was ". . . more spectacular than useful. They didn't help get the Red Sox out of sixth place." Ruth hit 54 home runs in 1920 for New York, and the Yankees drew a record 1,289,422 fans to the ballpark while Boston suffered through a 72-81 campaign that was witnessed by 402,445 disappointed fans.

472 The slugging percentage (.472) for Trot Nixon in 1999. He was a rookie who hit 15 home runs in 381 at bats—but on July 24, Nixon led Boston to an 11-4 victory vs. Detroit by hitting three bombs with five RBI from the nine spot in the lineup. Boston hit seven homers in the game, including one by fellow rookie Brian Daubach. Boston's four home runs hit by rookies tied a major league record done many times—but it was broken when the Florida Marlins hit five rookie home runs on September 11, 2006.

473 The slugging percentage (.473) for Dwight Evans from 1972-90. He got 925 extra-base hits for Boston, and his career slugging percentage with the club ranks him among the top 20 in franchise history—ahead of big names like Greenwell, Boggs, Yaz, Doerr, Scott, and DiMaggio.

474 Dwight Evans hit (474) doubles for the Red Sox. He never led the league in doubles and was only among the top ten leaders five times—but Dewey closed out his career with the third highest total in franchise history.

475 The number of times (475) Boston walked in 1980. One of the many factors that contributed to Don Zimmer's downfall was a club that hit a lot of home runs but struggled to get on base otherwise. The walk total was the tenth lowest out of 14 teams—but they struck out the ninth highest number of times. On the flipside, Boston's pitchers issued the fifth highest walks total while striking out fewer batters than all but two teams in the league. In the end, the offense was only the sixth highest scoring in the league despite being third in home runs and third in average—and the pitching staff gave up the 11th highest number of runs, which spelled disaster for the fifth place club.

476 The on-base percentage (.476) for Wade Boggs in 1988. It was the fifth time he led the league in on-base percentage, and he did so with a career high number. Boggs also entered the franchise record book with the tenth highest on-base percentage in team history—but the only player who posted a higher on-base percentage for a season than Boggs was Ted Williams, who owns spots one through nine in the franchise record book.

477 The slugging percentage (.477) for Johnny Damon in 2004. He hit 20 home runs from the leadoff spot, but his best slugging came in the postseason when the club benefited from it the most. Damon hit a grand slam and a two-run homer in Game 7 of the League Championship Series against the Yankees—and then he posted a .619 slugging percentage against the Cardinals in the World Series. Damon led off Game 4 with a home run again Jason Marquis—and that was the only run Boston would need to complete the sweep in a 3-0 victory. Only 16 times previously had a batter led off a World Series game with a home run.

478 The number of at bats (478) for Carlton Fisk in 1980. He hit .289 and posted good power numbers—but Red Sox fans were heartbroken in the off-season when GM Haywood Sullivan neglected to mail Fisk his contract by the obligatory December 31 deadline. That snafu made Fisk a de-facto free agent, and he left the club to sign with the Chicago White Sox.

479 The on-base percentage (.479) for Ted Williams in 1956. It was the tenth time he led the league in OBP, but it was only the ninth highest OBP of his career.

480 The slugging percentage (.480) for Carlton Fisk during the 1975 World Series. He hit only .240, but no one remembers that—everyone does recall the image of Fisk willing his hooking drive to stay fair in the twelfth inning of Game 6, and of course it did. Fisk came to bat at 12:34 a.m. against Pat Darcy, and the image of what he did is one of the most recognizable in sports history—not just baseball. Peter Gammons wrote of that moment in the *Boston Globe*, saying, "And all of a sudden the ball was there, like the Mystic River Bridge, suspended out in the black of the morning."

481 The slugging percentage (.481) for second baseman Dustin Pedroia after hitting a grand slam in Boston's 11-3 victory over New York at Yankee Stadium on August 27, 2008. Tris Speaker hit the first grand slam in Yankee Stadium history while playing for the Indians on June 9, 1923, after only 18 games played at the venue. Pedroia hit his with only 14 games left in the old Yankee Stadium, giving Boston 17 grand slams in Babe's House—the most of any visiting franchise—but it was also a decisive blow that for all intents and purposes removed any lingering hope for New York to make the postseason, which made it especially sweet. Pedroia's blast came in game number 132 for Boston, but it was his fifth homer in ten games—raising his slugging percentage to its highest level of the season since April 24.

482 The on-base percentage (.482) for Ted Williams. His career OBP and the 12 times he led the league in OBP are both major league records.

483 The slugging percentage (.483) for Bernie Carbo in 1975. He hit only 96 home runs in his career, but he hit 15 in limited action (only 319 at bats) for Boston in 1975. When Boston won the pennant it gave Carbo a second shot at the Fall Classic, and anything would be an improvement over his performance for Cincinnati in 1970 (0 for 8, three strikeouts). He definitely outdid himself—posting a staggering 1.429 slugging percentage after hitting not one, but two dramatic pinch-hit home runs against his former club. The second home run sent Game 6 into extra-innings, and teammate Rick Wise later said, "Bernie Carbo has never been given the credit for that homer—after fighting off pitches and barely staying alive there, he put us in the position to win."

484 The slugging percentage (.484) for Freddy Parent during the 1903 World Series. He was Boston's starting shortstop during the first World Series in baseball history—and he hit .290 with three triples during the eight-game series against Pittsburgh. He also scored eight runs as Boston won the series, a total that stood as the World Series record until Babe Ruth scored nine runs during the 1928 World Series.

485 The number of runs (485) Smoky Joe Wood gave up during eight seasons pitching for Boston. Only 313 of those runs were earned, but he was on the mound for 1,418 innings—and his 1.99 earned run average for the club is a franchise record.

486 The winning percentage (.486) for Cy Young in 1905. He was only 18-19, but he completed 31 of 33 starts and he also earned a decision in 37 of 38 games (he made five relief appearances). Young gave up 248 hits that season—but he also faced 1,238 batters, striking out 210 but issuing only 30 walks in 320-plus innings of work. That gave him an astounding ratio of .867 walks plus hits per innings pitched—one which stood as the franchise record until Pedro Martinez broke it in 2000.

487 The number of at bats (487) for Olaf Henriksen from 1911-17. He was a seldom used outfielder who hit just one career home run, although he did post exceptionally high on-base percentages when he got into games—posting a .392 OBP for his career. Henriksen was the first Danish born player in the major leagues and by our accounting the only one to play for Boston. Among his notable achievements are three World Series titles with Boston (1912, 1915, and 1916) and he was once used as a pinch-hitter for none other than Babe Ruth.

488 The slugging percentage (.488) as members of the Red Sox for Tony Conigliaro and Brian Daubach. Conigliaro was among the top ten league leaders in slugging three times for Boston, and Daubach posted four consecutive 20 home run seasons for the club from 1999-2002.

489 The number of at bats (489) for Reggie Jefferson in 1997. He got a career high 156 hits that season and led the club with a .319 average that was eighth best in the league.

490 The on-base percentage (.490) for Ted Williams in 1949. It was the fourth consecutive season that he led the league in OBP after returning from the war, and he also earned his second MVP in four seasons.

491 The slugging percentage (.491) for Boston in 2003. That number was the best in the league thanks to a franchise record 238 home runs. The Red Sox offense dominated opposing pitchers and led the league in several other categories as well: runs (961), hits (1,667), doubles (371), RBI (932), batting average (.289), and on-base percentage (.360).

492 The slugging percentage (.492) as a member of the Red Sox for Vern Stephens. In five seasons he was among the top five league leaders in home runs and extra-base hits three times, and his slugging percentage for Boston ranks among the top ten in franchise history.

493 The number of walks (493) Boston pitchers gave up in 1983 and again in 1988. In 1983 it was the seventh highest total among 14 teams in the league, and the club placed just sixth in the division. In 1988 it was the sixth highest total among 14 teams in the league, but the club won the division. So what made the difference? Could be the strikeout totals—in 1983 the club fanned only 758 batters for the tenth lowest total in the league, but in 1988 Boston pitchers struck out a league high 1,085 batters. Give credit to the 1988 offense as well—the club was first in the league in receiving walks, but also struck out fewer times than any other team in the league.

494 The winning percentage (.494) for Al Nipper from 1983-87. He was seventh in Rookie of the Year balloting during his first full season of 1984, when he posted an 11-6 record—but unfortunately that was his only winning season with the club. He was 42-43 overall during parts of five seasons—and Red Sox Faithful also remember Nipper for losing Game 4 of the 1986 World Series (though in that game he did not pitch bad), and for also giving up the Darryl Strawberry eighth inning home run that put away Game 7.

495 The number of runs (495) Larry Gardner scored from 1908-17. His best season total for Boston was 88 in 1912, and his career total is among the top 35 in franchise history. The most important runs he scored for Boston came in the postseason, however, as Gardner scored eight times in World Series play and won three titles: 1912, 1915, and 1916.

496 The number of at bats (496) for switch-hitter Carl Everett in 2000. The outfielder made his first career All-Star team after using those at bats to lead the club with 34 home runs and 108 RBI. Everett also posted a .587 slugging percentage that was eighth best in the league.

497 The on-base percentage (.497) for Ted Williams in 1946 and 1948. He led the league both times—and his percentage remains the sixth highest of his career, and the sixth highest in franchise history.

498 The number of times (498) Reggie Smith struck out from 1966-73. He was the runner-up in Rookie of the Year balloting in his first full season of 1967, and he only got better with time. He was a switch-hitting outfielder with power—and while he often struck out, he also frequented the league's top ten leader boards for some very important offensive categories: three times for average, twice for on-base percentage, five times for slugging, four times for runs, three times for hits, three times for total bases (including a league best 302 in 1971), four times for doubles, three times for triples, twice for home runs, five times for extra-base hits (including a league best 65 in 1971), and twice for RBI.

499 The on-base percentage (.499) for Ted Williams in 1947. His percentage led the league, as did his average, slugging percentage, OPS, runs, total bases, home runs, RBI, walks, times on base, and extra-base hits. Williams won his second Triple Crown, but placed second in MVP balloting behind Joe DiMaggio for the second time as well. DiMaggio also won the award when Williams hit .406 in 1941.

500 The stolen base percentage (.500) for Ted Williams in 1960. He was 1 for 2 in his final big league season. Williams only stole 24 bases throughout his career, and he was caught stealing 17 times—but that last steal in 1960 made him the first major league player in history to swipe a base in four different decades.

Jim Rice—1978 A.L. Most Valuable Player recipient.
(Courtesy National Baseball Hall of Fame Library, Cooperstown, NY)

"I knew he was capable of a lot—but contending for the MVP every year? That's amazing."
— *Johnny Damon, on his former teammate David Ortiz*

Chapter 6

The Most Valuable Players

BIG PAPI PLACED among the top five in Most Valuable Player balloting during his first five seasons with the Red Sox. His best finish in that span was second place in 2005, just losing out to Alex Rodriguez of the New York Yankees. It was A-Rod, however, who suggested he'd gladly trade his hardware for the ring Ortiz won in 2004. A-Rod got the hardware for MVP again in 2007, but it was Ortiz who got another ring.

Boston does have a long history of award winners, however, and Ortiz is no exception—he won the Thomas A. Yawkey Award as Boston's Most Valuable Player three consecutive seasons from 2004-06, he won the 2004 American League Championship Series MVP Award, and he won the 2005 Hank Aaron Award as the best hitter in the American League.

Other multiple winners of the Yawkey Award include: Mo Vaughn, Roger Clemens, Pedro Martinez, Carl Yastrzemski, Dwight Evans, and Ted Williams—while Manny Ramirez is a two-time recipient of the Hank Aaron Award (1999, 2004).

Tris Speaker won league MVP honors in 1912, making him the first player in franchise history to earn that title. Jimmie Foxx, however, is generally credited with being Boston's first league MVP. Foxx won the award in 1938, which is significant because the Baseball Writers Association of America began voting on the award in 1931, and that is the origin of the award still given today.

Who else has won league MVP honors for Boston?

Ted Williams won the award in 1946 and 1949. Other recipients include: Jackie Jensen (1958), Carl Yastrzemski (1967), Fred Lynn (1975), Jim Rice (1978), Roger Clemens (1986), and Mo Vaughn (1995).

In addition to Ortiz, who else has won postseason MVP honors for Boston?

Manny Ramirez won World Series MVP honors in 2004, and Mike Lowell won World Series MVP honors in 2007. Josh Beckett won the award for the 2007 League Championship Series, the same award Marty Barrett won back in 1986.

Incidentally, Ted Williams was a five-time Major League Player of the Year recipient, despite winning league MVP honors only twice. Carl Yastrzemski and Roger Clemens are the only other members of the Red Sox to be named Major League Player of the Year during the 20th century. Yaz won Player of the Year honors and the MVP during his 1967 Triple Crown season. Williams won two Triple Crowns, but was second in MVP balloting both times.

Boston is traditionally well represented in the All-Star Game. J.D. Drew, Pedro Martinez, Roger Clemens, and Carl Yastrzemski all won MVP honors for Boston during the mid-Summer Classic.

This chapter is filled with award winning members of the Boston Red Sox—but be on the lookout for these outstanding performances as well: Billy Rohr's near no-hitter in the Bronx, Joe DiMaggio winning the pennant for *Boston*, not the Yankees, Pedro's near no-hitter in the midst of a brouhaha with the ~~Devil~~ Rays, Yaz and Jim Lonborg carrying the team on the season's final day to complete the Impossible Dream in 1967, and Lou Clinton, a .247 career hitter who acted like he was Babe Ruth for two weeks in 1962.

Moving on to the sixth...

501 The number of RBI (501) for Tony Conigliaro while playing for Boston. His best season total was 116 in 1970, second best in the league. Conigliaro's career total with the club still ranks among the top 35 in franchise history.

502 The slugging percentage (.502) for Jim Rice. He led the league in slugging twice (1977, 1978) and was among the league's top ten leaders eight times overall. His career slugging percentage is also among the top ten in franchise history, but among players with at least 5,000 at bats for Boston, only Ted Williams ranks higher.

503 The winning percentage (.503) for Oil Can Boyd. He was 78-77 during his big league career. His best seasons came in Boston where he won 43 games from 1984-86, but he also played briefly for Montreal and Texas. He was a colorful figure who often made headlines for his off the field antics. Tim Kurkjian wrote in *ESPN The Magazine*, "It was the Can who was not allowed to leave spring training in Winter Haven until he returned some overdue adult movies, which he eventually did, but not before one member of the Red Sox family, in the greatest line ever, called the incident The Can Film Festival."

504 The number of RBI (504) for Buck Freeman from 1901-07. He posted season totals of 114, 121, and 104 from 1901-03. In that same span he was the league runner-up in home runs twice, and he won the home run title once. Freeman's RBI total for Boston still ranks among the top 35 in franchise history.

505 Oil Can Boyd struck out (5.05) batters per nine innings during parts of eight seasons with Boston from 1982-89. Boyd's highest strikeout total was 154 in 1985. His best ratio was 6.10 per nine innings in 1984, the sixth highest ratio in the league.

506 The winning percentage (.506) for Mickey Harris during six seasons from 1940-49. Harris served four years in the Army during that time as well. He was 43-42 overall but his best season was 1946, when he posted a 17-9 record for the sixth best winning percentage in the league. His performance helped Boston win the pennant that year, but unfortunately, Harris was the losing pitcher in Game 2 and Game 6 of the 1946 World Series—the only one he ever played in.

507 The number of extra-base hits (507) for Nomar Garciaparra from 1996-2004. Six times he was among the top ten league leaders in extra-base hits while paying for Boston and his career total is among the top ten in franchise history.

508 The winning percentage (.508) for Herb Pennock after posting a 61-59 career record for Boston. Pennock was sold by owner Harry Frazee to the Yankees in 1923 for $50,000 and three players: Camp Skinner, Norm McMillan, and George Murray—who combined to play just 205 games for the Red Sox. Pennock pitched 346 games for New York and posted a 162-90 record on his way to the Hall of Fame (and four pennants in the Bronx).

509 The number of runs (509) Doc Cramer scored from 1936-40. He was a four-time All-Star during five seasons with the club. Cramer scored 116 runs in 1938 for a career high, and his total with the club remains among the top 35 in franchise history.

510 The earned run average (5.10) for Billy Rohr in 1967. He made his big league debut that season on April 14. Rohr got the nod against the Yankees—in the Bronx—with fellow lefty and Hall of Fame legend Whitey Ford taking the mound for New York. Rohr gave up five walks, but he held the first 31 batters he faced hitless—and he was one strike away from a no-hitter when Elston Howard singled to right with two outs in the bottom of the ninth. Rohr got the next batter out to complete the one-hitter and a 3-0 victory at Yankee Stadium—which was an extraordinary way to begin his career, to say the least—but he never demonstrated that form again, and in fact, he won only two big league games afterwards.

511 The slugging percentage (.511) for Joe DiMaggio in 1946. The Hall of Fame legend for the Yankees hit 25 home runs that season, but none more important than the one that gave the pennant to the Red Sox. That's right—on September 13, 1946, DiMaggio hit a game-winning home run as the Yankees beat the Detroit Tigers 5-4, and coupled with a Red Sox victory earlier in the day, that win by the Yankees eliminated the second place Tigers from the pennant race and gave the title to Boston. Dom DiMaggio and some of his Red Sox teammates sent a telegram to his brother Joe, saying, "Thanks a lot for that home run, pal."

512 The winning percentage (.512) for Boston in 1976. The club was only 83-79 and fell to third in the division after winning the pennant and taking Cincinnati to seven games in the World Series the previous year. The season began with high hopes that soured quickly when Carlton Fisk, Fred Lynn, and Rick Burleson held out during spring training, asking for an increase in pay. Things only got worse from there, as owner Tom Yawkey died on July 9. Less than ten days later, and with the club 13 games out of first, manager Darrell Johnson was fired and replaced by third base coach Don Zimmer.

513 The on-base percentage (.513) for Ted Williams in 1954. It was the ninth time he led the league in on-base percentage, and it represents both the third highest percentage of his career and the third highest in franchise history.

514 The winning percentage (.514) for Boston in 2000 during games considered to be a blowout—which are games decided by five or more runs. Boston was only 18-17 in blowouts, but they did win one of the most exciting blowouts of the season on August 29, against Tampa Bay. Pedro Martinez hit Gerald Williams leading off the first for Tampa, but then he retired the next 24 batters he faced. He carried a no-hitter into the ninth inning but it was broken up by Rays' catcher John Flaherty. Pedro settled for a one-hit shutout and 13 strikeouts as Boston won 8-0, and in that game there was also a bench-clearing incident that resulted in eight members of the Devil Rays being ejected.

515 Joe Cronin hit (515) career doubles—including 270 as a member of the Red Sox. He led the league twice (1933, 1938), once for Washington, once for Boston, and placed among the top ten leaders eight times. His career total is among the top 40 in baseball history, and his Red Sox total is among the top 15 in franchise history.

516 The winning percentage (.516) for pitchers other than Mel Parnell and Ellis Kinder on the Red Sox staff in 1949. Parnell and Kinder combined to go 48-13 (a .787 winning percentage). The rest of the staff combined to go 48-45. In fact, Parnell and Kinder were the first teammates to win 20 games and be at least 17 games over .500 (Parnell was 25-7, Kinder was 23-6) since 1910—a feat no MLB teammates replicated the rest of the century.

517 The number of RBI (517) for Jim Tabor from 1938-44. The third baseman surpassed the century mark once, driving home 101 runs in 1941. He drove home at least 75 runs every year from 1939-43, however, and his career total with the club remains among the top 30 in franchise history.

518 Josh Beckett struck out (518) batters during his first 89 starts for Boston. Beckett's 89th start came on September 16, 2008, against Tampa Bay. He began that game tied with Ray Collins at 511 strikeouts—but after tossing three-hit ball over eight innings and striking out seven, Beckett moved into the top 35 for Boston's all-time strikeout leaders in only his third season with the club.

519 The number of runs (519) Freddy Parent scored from 1901-07. He scored 87 as a rookie, and then scored a career best 91 in 1902. Parent is best remembered for scoring eight runs during Boston's 1903 World Series triumph, but his career runs total remains among the 30 best in franchise history.

520 The slugging percentage (.520) as a member of the Red Sox for Fred Lynn. He led the league in slugging twice (1975, 1979) while playing for Boston, and his career mark with the Red Sox is among the ten best in franchise history.

521 Hall of Fame legend Ted Williams hit a franchise record (521) career home runs. He hit 43 home runs in 1949 to set a career high, and he hit 30 or more home runs eight times. His final season was 1960, and he began it by hitting a prodigious blast on opening day, and he closed it out with a home run on September 28, during the final at bat of his career.

522 The number of games (522) Hall of Fame catcher Rick Ferrell played for Boston. He hit .302 for the club, well above his .281 career average. Ferrell was with the Red Sox from 1933-37, and during that stretch he hit 16 of his 28 career home runs—including a career high eight in 1936. His best offensive years came in Boston, where he was a four-time All-Star—and where he played with his brother, hurler Wes Ferrell, who won 25 games for the Red Sox in 1935. Both the Ferrell's left the club in 1937, when they were traded together to the Washington Senators.

523 Carl Yastrzemski hit (.523) during the final two weeks of play in 1967. He also belted five home runs, scored 14, and drove home 16. His torrid finish gave him the Triple Crown, but of greater significance, it gave Boston a shot at winning the pennant. Boston trailed Minnesota by one game with two to play, and Detroit was also in the mix—but as fate would have it, the Twins and Red Sox were scheduled to play the final two games of the season head-to-head at Fenway. Yaz hit a three-run homer to propel Boston to a 6-4 victory in the first game. He said afterwards, while walking through the clubhouse door, "I want the feeling of coming through that door with the pennant won." Jim Lonborg got the start for Boston on the season's final day—and legend has it he wrote "$10,000" on the inside of his glove, reminding himself how much a postseason share was worth in monetary terms. Lonborg tossed a complete game, Yaz went 4 for 4, and the Red Sox 5-3 win, coupled with a Detroit loss vs. California, gave Boston the pennant.

524 The number of strikeouts (524) for Boston's pitching staff in 1944. That total was only fifth best out of eight teams in the league—but the staff gave up 592 free passes, the second highest total among those same teams. Tex Hughson was the only Boston hurler to pitch at least ten innings and record more strikeouts (112) than walks (41). The other 12 pitchers with at least ten innings combined to strikeout only 412 batters, while walking 551. Hughson won 18 games, but Boston was 77-77 despite having the highest scoring offense in the league.

525 Ted Williams hit (525) career doubles. The Kid led the league in doubles twice (1948, 1949) and placed among the top ten leaders ten times. His career total is among the top 35 in baseball history, but it is the second highest in franchise history.

526 The on-base percentage (.526) for Ted Williams in 1957. It was the second highest OBP of his career and the 11th time he led the league—and it remains the second highest OBP in franchise history.

527 The number of at bats (527) for Mo Vaughn in 1997. The Hit Dog used his big stick to clobber 35 home runs, while reaching base at a .420 clip that led the team and was fourth best in the league.

528 The slugging percentage (.528) for second baseman Bobby Doerr in 1944. His .399 on-base percentage was third highest in the league and his .325 batting average placed him second in the batting title race. Doerr led the league in slugging though, and as a result he was named *The Sporting News* A.L. Player of the Year.

529 The slugging percentage (.529) for Tigers All-Star outfielder Willie Horton in 1974. He was particularly brutal at Fenway that season—although his numbers hardly back up that claim. He hit only .143 with no home runs, runs, or RBI, and a paltry .143 slugging percentage in Boston's home park. His brutality, however, occurred with one weak swing of the bat. He hit a foul pop straight up that caught a low-flying pigeon square on the noggin, and the pigeon fell dead from the sky and landed just in front of home plate. To date, this is the only known bird fatality at Fenway.

530 The length in hours and minutes (5:30) for both ends of a doubleheader vs. Cleveland on April 12, 1992. The first game lasted 2:37 as Boston out hit the Indians 9-0, but lost the game by a score of 2-1. The second game lasted 2:53 as Boston out hit the Indians 9-2, and won the game by a score of 3-0. Matt Young tossed a no-hitter and lost, and Roger Clemens tossed a two-hit shutout to earn the split—as Boston out hit Cleveland 18-2 and set a major league record for the fewest hits allowed in a doubleheader.

531 The slugging percentage (.531) for outfielder Tony Armas in 1984. Armas, who is a member of the Venezuelan Baseball Hall of Fame, led the league with 43 home runs and set career highs in doubles, home runs, slugging, total bases, and RBI.

532 The slugging percentage (.532) for Dwight Evans in 1984. He was among the top ten league leaders in slugging, on-base percentage, OPS, runs, hits, total bases, times on base, doubles, triples, home runs, RBI, and walks—and he led the league with 77 extra-base hits. He posted solid and consistent numbers, but somehow he actually placed *outside* of the top ten in MVP balloting. He was clutch all year, as well—as demonstrated by his numbers against Seattle on June 28, when he was 4 for 7, with a double, triple, four runs, three RBI, and a walk-off game-winning home run that gave him the cycle.

533 The slugging percentage (.533) for John Valentin in 1995. The shortstop won his only career Silver Slugger Award as he set career highs in slugging, home runs (27), and RBI (102).

534 The slugging percentage (.534) for Nomar Garciaparra in 1997. He led the club and was second in the league with 85 extra-base hits and 365 total bases—both career highs. Nomar tallied 2,194 total bases for Boston before being traded to the Cubs in 2004, giving him one of the top 15 totals in franchise history.

535 The winning percentage (.535) for Ike Delock from 1952-63. He pitched 322 games during 11 seasons with Boston, one of the ten highest totals in franchise history. Delock started 147 of those games and overall he posted an 83-72 record, giving him a winning percentage that ranks among the top 40 in franchise history.

536 The number of RBI (536) for Reggie Smith from 1967-73. Twice in that span he was among the league's top ten leaders and his career total for Boston remains among the top 25 in franchise history.

537 The number of extra-base hits (537) for Manny Ramirez during seven-plus seasons with Boston. Manny, in his eighth season with the club, got 43 extra-base hits during 2008 prior to being traded to the Dodgers. That total moved him past Nomar Garciaparra and into seventh place in the franchise record book—but at the time of the trade, Big Papi was lurking not far behind.

538 The slugging percentage (.538) for Carlton Fisk in 1972. He hit 22 home runs as a rookie, but the man affectionately known as Pudge would have been suiting it up for the Boston Celtics if things had gone the route of his childhood dreams. "I didn't grow into a power forward," he quipped. Just as well, he became a Hall of Fame catcher instead.

539 The number of singles (539) for Jody Reed from 1987-92. Reed, a middle infielder of slight stature who came out of Florida State University, did lead the league with a career best 45 doubles in 1990—but at the end of the day he was a singles kind of guy. He hit 249 singles from 1990-91, and his total after 715 games with the club ranks among the top 50 in franchise history.

540 The slugging percentage (.540) for Lou Clinton in 1962. Clinton hit only .247 with 65 home runs during parts of eight major league seasons—but for two weeks in 1962 he was the best player in baseball. The Red Sox outfielder began play with a .100 average on June 29, but on that day he hit two home runs and drove home six. Two weeks, 13 games, 30 hits, and nine home runs later, Clinton was up to .316 for the season. Only five players since Clinton have put together at least 29 hits and seven or more home runs in a 13-game stretch: Kent Hrbek (Twins, 1986), Ivan Rodriguez (Rangers, 1999), Richard Hidalgo (Astros, 2000), Chipper Jones (Braves, 2006), and Lance Berkman (Astros, 2008).

541 Joe Bush posted a (.541) winning percentage while pitching for Boston. That number is among the top 40 in franchise history, but it is worth mentioning more so because of the odd numbers he posted to get it. He was 15-15 in 1918—his first season in Boston—but the following year he did not record any decisions after pitching in only three games due to injuries. Bush returned in 1920 and was again 15-15. He improved to 16-9 in 1921, so he was promptly traded by owner Harry Frazee to the Yankees where he won 26 games for the Bronx Bombers in 1922. Bush is also known for having won the World Series for three different teams: the Athletics (1913), Red Sox (1918), and Yankees (1923).

542 The slugging percentage (.542) as a member of the Red Sox for Mo Vaughn. He posted a career high .591 slugging percentage in 1998, his final season with the club. Vaughn ranked among the top ten league leaders in slugging during six consecutive seasons in Boston from 1993-98, and his career mark is among the top ten in franchise history.

543 The number of strikeouts (543) for George Winter during eight seasons pitching for Boston. He was there from the very beginning, posting a 16-12 record for the Boston Americans in 1901. Winter was part of the 1903 club that won the World Series, though he did not pitch in the series. He won 16 games again in 1905, the same year he struck out a career high 119 batters, but he also lost 17 games, and he subsequently lost 18, 15, and 19 games (the last five for Detroit) from 1906-08. Winter's career strikeout total with Boston, however, remains among the top 35 in franchise history.

544 Boston gave up (544) runs in 1912 for the second lowest total among eight teams in the league. That works out to a very tidy 3.53 runs per game. The offense scored a league best 799 runs, or 5.19 per game, and that combination of pitching and offense led to 105 wins in the regular season—and four more vs. the Giants in the postseason to win the 1912 World Series.

545 The number of hits (545) for Steve Lyons during nine big league seasons. He was a first-round draft choice of the Red Sox in 1981, who later established himself as a utility man that could play any position. He got 98 hits as a rookie in 1985, his highest during three stints and five seasons wearing a Red Sox uniform. Lyons became well-known for many things. He once played one inning at every position in an exhibition game between the Cubs and White Sox, and there was also the time he dropped his pants while standing on first base to shake the dirt out of them—much to the delight of the crowd. Lyons and the term "antics" were used frequently in close proximity, but occasionally they produced on the field, such as on May 13, 1991, when he successfully used the "hidden ball trick" against former White Sox teammate Ozzie Guillen.

546 Josh Beckett gave up (546) hits during his first 89 starts for Boston. Beckett tossed 573-plus innings during those starts and posted a 48-27 record. In his third season with the club, those numbers moved him into the franchise record book in two categories among pitchers with at least 500 innings: a ratio of 8.57 hits per nine innings that ranks among the top 35, and a .640 winning percentage that ranks among the top ten.

547 The winning percentage (.547) for Bruce Hurst from 1980-88. He nearly won MVP honors during the 1986 World Series and he nearly won Cy Young honors during his final season with the club after posting an 18-6 record in 1988—neither of those awards worked out for the lefty, but he had a solid career in Boston and his winning percentage with the club ranks among the top 35 in franchise history.

548 The winning percentage (.548) for Boston in 1972. Bad luck and poor play against Detroit gave the Tigers some measure of revenge for the pennant race Boston won in 1967 by a single game over Detroit and Minnesota. There was a players' strike in 1972 that erased seven games from Boston's schedule, but that took only six games away from Detroit. Boston was only 5-9 vs. Detroit, and the Tigers beat Boston two out of the final three games of the season after the Red Sox came into the series with a half-game lead in the division race. Boston was 85-70 on the season, Detroit was 86-70, and that extra game the Tigers got to play gave them the division title by half a game in the standings.

549 The number of at bats (549) for David Ortiz in 2007. Big Papi used them well, posting a .621 slugging percentage that was third best in the league despite nagging shoulder, back, and knee injuries that plagued him all season. During the postseason Ortiz said, "When one has been playing this game for a long time, you learn to deal with pain." He dealt with it better than most, as he also legged out a team high 52 doubles.

550 Boston scored only (550) runs in 1916—the lowest total in baseball history for a pennant-winning team. The pitching staff gave up only 480 runs in the regular season and just 13 runs in the World Series, as Boston defeated Brooklyn to win the fourth championship in franchise history.

551 The winning percentage (.551) for Hugh Bedient from 1912-14. He was 20-9 as a 22-year-old rookie but only 23-26 in his next two campaigns. Bedient also began his career by playing a key role for the club during the 1912 World Series triumph—but he was out of baseball less than four years later. Despite that, among players with at least 500 innings his winning percentage remains among the top 35 in franchise history.

552 The number of games (552) Bob Stanley pitched in relief. He spent 13 seasons with the club from 1977-89, and he was the first pitcher to appear in 500 games for Boston. He made a few starts, making his 552 relief jobs and 637 total games both franchise records. All that work, it makes sense he won a few—and his 115 career wins still puts him among the top ten in franchise history on that list as well.

553 The on-base percentage (.553) for Ted Williams in 1941. It was the second of a major league record 12 times that Williams led the league in OBP. His mark is also a franchise record, and it was the major league record until Barry Bonds surpassed it in 2002.

554 The number of extra-base hits (554) for Wade Boggs from 1982-92. The Hall of Famer is among the top 30 in baseball history for hits and doubles, and three times he was among the top ten league leaders in extra-base hits. His total for Boston is also among the top ten in franchise history.

555 Boston scored (555) runs in 1917. Harry Hooper led the team with 89, but the club total was only the fourth best among eight teams in the league. The pitching was much better, giving up 454 runs for the lowest total in the league, but that wasn't enough for Boston to catch the Chicago White sox. Chicago had the highest scoring offense and the second best pitching staff in the league, and they won the pennant by nine games over the second place Red Sox.

556 The number of innings (556) for Jose Santiago. He made 28 starts and was on the mound for a career high 172 innings in 1966, but it was primarily as a reliever in 1967 that he posted a 12-4 record and led the league with a .750 winning percentage. He did make 11 starts in 1967, and his 145-plus innings nearly equaled his workload from the previous season. In 1968 he was back in the rotation fulltime. He began that season 9-4 with a 2.25 earned run average in 124 innings of work—but then he tore a muscle in his pitching arm. He never won another game. Santiago only took the mound for 19 innings over the next two seasons, and then his career was over.

557 The number of hits (5.57) per nine innings that Dutch Leonard gave up in 1914. He faced 846 batters during 224-plus innings of work, but he gave up only 139 hits and 24 earned runs. Leonard led the league and set a franchise record for fewest hits per nine innings that lasted 86 years.

558 The number of at bats (558) for David Ortiz in 2006. Big Papi replied to a reporter's mid-season question about his big numbers, "I just swing hard in case I hit it—that's it." Well, it worked. Ortiz used his at bats to slug 54 home runs, 137 RBI, and 355 total bases—all league leading numbers—and he earned the Thomas A. Yawkey Award for being the Red Sox Most Valuable Player for the third consecutive season. Other multiple winners of the Yawkey Award include: Mo Vaughn, Roger Clemens, Pedro Martinez, Carl Yastrzemski, Dwight Evans, and Ted Williams.

559 The number of at bats (559) for Walt Dropo in 1950. Dropo was a 27-year-old rookie who used his at bats exceptionally well, tying teammate Vern Stephens for the league lead with 144 RBI—a total that at the time was the third best in franchise history. Manny Ramirez equaled that total in 2005, and it remains among Boston's ten best all-time.

560 The winning percentage (.560) for Derek Lowe while pitching for Boston from 1997-2004. He was an integral part of the staff during that time period, but perhaps never more so than in his final year when he went 3-0 during Boston's historic October. Lowe is among the top 30 in franchise history for both wins and winning percentage.

561 The number of at bats (561) for Ted Williams in 1940. He used them to hit a career high 14 triples, giving him 25 total after his first two seasons. Williams only hit 46 more after 1940—but his career total of 71 is among Boston's ten best all-time.

562 The number of runs (562) Boston scored in 1926. That total was dead last in the league—and the 835 runs the club gave up was the second highest total in the league. It was a disastrous combination as the club was 46-107 and placed dead last—44.5 games in back of the Yankees. To make things worse there was a fire at Fenway Park on May 8 that destroyed the bleachers down the left field foul line. The club was an abysmal wreck because their best players had been sold to the Yankees—but they still had no money, and the stadium went unrepaired until 1934.

563 The number of strikeouts (563) for Jack Wilson from 1935-41. He set career highs with 16 wins and 137 strikeouts in 1937. Wilson was 67-67 while pitching in 258 games for Boston, and he remains among the top 50 in the franchise record book for starts, complete games, wins, games, innings—and strikeouts.

564 The number of at bats (564) for Nick Esasky in 1989. He used them well, leading the team in slugging, total bases, home runs, RBI, and extra-base hits—and he was among the league's top ten leaders in every one of those categories as well.

565 The winning percentage (.565) for Hideo Nomo in 2001. He led the team in wins and winning percentage after posting a 13-10 record.

566 The number of at bats (566) for Ted Williams in 1949. He won his second Most Valuable Player Award after setting career highs with 194 hits, 43 home runs, and 368 total bases. His 43 home runs and 368 total bases also rank among the top ten efforts in franchise history.

567 The slugging percentage (.567) for Tris Speaker in 1912. He was third in the league in slugging, but he was first with 75 extra-base hits and ten home runs. It was the only home run title Speaker ever won, and it was the second time in three seasons that a Red Sox player won the title while hitting just ten homers. Jake Stahl did it in 1910—and both Stahl and Speaker share the distinction of having hit the lowest home run total during a season in which a Boston player led the league.

568 The number of at bats (568) for Pete Runnels in 1958. It was his first season in Boston and he used them well, setting career highs with 103 runs and 183 hits. Runnels posted a .320 average during five seasons in Boston, a number that ties him with Jimmie Foxx for one of the ten best in franchise history.

569 The slugging percentage (.569) for Dwight Evans in 1987. It was a career high, as were his 34 home runs, 123 RBI, .305 average, .417 on-base percentage, and .986 on-base plus slugging percentage—but he did not lead the league in any of those categories. In fact, he was second on the team in slugging, OBP, and OPS behind Wade Boggs—who out of nowhere hit 24 home runs that season to go along with his usual 200 hits.

570 The slugging percentage (.570) for 23-year-old rookie Mike Greenwell in 1987. He hit 19 home runs in 412 at bats for a career high mark in slugging, on his way to placing fourth in Rookie of the Year balloting.

571 The winning percentage (.571) for pitcher Joe Dobson. He spent parts of 14 seasons in the majors from 1939-54, and a good part of that time he was in Boston. He was the winning pitcher during Game 5 of the 1946 World Series, and he won a career high 18 games for Boston in 1947. Dobson was 137-103 in his career, but he won 106 of those games for the Red Sox, and that total puts him among the top ten in franchise history.

572 The winning percentage (.572) for Boston from 1998-99. The club won 186 games under the guidance of skipper Jimy Williams, but could not unseat the Yankees on top of the division standings. The club did win the Wild Card, however, in consecutive seasons—and it marked the first time since 1915-16 that Boston made two consecutive postseasons.

573 The number of at bats (573) for Jesse Burkett in 1905. It was the only season the Hall of Fame outfielder played for Boston, and it was the last season of his career. He hit just .257, well below the .338 mark that got him a ticket to Cooperstown.

574 The winning percentage (.574) for Boston during the first half of 1995. The club was 39-29 at the break and held a three-game lead over the Detroit Tigers. After a mediocre July, Boston was a smoking 23-7 in August, which led to a second half 47-29 record that was good for a .618 winning percentage. On September 6, the lead was over 15 games as Boston cruised to the division crown.

575 The winning percentage (.575) for Ray Collins. He was a lefty who tossed a complete game shutout against the Detroit Tigers on July 25, 1909, in only his second major league start. Collins was 84-62 during seven seasons with Boston—giving him a winning percentage that ranks among the top 30 in franchise history.

576 The slugging percentage (.576) for Mo Vaughn in 1994. He hit 26 home runs and 82 RBI in only 394 at bats during the strike-shortened season. Vaughn led the club with the sixth best slugging percentage in the league.

577 The winning percentage (.577) for Boston during September, 1967. Back in spring training, first-year skipper Dick Williams was not real popular with the players when he repeatedly made the team practice fundamentals such as bunting, base running, and throwing to the cut-off man from the outfield—but those same players were a ninth place club the previous season and he was determined to bend them to his way of thinking: "I had a one-year contract, so if I was crazy I was going to be crazy all year and give it the best I had." That September the club played some of their best fundamental ball of the season when it counted the absolute most—and when the club beat Minnesota two in a row to close out the season, they won the pennant by a single game over the Twins and the Tigers.

578 The slugging percentage (.578) for Trot Nixon in 2003. Nixon hit 28 home runs and was fifth among league leaders in slugging, but he was only third in slugging on his own team. Big Papi, Manny, and Nixon were first, second, and third on the club—and third, fourth, and fifth among league leaders.

579 The number of at bats (579) for Carl Yastrzemski in 1967. To say he used them well is quite an understatement—he got 189 hits, 44 of which left the yard—and when all the numbers were tallied at the end of the season, Yaz batted .326 and won not just the league batting title, but also the Triple Crown and the hardware for MVP.

580 The winning percentage (.580) for Boston in 1999. Jimy Williams guided the club to a 94-68 record that was good enough to win the Wild Card. Boston lost the pennant to the hated Yankees in a five-game series, but Williams earned Manager of the Year honors for getting the club to the postseason.

581 The earned run average (5.81) for the Red Sox staff during August, 2006. Boston gave up 179 runs, but scored just 132 as they struggled to a 9-21 record. The club was tied for the division lead on August 1, but they trailed by eight games on September 1. It was the highest ERA by the Red Sox staff in any calendar month since June, 1994—and it led to the club missing the postseason for the first time since 2002.

582 The number of games (582) for utility player Dave Stapleton. He got off to a fine start as a 26-year-old rookie second baseman in 1980. Stapleton did not make his debut until May 30, but he hit .321 and collected 144 hits in 106 games the rest of the season. He also led the majors with 50 hits during the season's final 34 games—and to give you an idea how rare a feat that is, the next time a rookie led all of baseball in hits during the season's final month was 2006, when Hanley Ramirez got 43 hits for the Marlins.

583 The slugging percentage (.583) for first baseman Walt Dropo in 1950. He was a star basketball player at the University of Connecticut who was drafted for both the NFL and the BAA (Basketball Association of America), but he chose instead to sign with the Red Sox. He made it look like the right decision as a rookie in 1950 when he led the league with 326 total bases and 144 RBI. He was also among the league leaders in runs, hits, triples, home runs, slugging, average, and OPS. He made the All-Star team and easily won Rookie of the Year honors ahead of Whitey Ford—but unfortunately, his rookie numbers in each of those categories were also the best numbers of his career, and he never made another All-Star team, won another award, or played in the postseason.

584 The winning percentage (.584) for Dutch Leonard from 1913-18. He won at least 14 games during five consecutive seasons from 1913-17, and he never posted a losing record for Boston. Three times during his tenure with the club he ranked among the top ten league leaders in earned run average, three times he was in the top ten for wins, and three times he was in the top ten for winning percentage—and his career winning percentage with the club ranks among the top 30 in franchise history.

585 Jimmie Foxx hit 41 home runs in (585) at bats in 1936—his first season in Boston. Mel Harder, who pitched for Cleveland, once said, "I saw him hit one in the upper deck at the stadium and that was one of the longest balls I ever saw. Nobody was stronger than Foxx." Double-X hit 36 or more home runs his first five seasons in Boston.

586 The winning percentage (.586) for Boston during August, 1974, after posting a 17-12 record. The club struggled in July, but rallied to take a seven-game lead over the Yankees and Orioles on August 23. The Fenway Faithful started preparing for October—but then September happened. The club fell hard: 11-18, a .379 winning percentage in the home stretch marred by an eight-game skid that began on August 30, and for the second time in three seasons fans were left in sheer agony as Baltimore claimed a division title that Boston should easily have won.

587 The slugging percentage (.587) for Manny Ramirez in 2003. That was the fourth highest slugging percentage in the league, but it was only the second best on the club behind teammate David Ortiz. Manny hit 37 home runs and Ortiz hit 31, but they both trailed the league leading .600 slugging percentage and 47 home runs for Rangers' shortstop Alex Rodriguez.

588 The slugging percentage (.588) for Manny Ramirez during the 2004 World Series. He batted 7 for 17, including one home run and four RBI, during a four-game sweep of the Cardinals. It was his third trip to the World Series, but it was the first time he got a ring. He also got the hardware for series MVP.

589 The slugging percentage (.589) for Rico Petrocelli in 1969. The All-Star second baseman hit a career high 40 home runs, which resulted in a career high slugging percentage that was also second best in the league. Petrocelli, who played his entire career in Boston, hit 210 home runs overall—a total that ranks among the top ten in franchise history.

590 The winning percentage (.590) for Boston in 1986. John McNamara guided the club to a 95-66 record, a division title, and a thrilling comeback in the American League Championship Series against the Angels—but the club lost in heartbreaking fashion to the Mets in the World Series. McNamara did pick up Manager of the Year honors.

591 The winning percentage (.591) for Boston in 1916. Bill Carrigan managed the club to a 91-63 record that was the best in the league—and the Red Sox went on to defeat Brooklyn in five games to earn their second consecutive World Series title, and the fourth title overall in franchise history.

592 The winning percentage (.592) for player-manager Jack Barry in 1917. He won three World Series titles as a player with the Philadelphia Athletics, and then he won two more with Boston in

1915 and 1916, before taking over the managerial duties from Bill Carrigan and guiding the club to a 90-62 record in 1917. He was only the manager for one year, however, because after the season he enlisted in the Navy where he served honorably during World War I. He returned for 31 games in 1919, but then retired from the game. Barry later coached his alma mater, Holy Cross, from 1921-60, and he led the club to victory in the 1952 College World Series.

593 The slugging percentage (.593) for Jim Rice in 1977. It was the first of back-to-back seasons during which Rice led the league in both slugging and home runs. He went yard 39 times on the season.

594 The winning percentage (.594) for Oakland from 1971-75. The Athletics won five consecutive division titles and averaged 95 wins per season. The club won three consecutive World Series from 1972-74, and they were the favorite to beat Boston in the 1975 League Championship Series and make a run at a fourth consecutive World Series. Boston won the first two games in the best-of-five series at home, however, prompting owner Tom Yawkey to close Fenway Park and fly every Red Sox employee to Oakland for Game 3—where Boston finished the sweep, 5-3.

595 The winning percentage (.595) for Boston in 1918. Ed Barrow, who was elected into the Hall of Fame as a baseball executive/pioneer in 1953, managed the club to the pennant with a 75-51 record during his first year at the helm. Boston then beat the Cubs in six games to win the fifth World Series title in franchise history.

596 The winning percentage (.596) for Joe Dobson from 1941-50. He won at least 13 games five consecutive seasons from 1946-50. Three times during that stretch he was among the top ten league leaders in earned run average, three times he was among the top ten in wins, and three times he was among the top ten in winning percentage—and his career winning percentage with Boston ranks among the top 25 in franchise history.

597 The winning percentage (.597) for Boston during the second half of 1988. The club was 43-42 at the break and nine games out of first. John McNamara was fired as manager, and Joe Morgan was given the job on an interim basis. He went 12-0 to start the second half, closing to within 1.5 games of New York before finally losing one. Morgan led the club to a 46-31 record in the second half, despite losing six of seven to close the season, and held on to win the division by one game over Detroit, two games over Milwaukee and Toronto, and 3.5 games over New York.

598 The ratio (5.98) of strikeouts per walk for Pedro Martinez in 2002. It was the third time since joining the club that Martinez led the league in this category, and when he left the club after 2004, his career ratio of 5.45 was the best in franchise history.

599 The slugging percentage (.599) for Nomar Garciaparra in 2000. He led the club with the seventh best slugging percentage in the league—and it came on the strength of a team best 51 doubles and 317 total bases.

600 The slugging percentage (.600) for outfielder Jim Rice in 1978. He led the league in slugging as he put up monstrous numbers that season: .315 average, 46 home runs, and 139 RBI. Rice took home MVP honors for his performance. The next spring, Ted Williams predicted, "They'll pitch to him a little differently this time." Well they tried, but Rice backed up his well-deserved hardware with a .325 average, 39 home runs, and 130 RBI in 1979.

Mo Vaughn—one of the top 100 sluggers in baseball history. (Courtesy National Baseball Hall of Fame Library, Cooperstown, NY)

"He had great powerful arms, and he used to wear his sleeves cut off way up, and when he dug in and raised that bat, his muscles would bulge and ripple."
— Ted Lyons, on Hall of Fame legend Jimmie Foxx

Chapter 7

The Sluggers

MANNY RAMIREZ, JIM Rice, Fred Lynn, Carl Yastrzemski, Ted Williams, Bobby Doerr, Jimmie Foxx, and Babe Ruth all led the league in slugging at least once while playing for Boston. Williams led the league in slugging nine times—the second most times in history behind Babe Ruth.

Seemingly every year at least one of the league's top sluggers can be found in Boston's lineup—and often times more than one. David Ortiz was second or third in slugging five consecutive seasons from 2003-07. Manny Ramirez was in the top five in slugging six consecutive seasons from 2001-06. Manny and Big Papi were one-two in slugging in 2004, and from 2003-06 Boston's big bats gave the club two of the league's top five sluggers—something no other team in the league could boast.

Trot Nixon was also among the league's top five leaders for slugging in 2003, meaning three of the top five league leading sluggers were in Boston's lineup.

No question about it—Boston has always been home to big bats.

Jim Rice led the league in slugging twice (1977, 1978) and was among the league's top ten leaders eight times from 1975-86. Fred Lynn also led the league in slugging twice (1975, 1979)—and in fact, Jim Rice was second in the league behind Reggie Jackson in 1976, or the league's leading slugger would have come from Boston every year from 1975-79.

Several players who either spent their entire career or a significant portion of it with the Red Sox are among Baseball's top 100 sluggers of all-time: Ted Williams, Jimmie Foxx, Manny Ramirez, David Ortiz, Nomar Garciaparra, Mo Vaughn, Ellis Burks, Jim Rice, and Tris Speaker.

This chapter is all about the sluggers: from Big Papi and his monster numbers in 2005 to Hall of Fame legend Jimmie Foxx, the unbelievable 1949 season for shortstop Vern Stephens to the equally impressive numbers by his teammate Ted Williams, the league best slugging for Manny in 2004 to his chase for the home run title against teammate David Ortiz that same season, Yaz and his Triple Crown performance in 1967 to the slugging prowess of Jim Rice a decade later, Williams and his batting title in 1942 to Manny and his batting title in 2002, Babe Ruth's big numbers just before getting sold to New York to Williams' big numbers upon his return from World War II, the Kid putting on a show in the 1946 All-Star Game to an unheralded Mark Bellhorn putting on a show in the 2004 World Series, and the consistency of Bobby Doerr to the Hit Dog himself, Mo Vaughn—those stories are all here.

Also in this chapter are some memorable teams and more great individual performances—among our favorites: Terry Francona and the 2004 club, Manny vs. Anaheim in the 2007 Division Series, Doc Cramer's four-year power outage, Dwight Evans' dominant 1984 campaign, the 1903 club that won the first modern World Series, a home run title for Tony Armas, a legendary Ted Williams in his final season, some strong numbers but incredibly bad timing for catcher Mike Stanley in 1997, and the 1918 club that won the last title of the 20th century for Boston.

It's stretch time...

601 The winning percentage (.601) for Luis Tiant during 274 games for Boston. He started 238 of those games and he posted a 122-81 record from 1971-78. He left the club with the third most wins in franchise history—and though he has since been surpassed by Roger Clemens and Tim Wakefield, his total remains the fifth highest.

602 The winning percentage (.602) for Boston in 1977. The club was 97-64, but tied for second 2.5 games back of the Yankees after spending 44 days in first throughout the season. Early in 1976, team owner Tom Yawkey was prepared to buy outfielder Joe Rudi and reliever Rollie Fingers from Oakland, but Baseball Commissioner Bowie Kuhn stepped in and prevented the transactions from occurring—prompting many fans to wonder what their impact might have been, and many old-timers to lament the fact that Kuhn had not been around when Harry Frazee was selling Babe Ruth and other Red Sox stars to New York.

603 The number of at bats (603) for Carl Yastrzemski in 1969. Boston finished 19 games back of the division champion Orioles, but it wasn't because of a lack of effort from Yaz. He suited it up and played all 162 games, but it was only the third and final time that his at bats total cracked the top ten league leaders—which is surprising, because his career at bats total (11,988) are a franchise record, and the third highest total in baseball history behind Pete Rose (14,053) and Hank Aaron (12,364).

604 The slugging percentage (.604) for David Ortiz in 2005. He hit 47 home runs and led the league with 88 extra-base hits. Ortiz also led the club with 363 total bases, the third highest number in the league.

605 The winning percentage (.605) for Boston in 2004. Terry Francona managed the club to a 98-64 record, and though that was only good for second in the division, it was easily enough to win the Wild Card. Once in the postseason, Boston swept the Angels, nearly got swept by the Yankees, and then swept the Cardinals to win the sixth World Series title in franchise history.

606 The number of earned runs (606) Cy Young gave up from 1901-08. He tossed 2,728-plus innings, and Young was among the top six leaders in earned run average seven times in eight seasons while pitching for Boston.

607 The winning percentage (.607) for Boston in 1978. The Red Sox led the division by ten games on July 8, and they led the Yankees by 14 games on July 19, but the season became a nightmare after New York completed a four-game sweep at Fenway on September 10, leaving the rivals tied on top of the standings. They were tied at 99-63 at season's end—and Boston lost the one-game playoff to finish at 99-64. The *Washington Post* reported that Yankees' owner George Steinbrenner said after the game, "How could any World Series offer more? I just think it's a shame that the two best teams in the world had to end up in the same division. By 1980, I think you'll see interdivisional play between both leagues with Wild Card teams."

608 The winning percentage (.608) for Wes Ferrell as a member of the Red Sox. He was with the club from 1934-37, when he was traded mid-season to the Washington Senators (along with his brother, catcher Rick Ferrell) in a deal that brought Bobo Newsom to Boston (Newsom has the distinction of being the player traded the most times in major league history: 16). Ferrell's best numbers with Boston came in 1935, when he led the league in wins after posting a 25-14 record. Only Cy Young and Smoky Joe Wood have won more than 25 games in a season for the Red Sox. Ferrell won another 20 games in 1936, and his winning percentage with the club ranks among the top 20 in franchise history.

609 The slugging percentage (.609) for Hall of Fame legend Jimmie Foxx. He spent 20 seasons in the majors and his career slugging percentage is among the top ten in baseball history. Foxx, who posted a .605 slugging percentage during six-plus seasons for the Red Sox, led the league in slugging twice during his tenure with the club.

610 The number of at bats (610) for Vern Stephens in 1949. The All-Star shortstop set career highs with 39 home runs and 159 RBI. Stephens and teammate Ted Williams tied for the league lead in RBI with a total that remains the second highest in franchise history.

611 Boston gave up (611) runs in 1968. That was the eighth highest total out of ten teams in the league—but in 1967 the club was seventh in the league after giving up 614 runs and yet still won the pennant. In 1968 Boston fell to fourth place, 17 games out, and to find out why see number 614.

612 The number of at bats (612) for Marty Barrett in 1988. Barrett spent two more seasons with the club, but 1988 was the last time he played a full year. He hit .283 in the regular season but the magical postseason success he experienced two years earlier did not return when Boston met Oakland in the League Championship Series. Barrett hit just .067, going 1 for 15 in that series after going 24 for 60 during his incredible 1986 postseason run.

613 The slugging percentage (.613) for Manny Ramirez in 2004. He led the league in slugging after posting 87 extra-base hits—one of the ten highest totals in franchise history. Ramirez also led the league with 43 home runs—but his extra-base hits total was actually just the second best on the team, trailing the 91 for David Ortiz.

614 Boston scored (614) runs in 1968. The club won the pennant in 1967 after the offense led the league with 722 runs scored. Scoring 108 fewer runs made a huge difference—in 1967 the club was 20-8 in games decided by five or more runs, but in 1968 that record fell to just 16-19.

615 The on-base percentage (.615) for Manny Ramirez during the 2007 Division Series vs. the Angels. Manny hit .375 with two home runs. He was 3 for 8, but he also walked five times, scored three runs, and drove home four runs as Boston swept the series in three games.

616 The number of plate appearances (616) for Doc Cramer in 1937. He hit .305, scoring 90 runs after going 171 for 560 at the plate—but it was the second of four consecutive seasons that he made at least 600 plate appearances for Boston and did not hit a single home run.

617 The winning percentage (.617) for Boston in 1904. The club lost 9-1 to Cleveland on September 3, and fell a half-game back of the New York Highlanders in the standings. Boston and New York traded places on top of the standings 15 times during the final four weeks of the season, as the two clubs prepared to do head-to-head battle in the final five games of the season to see who would win the pennant. Boston won three out of five from New York to end the season—and the Red Sox won the first-ever pennant race that involved the two historic franchises.

618 The number of RBI (618) for Dom DiMaggio. Affectionately dubbed The Little Professor, Dom drove home a career best 87 runs in 1948. His career total ranks among the top 25 in franchise history.

619 The winning percentage (.619) for Boston in 1948 after posting a 96-59 record. On October 2, New York and Boston were tied for second place, one game behind the Cleveland Indians—and the Red Sox and Yankees were scheduled to play the season's final two games head-to-head at Fenway Park. Boston won both games: 5-1, and 10-5. New York was eliminated from the pennant race, and because Cleveland lost their final game against Detroit, the Indians and Red Sox met at Fenway on October 4, for the first one-game playoff in league history. The Indians, unfortunately, won that game 8-3, and they went on to win the World Series.

620 The winning percentage (.620) for Jesse Tannehill while pitching for Boston from 1904-08. The lefty, who stood a very unintimidating 5' 8" in his spikes, was effective nonetheless—twice winning 20-plus games for Boston and posting a winning percentage that ranks among the top 20 in franchise history.

621 The winning percentage (.621) for Roger Clemens in 1992. He posted an 18-11 record for the best winning percentage on the club. Clemens, who only placed third in Cy Young Award balloting, also led the league with a 2.41 earned run average. It was the third consecutive season that he led the league in ERA.

622 The slugging percentage (.622) for Carl Yastrzemski in 1967. It was a career high, and the second of three times he led the league in slugging. Yaz posted prolific numbers that season—79 extra-base hits, 284 times on base, 360 total bases, and 189 hits—all numbers that led the league and that culminated in Yaz taking home the hardware for league MVP.

623 The winning percentage (.623) for Boston in 1949 after posting a 96-58 record. Unlike 1948, when Boston and New York trailed the Indians by one game with two remaining, in 1949 the Red Sox led the Yankees by one game and no one else was in the picture—but this time the final two games were played at Yankee Stadium. The media and fans were so certain Boston would win that the *Boston Herald* headlines read, "Sox Send Parnell to Clinch Flag Today." Boston led 4-0, but lost 5-4 in the first game. Boston never led on the season's final day. They scored three in the ninth to make it close, but the Yankees won the pennant 5-3, and they went on to beat the Dodgers in the World Series.

624 The number of times (624) Jimmie Foxx walked as a member of the Red Sox. The Hall of Fame legend is among the top 25 in baseball history with 1,452 walks—and the 624 he got during six-plus seasons in Boston is among the top 15 totals in franchise history.

625 Boston scored (625) runs at Fenway Park in 1950. The club led the league with 1,027 total runs and the home total set a record for the most in major league history. Boston was 55-22 at Fenway, but only 39-38 on the road—and despite 94 victories the club was four games back of New York at season's end.

626 Smoky Joe Wood struck out (6.26) batters per nine innings from 1908-15. Wood placed among the top ten league leaders in this category four times during that span. He led the league in 1911, and twice was second in the league, in 1910 and 1912. Wood's ratio for the club is among the top 15 in franchise history.

627 Earl Wilson struck out (6.27) batters per nine innings during parts of seven seasons with Boston from 1959-66. His best ratio came in 1964, when he struck out 7.38 batters per nine innings. Wilson was among the top ten league leaders in this category three times, and his ratio as a member of the Red Sox is among the top 15 in franchise history.

628 The number of at bats (628) for Vern Stephens in 1950. Buster, as he was known, completed a remarkable three-year run during which he posted RBI totals of 137, 159, and 144—and like other Red Sox stars of that era he was enormously popular with the media, especially those based out of New York, seeing as he placed fourth, seventh, and 24th in MVP balloting those same three seasons. His numbers: .269, 29 HR, 137 RBI; .290, 39 HR, 159 RBI; and .295, 30 HR, 144 RBI.

629 The winning percentage (.629) for Lefty Grove from 1934-41. The Hall of Fame legend pitched eight seasons in Boston, and during that stretch he led the league in winning percentage once while placing among the top ten league leaders three times. Lefty posted a .680 career winning percentage that is among the top ten in baseball history, and his percentage for the Red Sox is among the top 15 in franchise history.

630 The number of at bats (630) for Dwight Evans in 1984. Dewey got on base that season at a .388 clip, but he was also third in the league with a .532 slugging percentage. That combination led to a .920 on-base plus slugging percentage and 121 runs scored—both the best numbers in the league.

631 The number of batters (631) faced by Joe Hesketh in 1991. The lefty posted an 0-4 record in 12 games with the club in 1990, but in 39 games in 1991—including 17 starts—he turned things around and posted a 12-4 record and a league best .750 winning percentage. Only 56 of those batters he faced reached base and scored an earned run against him.

632 The winning percentage (.632) for Cy Young during 327 games for Boston. Young and Roger Clemens are tied for the most wins in franchise history. Young posted a record of 192-112, while Clemens posted a record of 192-111. Clemens made 85 more starts for Boston than did Young, but appeared in only 56 more games.

633 The number of plate appearances (633) for Trot Nixon in 2001. He hit .280 with 27 home runs, and he scored exactly 100 runs—the only time in his career that he reached the century mark.

634 The slugging percentage (.634) for Ted Williams. It is a franchise record, and the second highest career slugging percentage in baseball history behind Babe Ruth. Williams is also second all-time behind Ruth for career OPS, and Ruth is the only player in history to lead the league in slugging and OPS more times than Williams did.

635 The distance in feet (635) from home plate to center field at Huntington Avenue Grounds, where Boston played their home games from 1901-11, and where the first game in World Series history was played on October 1, 1903. It was also the site of the first title-clenching game in World Series history, and to see Boston win in person on October 13, 1903, you could have sat on the rooftops that looked over the field, paid $1 admission at the gate, or paid as much as $5 if you bought your ticket from a scalper. Scorecards were sold at the game for 15 cents—an exorbitant price that the *Boston Herald* said was "squeezing the dear public hard."

636 The winning percentage (.636) for New York vs. Boston in 1923. Boston team owner Harry Frazee began selling off top players—beginning with Babe Ruth—to the New York Yankees in 1920 in exchange for cash in order to keep his other interests (such as theater productions) solvent. The result was predictable. New York was 14-8 against Boston in 1923 and won the pennant—37 games in front of the last place Red Sox. New York beat the Giants to win the Yankees' first World Series title—but they did it with a roster that included 11 former Red Sox players as well as Boston's top farmhand from the previous season (George Pipgras). Eight members of New York's 1923 championship club previously had won a World Series title with the Boston Red Sox.

637 The winning percentage (.637) for both Ernie Shore and Rube Foster as members of the Red Sox. Foster was 58-33 during a brief five-year career, all of it in Boston. Shore was 58-33 during four seasons with the club, prior to being traded to the Yankees in 1918. They share a winning percentage that ranks among the top ten career efforts in franchise history.

638 Dutch Leonard gave up (6.38) hits per nine innings of work in 1915. He was 15-7, but he only pitched 183-plus innings because 11 of his 32 games were in relief. Leonard gave up just 130 hits, despite facing 705 batters. His ratio of hits per nine innings led the league and it remains among the top five in franchise history.

639 The number of at bats (639) for Tony Armas in 1984. He used them to hit a career high and league leading 43 home runs—and he won his only career Silver Slugger Award.

640 The winning percentage (.640) for Joe Bush in 1921. He posted a 16-9 record for the best winning percentage on the club—one that was good enough to generate interest from Yankees' owner Jacob Ruppert, who after the season got Bush along with Everett Scott in a trade with Harry Frazee, the cash-strapped owner of the Red Sox. Bush then won 26 games for New York in 1922 and he led the league with a .788 winning percentage. He won 62 games in three seasons with New York.

641 The number of runs (641) for Frank Malzone from 1955-65. He scored two runs in six games after a September call-up in 1955, and he scored a career high 90 runs for the club in 1959. Twice he was among the league's top ten leaders for runs, and his career total with the club is among the top 25 in franchise history.

642 The number of RBI (642) for David Ortiz from 2003-07. He surpassed the century mark each season, and twice (2005, 2006) he posted the highest total in the league. Big Papi also hit 208 home runs during that stretch—a total that put him among the top ten in franchise history after only five seasons in Boston.

643 The earned run average (6.43) for Derek Lowe vs. New York in the 2003 League Championship Series. It was his clutch save in Game 5 of the Division Series that gave Boston a shot at the pennant, but against the Yankees neither Lowe nor Pedro Martinez could win a game. Pedro posted a 5.65 ERA and combined they were 0-3. The best starter for the Red Sox was Tim Wakefield, who was masterful in winning both Game 1 and Game 4—but Wakefield is also the one who gets remembered for the most devastating loss in that series, for he gave up the pennant-winning blast to Aaron Boone.

644 The number of at bats (644) for Jim Rice in 1977. The Red Sox slugger posted a .593 slugging percentage on the strength of 83 extra-base hits. His power also produced a league best 382 total bases—a number that remains the third highest in franchise history.

645 The slugging percentage (.645) for Ted Williams in 1960. He was a 41-year-old veteran in his final season when he batted .316 with 29 home runs in only 310 at bats. Williams got his first long ball of the season on opening day, and the last home run of his career in his final at bat of the season—but he did not get enough at bats to qualify for any of the league leader categories, and so Roger Maris (who hit 39 home runs) led the league with a .581 slugging percentage.

646 Carl Yastrzemski hit a franchise record (646) career doubles. In 23 seasons from 1961-83, Yaz led the league in doubles three times (1963, 1965, 1966) and placed among the top ten leaders nine times. His career total is the eighth highest in baseball history.

647 The slugging percentage (.647) for Manny Ramirez in 2002. He hit .349 to win his first career batting title, but he also tagged opposing pitchers for 31 doubles and 33 home runs in only 120 games. The result was the second highest slugging percentage in the league and one of the ten best in franchise history. Only three players have posted a higher number for the club: Hall of Fame legends Ted Williams, Jimmie Foxx, and Babe Ruth.

648 The slugging percentage (.648) for Ted Williams in 1942. His average went down 50 points from the previous season—but he still hit .356, good enough to win a second consecutive batting title. He also hit a league best 36 home runs and led the league in slugging.

649 The number of at bats (64.9) per strikeout for Stuffy McInnis in 1921. He struck out only nine times all season—in 584 at bats—and his ratio of at bats per strikeout is a franchise record. McInnis hit .307 with 76 RBI that season, but no home runs.

650 The slugging percentage (.650) for Ted Williams in 1949. He hit 43 home runs, setting a career high as he led the league for the fourth and final time of his career. It was also the sixth consecutive season that he led the league in slugging—not counting 1943-45, seasons he did not play—and he would go on to lead the league in slugging nine times during his career.

651 The offensive winning percentage (.651) for Mike Stanley while playing for Boston in 1997. The catcher was in the midst of another fine offensive season for the Red Sox (.300, 13 HR, 53 RBI, in 97 games) when the club traded him that August to the New York Yankees—his former club. Stanley's numbers and his track record in the Bronx made the move a good one for the Yankees as they tried to defend their 1996 World Series title. In retirement, Stanley says people don't believe him when he says he never won a ring—fans point to his career with Boston and New York and assume he has several, when in fact, Stanley lost the 1995 Division Series with New York; Stanley was with Boston when the Yankees won the 1996 World Series; Stanley lost the 1997 Division Series with New York; Stanley lost the 1998 Division Series after returning to Boston; and Stanley lost the 1999 League Championship Series with Boston, against his former club, the Yankees, who went on to win the World Series.

652 The slugging percentage (.652) for Ted Williams during the mid-Summer Classic. The Splendid Splinter gave his best slugging performance in front of a partisan crowd at Fenway Park on July 9, 1946, in an All-Star Game that featured eight members of the Red Sox. Williams went 4 for 4, with two home runs, four runs, five RBI, and a walk. The A.L. won the game 12-0.

653 The number of at bats (653) for Wade Boggs in 1985. His total is one of the ten highest in franchise history, and he used them to get a franchise record 240 hits. Boggs hit .368 to win the first of four consecutive batting titles.

654 The winning percentage (.654) for Bill Lee in 1975. He was 17-9, and it was the third consecutive season the lefty won 17 games. It was also his best chance to win 20 games. In late August, however, Boston pitchers began taking batting practice. In case the team won the pennant, they wanted the pitchers to be prepared to hit in the World Series. Lee injured his elbow trying to hit home runs during BP, and he was ineffective the rest of the regular season, going 0-2 during his final eight appearances.

655 Boston scored (655) runs in 1966. It was the fourth highest total in the league, but the pitching was horrendous—allowing 731 runs for the highest total in the league. The result was a disastrous 72-90 record and a ninth place finish. The only remnant of a silver lining to be found is that Boston was a half-game better than the team in dead last that season—the New York Yankees.

656 Boston scored (656) runs in 1953. The club placed fourth in the pennant race behind New York, Cleveland, and Chicago, but if they could have somehow scheduled a few more contests against Detroit then perhaps the Red Sox would have been in the pennant race right up until season's end. Boston outscored Detroit 117-75, but the offense was particularly brutal to the Tigers' pitching staff on June 17 and 18, when the club won 17-1 and 23-3 on consecutive days.

657 The slugging percentage (.657) for Babe Ruth in 1919. It was the second consecutive season that Ruth led the league in home runs and slugging—he hit 29 big flies, a number that broke the season record at the time—but after the season ended, Boston sold Ruth to the New York Yankees for $100,000. The next two seasons he posted home run totals of 54 and 59 for New York, becoming the only player in history to break the season home run record in three consecutive seasons.

658 The number of at bats (658) for Doc Cramer in 1938. His total led the league and remains tied with Nomar Garciaparra (2003) for one of the ten highest in franchise history. Cramer led the league in at bats seven times and ranks among the top 60 in baseball history for career at bats, but he hit only a grand total of 37 home runs in all or parts of 20 seasons—and 1938 was the third consecutive season that he didn't hit any home runs at all. Nomar, who hit a career high 35 big flies in 1998, settled for 28 during his 658 at bats in 2003.

659 The winning percentage (.659) for the Boston Americans in 1903. Hall of Fame player-manager Jimmy Collins led the club to a 91-47 record as Boston won the very first A.L. pennant in league history—and they went on to defeat the Pittsburgh Pirates in the very first official World Series played between the American and National Leagues.

660 The number of games (660) Vern Stephens played for Boston from 1948-52. He was a slugging shortstop who hit 122 home runs for the club in only five seasons—yet fewer than 60 players have taken the field for Boston more times in their careers than he did.

661 The number of at bats (661) for All-Star outfielder Doc Cramer in 1940. His total led the league and remains the fifth highest in franchise history. Cramer also led the league with 200 hits that season, his last as a member of the Red Sox. It was the third and final time in his career that he reached the 200 hits plateau.

662 The number of innings (662) for Ed Morris from 1928-31. Big Ed tossed 12 innings for the Cubs in 1922, but did not appear in the big leagues again until he resurfaced with the Red Sox in 1928. Morris won 19 games that season, tossing a career high 257-plus innings while picking up some votes in MVP balloting. Sadly, both his career and his life came to an abrupt end on March 3, 1932, when he was stabbed in a bar fight while on his way to Red Sox spring training in Florida.

663 The number of at bats (663) for shortstop Rick Burleson in 1977. His total led the league and set a franchise record at the time—and it remains among the five highest in club history. Burleson used his at bats well enough that he earned his first trip to the All-Star Game. He was among the top ten league leaders in hits, doubles, and times on base, but he went hitless in two at bats during the mid-Summer Classic.

664 The number of plate appearances (664) for Harry Hooper in 1913. The Hall of Fame outfielder scored 100 runs that season. It was the only time he hit the century mark for Boston, despite scoring 988 career runs for the club.

665 The number of times (665) the musical comedy *No, No, Nanette* was performed at London's Palace Theatre beginning on March 11, 1925. The Broadway production of *No, No, Nanette* ran for 321 performances, beginning on September 16, 1925. It was the first successful Broadway venture for Red Sox owner Harry Frazee, who made millions off the show—but the cash flow came too late for the franchise. Frazee sold the Red Sox just prior to his Broadway success, which ironically, he financed by selling off Boston's top players to the Yankees.

666 The number (666) that seems most appropriate for Bucky Dent on October 2, 1978, and for Aaron Boone in the early morning hours of October 17, 2003.

667 The slugging percentage (.667) for World War II veteran Ted Williams in 1946. He was only a 23-year-old kid when he batted .406 in 1941, but then the season ended and our country came under attack at Pearl Harbor—and by 1943 he was a Marine fighter pilot serving overseas who cheated death on several documented occasions. He came back in 1946, and he won his first career MVP after hitting 38 home runs. Williams was awarded the Presidential Medal of Freedom in 1991—our nation's highest civilian honor—by President George H.W. Bush, who said, "Ted Williams is an American legend, a remarkable figure in American sports and a twice-tested war hero. At the height of his athletic career, he answered the call of patriotism, serving in both World War II and the Korean War—a true champion."

668 The number of plate appearances (668) for Tris Speaker in 1914. The Hall of Famer led the club with a .338 average, .423 on-base percentage, .503 slugging percentage, .926 OPS, 101 runs, 193 hits, 287 total bases, 46 doubles, four home runs, 90 RBI, 42 steals, 68 extra-base hits, and 277 times on base. The crazy thing—by any standard, it was just a "normal" year for Speaker.

669 The winning percentage (.669) for Boston in 1915. Player-manager Bill Carrigan led the club to a 101-50 record and held off the Detroit Tigers (100-54) to win the pennant. Boston went on to beat the Phillies in five games to win the third World Series title in franchise history.

670 The number of times (670) Jim Rice walked. He was a free-swinging slugger who never got cheated at the plate and never walked more than 62 times in any one season. Rice struck out far more often than he walked—but so what? The fans paid to see him swing the lumber, and he did not disappoint. His career walks total, despite his free-swinging spirit, is among the top ten in franchise history.

671 The losers' share ($671) of the 1918 World Series. Boston beat the Cubs, and each Red Sox player took home a winners' share of $1,108—but both shares represent the lowest paid out in World Series history. The owners were trying to save money during the war by paying lower salaries and offering "bonuses" instead—but the bonuses were cut from the postseason shares and distributed to players on non-pennant winning teams. Players from both teams actually forced a delay of Game 5 in order to renegotiate, but in the end their efforts only alienated fans who saw such actions during wartime as inappropriate. In the end, members of the Red Sox did not even receive the medallions that were traditionally awarded to the champions (this was before the now-traditional championship rings)—and there wasn't even a victory parade. In 1993, however, the Boston Red Sox celebrated the 75th anniversary of the 1918 championship season by awarding the commemorative medallions to relatives of the players on that team.

672 The number of plate appearances (672) for Ted Williams in 1946. He used them well, obviously, as he won his first career MVP and the only pennant of his career. There were many impressive at bats for Williams that season, but perhaps none as impressive as one particular at bat that occurred on June 9, 1946, when The Splendid Splinter launched one of the longest home runs in Fenway Park history against Fred Hutchinson of the Detroit Tigers. It measured 502 feet—and when you visit Fenway, there is a seat in the right field bleachers that is painted red to mark the spot where it landed: Section 42, Row 37, Seat 21. The man sitting there took it on the noggin. Joseph Boucher later said, "The sun was right in our eyes. All we could do was duck. I'm glad I didn't stand up. They say it bounced a dozen rows higher, but after it hit my head I was no longer interested."

673 The number of at bats (673) for Bill Buckner in 1985. In his second season with the club, his total was the second highest in the league and remains the third highest in franchise history. Buckner, who came over from the Cubs the previous season in a trade for Dennis Eckersley, used his at bats to collect 46 doubles, 201 hits, and a career high 110 RBI—and he was also sixth in the league with 301 total bases.

674 Boston gave up (674) runs in 1945—the highest total out of eight teams in the league. Boston's offense was only fourth best in the league, and that combination led to a seventh place finish. The next season, however, the pitching staff gave up only 594 runs, which was the third lowest total in the league, while the offense scored the most runs in the league—and that combination led to a pennant.

675 The winning percentage (.675) for Boston in 1946. The club won their first pennant since 1918 after posting a 104-50 record, but when Ted Williams did not show up for the post-game celebration he was immediately criticized in the press for snubbing his teammates and fans. Until the truth came out, that is. Hy Hurwitz of the *Boston Globe* reported that Williams "sneaked out to an army hospital to sit at the bedside of a dying veteran who had requested that the Kid visit him. Williams ducked a nation-wide radio broadcast to perform a charitable act."

676 The winning percentage (.676) for Joe Wood during 218 games for Boston. Wood's winning percentage is the third best in franchise history. He posted a 117-56 record for the club, tying him with Pedro Martinez (117-37) for one of the top ten victory totals in franchise history as well.

677 The number of at bats (677) for Jim Rice in 1978. His total set a franchise record at the time, and it was also the first of two seasons that Rice led the league in at bats. To say he used them well is an understatement. Rice earned MVP honors after posting league best numbers in slugging, OPS, hits, total bases, triples, home runs, and RBI—and he was third in batting, just missing the Triple Crown.

678 Dick Radatz gave up (6.78) hits per nine innings of work for Boston. Radatz was with the club from 1962-66, and during that time he tossed 557-plus innings but gave up just 420 hits—which edges out Pedro Martinez (6.79) for the best ratio of hits per nine innings in franchise history.

679 The winning percentage (.679) for Boston in 2007 during games considered to be a blowout. Boston was 36-17 and outscored their opponents 405-242 during games decided by five or more runs. Boston beat Baltimore 13-4 at Fenway on May 12, but that particular blowout was an anomaly of sorts, as it was the first time since May 31, 1998, that Boston scored 13 or more runs but did not hit a homer. The 1998 game was at Yankee Stadium—the last time Boston had scored 13 or more runs without a homer at Fenway was even farther back, on May 29, 1993.

680 Derek Lowe gave up (6.80) hits per nine innings of work in 2002. He gave up just 166 hits during 219-plus innings on the mound. Lowe's ratio was the third best in the league and only second best on the club behind Pedro Martinez—but it remains one of the top 20 season efforts in franchise history.

681 The number of plate appearances (681) for Mo Vaughn in 1998. He used them to post a team best .337 average, .402 on-base percentage, .591 slugging percentage, .993 OPS, 205 hits, 360 total bases, 40 home runs, and 274 times on base. Oh yeah, he also led the club with 144 whiffs—but the Hit Dog was always fun to watch.

682 The winning percentage (.682) for Curt Schilling in 2006. He was 15-7, and his team best winning percentage was sixth among league leaders.

683 The number of runs (683) Bill Lee gave up from 1969-78. The Spaceman was 94-68 during a decade with the club. He pitched 1,503-plus innings and only 608 of those runs were earned, giving him a very respectable 3.64 earned run average during his tenure in Boston.

684 The number of at bats (684) for shortstop Nomar Garciaparra in 1997. He was a 23-year-old rookie when he led the league with a franchise record number of at bats. He used them exceptionally well, as he also led the league with 209 hits and was second with 122 runs. Garciaparra was the unanimous choice in Rookie of the Year balloting.

685 The number of batters (685) faced by Randy Johnson as a member of the Seattle Mariners in 1998. He struck out 213 of those batters, and then he was traded to the Houston Astros where he posted a 10-1 record down the stretch. It was apparent early on that Johnson was set for a dominant season—on April 10, he struck out 15 against Boston, and gave up just two hits in eight innings. The Mariners held a five-run lead so they went to the bullpen in the ninth. Seven batters, two singles, two walks, a double, a hit batter, and a Mo Vaughn grand slam later, Boston won 9-7.

686 Babe Ruth gave up (6.86) hits per nine innings of work in 1915. That ratio was the second best in the league, and it was also the first of four consecutive seasons that Ruth posted a ratio that placed among the top four league leaders—all four of which remain among the top 20 in franchise history.

687 The ratio (6.87) of hits per nine innings pitched for Daisuke Matsuzaka in 2008. Dice-K posted the best ratio in the league. He was also second in the league with a .857 winning percentage after posting an 18-3 record. With a win or a no-decision in his final start, Dice-K would have broken Bob Stanley's franchise record .882 winning percentage. Instead, he took the loss and tied Roger Clemens' 1986 mark for Boston's third best all-time.

688 The Texas Rangers scored (688) runs during their first 122 games on the 2008 schedule—a total that at the time was the best in the league and 56 more than Boston, the second highest scoring team in the league. In fact, games 120, 121, and 122 were against Boston, and the Rangers scored 21 runs in the three game set. The series was a sweep, but it was the Red Sox carrying the broom. Boston outscored Texas 37-21 in the series, and at one point in all three games Boston led by a score of at least 8-0. That feat was reported as a franchise first by the Elias Sports Bureau—which also noted that only one other team in the last 46 years held such commanding leads in three consecutive games.

689 Boston gave up (689) runs in 1988. That total was the seventh highest out of 14 teams in the league, but it was a big improvement over the 825 runs the club gave up the previous season—a total that was the 11th highest in the league. The improved pitching was exactly what the club needed to go along with an offense that scored the most runs in baseball, a combination that led to a division title.

690 The winning percentage (.690) for Boston during June, 1990, after posting a 20-9 record that included a pair of seven-game winning streaks and a 6-1 record vs. Baltimore. Jeff Gray, who got a cup of coffee with Cincinnati two years earlier but was a full-fledged rookie in 1990, earned his first big league win on June 23, when he came out of the bullpen in a 4-3 extra-inning victory over the Orioles. The very next day, on June 24, Gray came out of the bullpen again, this time earning his first big league save in a 2-0 victory that completed a three-game sweep of Baltimore and kept the club a half-game back of Toronto in the standings. The club took over first the next day when they won the first of four straight over Toronto.

691 The winning percentage (.691) for Boston in 1912. Player-manager Jake Stahl led the club to a 105-47 record for Boston's highest winning percentage of the 20th century. Boston went on to defeat the New York Giants in an eight-game series (4-3-1) to earn the second World Series title in franchise history.

692 Cy Young gave up (6.92) hits per nine innings of work in 1908. He was a 41-year-old veteran in his final season with the Red Sox, but his ratio was the sixth best in the league. The Hall of Fame legend was helped by his performance on June 30, against the Yankees, when he tossed his third career no-hitter, and his second as a member of the Red Sox.

693 The number of extra-base hits (693) for Bobby Doerr. Seven times he was among the top ten league leaders in total bases, seven times he was among the top ten league leaders in slugging percentage, and seven times he was among the top ten league leaders in home runs. Doerr was among the top ten league leaders in extra-base hits ten times—and his career total is the fifth highest in franchise history.

694 The slugging percentage (.694) for Jimmie Foxx in 1939. It was the fifth time in his career that he led the league in slugging, and he did it with the fourth highest percentage in franchise history. Foxx also led the league with 35 home runs—but that was his lowest total during his first five seasons with the club from 1936-40. His other totals were: 41, 36, 50, and 36.

695 The number of singles (695) Carlton Fisk hit for Boston. The slugger had bad knees or surely some of those would have gone for two bases, but either way, his total is the exact number Manny Ramirez had for Boston at the time he was traded to LA in 2008. It is one of the top 35 totals in franchise history.

696 Cy Young gave up (6.96) hits per nine innings of work in 1905. He gave up 248 hits total, but he was on the mound for 320-plus innings after completing 31 of 33 starts. Young's ratio of hits per nine innings was the third best in the league, and it remains among the top 20 season efforts in franchise history.

697 Carl Yastrzemski made (697) plate appearances in 1970—and he produced a league best .452 on-base percentage on the strength of a .329 average and 128 walks. His walks total from that season is the eighth highest in franchise history—but it is the highest total that does not belong to Ted Williams.

698 Boston gave up (698) runs in 1995. That was only the sixth best total out of 14 teams in the league, but only 630 of those runs were earned, giving the staff the third best earned run average in the league. On the offensive side, Mo Vaughn, Jose Canseco, and John Valentin all led an offense that was the fourth best in the league, but that was the best in the East—and in the end, that combination led to a division title for Kevin Kennedy's club.

699 Smoky Joe Wood gave up (6.99) hits per nine innings of work in 1912. That ratio led the team and was the second best in the league. Wood gave up 267 hits, but tossed 344 innings—and his ratio remains among the top 25 in franchise history.

700 The slugging percentage (.700) for Mark Bellhorn during the 2004 World Series. He hit just .091 in the Division Series vs. Anaheim and .192 in the League Championship Series vs. New York, but he hit .300 in the World Series vs. St. Louis—plus, he hit the game-winning home run in Boston's wild 11-9 victory over the Cardinals in Game 1 of the series. That game was the first in World Series history where the two teams combined to score 20 runs.

Boston Red Sox Career Wins Leaders

Player	Career Wins	Seasons
Roger Clemens	192	13
Cy Young	192	8
Tim Wakefield*	179	16
Mel Parnell	123	10
Luis Tiant	122	8
Pedro Martinez	117	7
Joe Wood	117	8
Bob Stanley	115	13
Joe Dobson	106	9
Lefty Grove	105	8

*still active in 2011

Boston Red Sox Single Season Wins Leaders

Player	Wins	Year
Joe Wood	34	1912
Cy Young	33	1901
Cy Young	32	1902
Cy Young	28	1903
Cy Young	26	1904
Wes Ferrell	25	1935
Dave Ferriss	25	1946
Mel Parnell	25	1949
Roger Clemens	24	1986
Babe Ruth	24	1917

"Curt Schilling's performance tonight will long live in New England baseball lore."
— Tim McCarver, FOX broadcaster after Game 6 of the 2004 ALCS

Chapter 8

Winning Pitchers

JOSH BECKETT, CURT Schilling, Pedro Martinez, Roger Clemens, Jim Lonborg, Frank Sullivan, Mel Parnell, Tex Hughson, Wes Ferrell, Joe Wood, and Cy Young all led the American League in wins while pitching for Boston. Clemens actually led the league twice (1986, 1987) with Boston while Young led the league three times (1901, 1902, and 1903). Young, of course, is the man for whom baseball's most prestigious pitching award is named—and Clemens is the man who has won that award a record seven times. That two of baseball's greatest legends from two very distinct eras are such an integral part of Red Sox history is neither a surprise nor a coincidence. People associate the Boston Red Sox with winners for one simple reason— because we are.

And it isn't just because some very good pitchers have led the league in wins while wearing a Red Sox uniform either—it's much more than that.

It's CC Sabathia winning the 2007 Cy Young Award for Cleveland, but getting lit up in the League Championship Series for two losses head-to-head against Boston's Josh Beckett. Sabathia got the Cy Young despite Beckett leading the league in wins, but Beckett was 4-0 in the postseason and got his second career ring.

Beckett is a winner.

It's Jon Lester clinching the 2007 World Series in his first career postseason start, and then shutting down a potent Anaheim offense not once, but twice during the 2008 Division Series. Lester tossed more than 20 innings of postseason baseball without allowing an earned run.

Lester is a winner.

It's Curt Schilling and his bloody sock staring down the Yankees in the Bronx. It's Derek Lowe taking the mound the very next night to complete the most improbable comeback in baseball history—and then seven days later clinching the World Series. It's Pedro Martinez and his six hitless innings of postseason relief against the Indians. Yes, it is also Cy Young and Roger Clemens, and the 192 wins in a Red Sox uniform that they share—the perfect game for Young, the 20 strikeout games for Clemens—but it is also Bill Dinneen clinching the 1903 World Series with a busted, bloody hand, and Jose Santiago shutting down Minnesota with two games left in the season to keep the 1967 Impossible Dream alive, and Jim Lonborg clinching the Impossible Dream the very next day, and Jim Lonborg again, tossing a one-hitter and a three-hitter in the 1967 World Series, and Luis Tiant in the 1975 postseason, shutting out Oakland and Cincinnati in back-to-back starts.

They are all winners.

They all stood toe-to-toe against the fiercest opponents in the game, in the direst of circumstances, with the hearts of Red Sox Nation hanging in the balance, and they won.

It's also the knuckleball of Tim Wakefield.

The man who was released by the Pittsburgh Pirates in 1995 only to find a new home and a new career in Boston, he closed out 2010 with 179 victories for the Red Sox—trailing only Cy Young and Roger Clemens in the franchise record book.

Wakefield is most definitely a winner.

Chapter eight is all about Boston's pitchers who dominated—for a game, for a season, or for a career—including: teammates Charley Hall and Smoky Joe Wood making history in 1910, Dutch Leonard racking up the Ks in 1914, Derek Lowe putting up Cy Young numbers in back-to-back seasons, Jim Lonborg and his incredible numbers in 1967, Luis Tiant winning 20 games in 1973, Roger Clemens' third Cy Young, and speaking of Cy Young, he is here as well, and so are Mel Parnell and his 21 wins in 1953, Smoky Joe Wood and his epic battle vs. Walter Johnson in 1912, Sam Jones, Carl Mays, and Babe Ruth, Josh Beckett, Bruce Hurst, Lefty Grove, Pedro Martinez, Tom Gordon, Dennis Eckersley, Tex Hughson, Ernie Shore, and Tim Wakefield.

Also in this chapter are players who raised their game to a new level when the pressure was the most intense—guys like Derek Lowe, who sealed Boston's comeback vs. Oakland in the 2003 Division Series after inheriting a 4-3 lead, two men on base, and no outs.

Lowe got the job done. He is a winner.

On to the late innings...

701 Dave Morehead struck out (7.01) batters per nine innings in 1963. He was a 20-year-old rookie who struck out 136 batters during 174-plus innings of work. That ratio placed him sixth among league leaders—but it was the best among Boston's staff, and it remains among the top 40 ratios in franchise history.

702 Smoky Joe Wood gave up (7.02) hits per nine innings of work in 1910. He gave up just 155 hits during 198-plus innings on the mound for a ratio that was the fifth best in franchise history at that time— but he was overshadowed by his teammate Charley Hall, who in 1910 set a new franchise record after giving up just 6.77 hits per nine innings. Today, Hall's ratio remains among the top 15 in franchise history, and Wood's ratio remains among the top 25.

703 The number of plate appearances (703) for Mark Loretta in 2006. That total led the team, and the second baseman also led the club with 181 hits. Loretta hit .285 and was an All-Star during his one-season stop in Beantown.

704 The slugging percentage (.704) for Hall of Fame legend Jimmie Foxx in 1938. He hit 50 home runs for a franchise record that stood until David Ortiz hit 54 in 2006. Foxx led the league in on-base and slugging percentage, total bases, extra-base hits, walks, and RBI—plus, he also batted .349 to win his second batting title, and third career MVP.

705 The number of strikeouts (7.05) per nine innings for Dutch Leonard in 1914. He struck out a career high 176 batters but gave up only 139 hits during 224-plus innings of work. His strikeout ratio was the best in the league.

706 Babe Ruth gave up (7.06) hits per nine innings of work for Boston. He logged 1,190-plus innings on the hill, but gave up just 934 hits. Ruth's hits per nine innings ratio was among the top four league leaders from 1915-18, including a league best 6.40 in 1916, and his career ratio with Boston remains among the top five in franchise history.

707 The number of plate appearances (707) for Carl Yastrzemski in 1969. Yaz used them to lead the club with 40 home runs and 111 RBI. Those totals gave him three consecutive seasons among the league's top ten leaders in both categories—and he made it four straight in 1970.

708 The winning percentage (.708) for Derek Lowe in 2003. He backed up his 20 wins from the previous season by posting a 17-7 record that gave him the sixth best winning percentage in the league.

709 The number of times (709) Ted Williams struck out. One of the most disciplined hitters in baseball history, Williams never posted more strikeouts than walks in any season. He is fourth in baseball history with 2,021 walks—a ratio of 2.85 walks per strikeout, which is so good that it's ridiculous, especially considering he also hit 521 home runs.

710 The winning percentage (.710) for Jim Lonborg in 1967. That gave him the third best winning percentage in the league and one of the top 50 in franchise history—and his league best 22 wins and 246 strikeouts earned him the Cy Young Award and his only career All-Star appearance.

711 The offensive winning percentage (.711) for Mo Vaughn in 1994. Boston was 54-61 and 17 games back of the Yankees when the strike brought 1994 to a halt. The offensive winning percentage is an estimate of how well a club would do if all nine spots in the lineup produced at the same level as a specific player—say Mo Vaughn in 1994. Boston posted a measly .470 winning percentage in 115 games that year, but Vaughn produced at such a high rate that fans could have expected a .711 winning percentage if his name could have been penciled into every spot in the batting order.

712 Norwood Gibson gave up (7.12) hits per nine innings of work in 1904. He posted a 17-14 record during his sophomore year with the club. Gibson gave up 216 hits but was on the mound for 273 innings. His ratio of hits per nine innings led the club and was the fourth best in the league, and it remains among the top 30 season efforts in franchise history. Gibson, unfortunately, won only four more games the rest of his career.

713 The number of batters (713) faced by Luis Tiant in 1972. He tossed 179 innings from the rubber but gave up just 128 hits. That gave him a team leading ratio of 6.44 hits per nine innings of work—a ratio that remains among the top ten in franchise history.

714 The on-base plus slugging percentage (.714) for Terrence Long vs. Derek Lowe in 22 career plate appearances. Primarily an outfielder for Oakland, Long batted 6 for 20 with a double and two walks against Lowe during six full seasons of big league play—but it was Lowe who won the most important match-up between the two. On October 6, 2003, Lowe completed Boston's rally from a two-game deficit to win the best-of-five Division Series by striking out Long with the potential tying and winning runs in scoring position—preserving a 4-3 victory after inheriting the two base runners with no outs.

715 The number of plate appearances (715) for Billy Goodman in 1955. He got 599 at bats that season for a career high, but the former batting champion and MVP runner-up did not hit a single home run.

He posted just a .352 slugging percentage, the lowest during his time with Boston.

716 The number of batters (716) faced by Ed Durham in 1931. He faced 43 of those batters in a single game against the Detroit Tigers on September 12. Durham tossed a complete game five-hit shutout—and it was a 13 inning game. He only struck out one batter, but he did not allow a hit after the fourth, and he did not walk any batters either.

717 The Louisville Bats scored (717) runs in 2008. The Triple-A affiliate of the Cincinnati Reds posted the second highest runs total in the International League, trailing only the Pawtucket Red Sox. Boston's Triple-A affiliate scored a league high 752 runs, averaging 5.26 runs per game. The Pawsox also hit a league best 176 home runs, led by Jonathan Van Every (26), Jeff Bailey (25), Chris Carter (24), and George Kottaras (22).

718 Luis Tiant gave up (7.18) hits per nine innings of work in 1973. That ratio was the fourth best in the league, but it was the best on the club for the 20-game winner—and it remains among the top 30 in franchise history.

719 The number of plate appearances (719) for Carl Yastrzemski in 1962. His total was only fifth highest in the league, but it was a career high for the man who would go on to make more trips to the plate than any other player in Red Sox history. Yaz stepped into the box 13,991 times during his Hall of Fame career. Pete Rose is the only player in baseball history with more career plate appearances (15,861).

720 Boston scored (720) runs in 1947. Led by Ted Williams (125) and Johnny Pesky (106), the Red Sox offense was the second highest scoring in the league—but unfortunately, the pitching staff was one of the worst in the league, and the club fell from first in 1946, to third in 1947.

721 Jimmie Foxx scored (721) runs as a member of the Red Sox. He is among the top 25 in baseball history with 1,751 career runs. Foxx surpassed the century mark five times for Boston—and his total with the club is among the top 15 in franchise history.

722 Boston scored (722) runs in 1967. That total was the highest in the league, and unlike the previous season, Boston also got production on the rubber. Okay, the team did give up 614 runs—the third highest total in the league—but Jim Lonborg won the Cy Young Award, and the club won 20 more games than they did the previous year. Only a half-game out of dead last in 1966, the 1967 club lived the Impossible Dream and won the pennant by a single game over the Tigers and Twins.

723 The average on-base plus slugging percentage (.723) for American League players in 1965. Boston's Tony Conigliaro did a touch better than the average player. The 20-year-old outfielder led the league with 32 home runs in only 138 games. He posted a .512 slugging percentage and a .850 OPS.

724 The winning percentage (.724) for Derek Lowe in 2002. He saved 81 games the previous three seasons, but he returned to the rotation and was second in the league in wins after posting a 21-8 record. His effort gave him one of the top 40 winning percentages in franchise history—and nearly won him the Cy Young Award.

725 The number of times (725) Mo Vaughn walked during his 12-year career. He preferred to swing the lumber and was never afraid to miss—seeing as he went down on strikes 1,429 times (but went yard 328 times).

726 Roger Clemens gave up (7.26) hits per nine innings of work in 1991. That ratio led the club and was fourth in the league, and it was a contributing factor towards Clemens' third Cy Young Award. His 1991 ratio also ranks among the top 35 in franchise history.

727 The winning percentage (.727) for Boston vs. Chicago in 1912. Boston was 16-6 against the White Sox on the season, but on June 1, the Red Sox trailed Chicago by three games as the club began a 25-game road trip. Boston lost two of three at home earlier in the season to Chicago, but after losing four of five to start their long road trip, the club got hot and posted a 17-8 record that included three wins in four games in Chicago—and when they got back home, Boston held a five-game lead that they never relinquished en route to winning the pennant, and the 1912 World Series.

728 Boston gave up (728) runs in 1954. The club struggled all season and won just 69 games, thanks in part to a pitching staff that gave up the second highest runs total in the league. Boston's offense was only middle of the pack, and that combination led to a disastrous finish—42 games back of Cleveland.

729 Cy Morgan gave up (7.29) hits per nine innings of work in 1908. The Red Sox hurler posted the tenth best ratio in the league, but there were two hurlers on the staff named Cy, and Morgan was nowhere near the team best 6.92 ratio posted by Young. Morgan and Young were the two best pitchers on the staff, however, and while Young's ratio from 1908 is among the top 20 in franchise history, Morgan's ratio is respectably within the top 35. It's worth mentioning that in 1909 Morgan got off to a 2-6 start and found himself pitching in Philadelphia after appearing in only 12 games for Boston. The rest of the season he was lights out, and in 1909 it was Morgan who posted a league best 6.26 hits per nine innings ratio.

730 The number of plate appearances (730) for Ted Williams in 1949. The Kid won the Most Valuable Player Award that season after setting career highs with 194 hits, 150 runs, 43 home runs, 159 RBI, and 162 walks.

731 The slugging percentage (.731) for Ted Williams in 1957. He led the league in slugging for the ninth time after posting the second highest percentage in franchise history.

732 The number of strikeouts (732) for Mel Parnell. He struck out a career high 136 batters in 1953 when he won 21 games. Twice he was among the top ten league leaders for strikeouts, and his career total is among the top 20 in franchise history.

733 The winning percentage (.733) for Washington Senators Hall of Fame pitcher Walter Johnson in 1912. He was 33-12, and he led the league with 303 strikeouts and a 1.39 earned run average. Johnson also set a league record by winning 16 consecutive games that season, and he nearly won the pitching Triple Crown. He came up one win short, however, because Boston's Smoky Joe Wood won 34 games that season—including a 1-0 match-up against Johnson and the Senators on September 6. That sterling performance also gave Wood 14 consecutive victories—and he posted two more to equal Johnson's mark of 16 straight.

734 The number of plate appearances (734) for Nomar Garciaparra in 1997. The 23-year-old shortstop led the club with 122 runs on his way to earning top rookie honors. Ken Griffey, Jr. scored 125 runs for the Mariners to edge out Nomar for the league lead. Nomar also led Boston in runs during 2003, scoring 120 in his last full season with the club—but this time it was Alex Rodriguez who edged him out for the league lead by scoring 124 runs.

735 The slugging percentage (.735) for Ted Williams in 1941. He batted .406 and hit 37 home runs—and set a franchise record for slugging. Williams earned Major League Player of the Year honors for the first of five times in his career.

736 The average on-base plus slugging percentage (.736) for American League players in 1975. A couple of Boston rookies did slightly better than the league average: Jim Rice (.309, 22 HR, 102 RBI) had a .841 OPS, while Fred Lynn (.331, 21 HR, 105 RBI) had a league leading .967 OPS.

737 The number of RBI (737) as a member of the Red Sox for Joe Cronin. He surpassed the century mark three times for the club and eight times overall. Cronin is among the top 75 in baseball history with 1,424 RBI, and the 737 he got for Boston was one of Boston's top ten totals until David Ortiz surpassed it in 2008.

738 Mickey McDermott gave up (7.38) hits per nine innings of work in 1951. The lefty divided his 34 games pretty evenly between starts and relief appearances, but regardless of how he was used he was definitely tough to hit. McDermott's ratio of hits per nine innings led the club and was second best in the league—and he also posted the best strikeouts per nine innings ratio in the league.

739 Sam Jones gave up (7.39) hits per nine innings of work in 1918. That ratio was the sixth best in the league, but it was only the third best on the team behind Carl Mays (7.06) and Babe Ruth (6.76), as three of the top 40 ratios in franchise history were recorded that season.

740 Roger Clemens gave up (7.40) hits per nine innings of work in 1988. He gave up 217 hits in 264 innings for the best ratio on the team, the sixth best ratio in the league, and one of the top 40 ratios in franchise history.

741 The winning percentage (.741) for Josh Beckett in 2007. He was the only 20-game winner in the league. Beckett's winning percentage was the best on the club, but it was only second in the league behind the .750 winning percentage for Justin Verlander (18-6 record) of the Detroit Tigers.

742 Bruce Hurst struck out (7.42) batters per nine innings in 1985. He set down 189 batters on strikes while taking the mound for 229-plus innings. That ratio was the second best in the league, trailing only Floyd Bannister of the Chicago White Sox—but it is also among the top 35 ratios in franchise history.

743 Lefty Grove struck out (743) batters while pitching for Boston. He was among the top four league leaders three times while with the club, but Lefty previously had led the league in strikeouts seven consecutive seasons from 1925-31 while pitching for Philadelphia. His career total is among the top 50 in baseball history, and his total for Boston is among the top 20 in franchise history.

744 The winning percentage (.744) for Cy Young in 1902. He was 32-11 after completing a staggering 41 of 43 starts. Young faced 1,527 batters in 384-plus innings on the mound—and after all that, he emerged with a winning percentage that remains among the top 30 in franchise history.

745 Boston gave up (745) runs in 2000. That was the lowest total in the league, but the offense was the third worst in the league—and after dropping two out of three to Tampa Bay to close out the season, Boston came in second 2.5 games back of the Yankees.

746 The offensive winning percentage (.746) for Dwight Evans in 1987. This estimate of what an all-Dewey offense would produce made him the third highest rated player in the league behind Mark McGwire and teammate Wade Boggs—which makes you wonder how Boston won just 78 games. Oh wait, pitching—got it.

747 The number of singles (747) for Marty Barrett from 1982-90. Barrett went 1 for 18 during a September call-up in 1982, with his first big league hit being a single. He got a lot of singles, in fact, that contributed to his .278 average for Boston—his total ranks among the top 25 in franchise history.

748 Barry Bonds hit career home run number (748) at Fenway Park. The blast to deep right field came against knuckleball artist Tim Wakefield on June 17, 2007, as Bonds moved closer in his historic quest to surpass Hank Aaron in the record book. It was a pretty good day to be a fan at the ballpark—36,137 got to see Bonds' only career home run at Fenway, but they also saw Manny go yard as Wakefield and Boston picked up a 9-5 win. To cap it off, it was Father's Day—and after the game the Red Sox invited kids in the stands out onto the field to play catch with their dads.

749 The number of singles (749) for Doc Cramer from 1936-40. He hit only one home run for Boston. It came in 1940, after four consecutive homerless seasons. Cramer did hit a lot of singles for the club—one of the top 25 totals in franchise history.

750 The number of times (750) Dom DiMaggio walked. He drew 101 bases on balls in 1948 to set a career high, and he posted more walks than strikeouts eight times during ten seasons. His total is among the ten highest in franchise history.

751 Jim Lonborg gave up (7.51) hits per nine innings of work in 1967. Lonborg tossed 273-plus innings but gave up just 228 hits for the best ratio on the club—just one of the eight major categories he led the staff in that season—and his ratio remains among the top 50 in franchise history.

752 The number of RBI (752) as a member of the Red Sox for Mo Vaughn. He surpassed the century mark four times during seven full seasons in Boston—including a league best 126 RBI in 1995. Vaughn drove home 1,064 runs during his career, and the 752 RBI that came for the Red Sox is among the top ten totals in franchise history.

753 Mickey McDermott gave up (7.53) hits per nine innings from 1948-53. In the Red Sox farm system he tossed two no-hitters and once struck out 20 batters in a single game. The best of his six seasons in Boston was 1953, when he posted an 18-10 record and gave up just 169 hits in 206-plus innings of work. That same season he was second in the league with a 7.37 hits per nine innings ratio— and his career mark with Boston is among the top ten in franchise history.

754 The offensive winning percentage (.754) for Manny Ramirez as a member of the Red Sox from 2001-08. Statistical models predict that an all-Manny lineup and a normal defensive unit would have won games at a .754 rate based on the numbers he produced for the Red Sox—not bad at all.

755 The on-base plus slugging percentage (.755) for Hall of Famer Bobby Doerr in 1946. That mark was well below his career .823 OPS, but after hitting 18 home runs with 116 RBI he was still third in MVP balloting.

756 The number of plate appearances (756) for Dom DiMaggio in 1948. That total set a franchise record that lasted until 1985.

DiMaggio used his plate appearances well, hitting .285 and scoring a team best 127 runs.

757 The winning percentage (.757) for Cy Young in 1903. He led the league after posting a 28-9 record, and his winning percentage remains among the top 25 efforts in franchise history. Young won enough games (119) from 1901-04 (33, 32, 28, and 26) to place him sixth among Boston's career leaders. Include his other four seasons from 1905-08, of course, and he has 192 wins—tied with Roger Clemens for number one.

758 The number of plate appearances (758) for Wade Boggs in 1985. He led the league and set franchise records for both hits and plate appearances on his way to a .368 average and his second career batting title. Boggs also made his first career All-Star team, but he only placed fourth in league MVP balloting and the Royals George Brett won the Silver Slugger Award for third basemen.

759 Roger Clemens struck out (7.59) batters per nine innings in 1992. He was third in the league with 208 strikeouts and sixth in the league with 246-plus innings, and his ratio of strikeouts per nine innings was the fourth best in the league. The Rocket also won 18 games while leading the league with a 2.41 earned run average—and he placed third in Cy Young balloting.

760 The winning percentage (.760) for Pedro Martinez during 203 games for Boston. Martinez posted a 117-37 record during seven seasons for the best winning percentage in franchise history.

761 Roger Clemens gave up (7.61) hits per nine innings in 1990. That ratio led the club and was third best in the league behind Nolan Ryan and Randy Johnson. The Rocket was 21-6, and he led the league with four shutouts and a 1.93 earned run average. If not for the 27 wins for Bob Welch, 1990 would have been another Cy Young year for Clemens.

762 The winning percentage (.762) for Sam Jones in 1918. In four previous seasons Jones had a 4-11 record with Cleveland and Boston, but in 1918 he completed 16 of 21 starts, tossed five shutouts, and posted a 16-5 record that left him with a winning percentage that not only led the league, but that also remains among the top 25 in franchise history—and more importantly, he was a key part of the 1918 team that won the World Series.

763 The average on-base plus slugging percentage (.763) for American League players in 1993. The team leader for Boston was Mo Vaughn, who was among the league's best with a .915 OPS that was way above your average player. Vaughn reached base at a .390 clip, while posting a .525 slugging percentage.

764 Tom Gordon gave up (7.64) hits per nine innings in 1997. That ratio led the club and was the fifth best in the league. Flash gave up 155 hits in 182-plus innings of work, divided between bullpen duty and the rotation. He took that success to the bullpen fulltime in 1998 and saved a career high 46 games.

765 Roger Clemens gave up (7.65) hits per nine innings from 1984-96. That ratio is among the top ten in franchise history. Clemens was among the top ten league leaders in this category nine times while playing for Boston, and he led the league twice (1986, 1994). The guys who got the most career hits off Clemens are: Paul Molitor (33), Harold Baines (32), Rafael Palmeiro (30), and B.J. Surhoff (30).

766 The number of batters (766) faced by Charley Hall in 1912. He faced a lot more hitters in the minors than he ever did at the major league level—after all, this is the guy who pitched in 701 minor league games. In the best year of his career, however, he was 15-8 for the Boston Red Sox and only 64 batters reached base and scored an earned run against him. Hall was only fourth on the staff in wins, but he was an integral part of the club that won the 1912 World Series.

767 The winning percentage (.767) for Cy Young in 1901. He led the league with 33 wins—one of which came vs. Philadelphia on May 8, when Boston beat the Athletics 12-4 at the Huntington Avenue Grounds in the very first home game in franchise history.

768 Boston gave up (768) runs in 2004. That total was the third lowest in the league thanks to a staff anchored by Curt Schilling, Pedro Martinez, Tim Wakefield, and Derek Lowe. Boston scored on average 5.86 runs per game, but gave up only 4.74 runs per game—and won 98 contests as a result.

769 The winning percentage (.769) for Boston vs. Toronto in 1990. The Red Sox posted a 10-3 record against Toronto—which was huge, because the two clubs battled it out all season for the division title. Boston won two of three from Toronto during the final week of the season, and when the dust settled the Red Sox won the A.L. East by two games over the Blue Jays.

770 The number of at bats (770) for Jim Lonborg from 1965-79. The pitcher got 105 hits for a career .136 average—hardly worth bragging about, even for a pitcher. Lonborg, however, who did hit three big league home runs, got one of the most important hits in Red Sox history on a bunt single. It ignited a five-run, sixth inning rally against the Twins on October 1, 1967, and Lonborg went the distance for a 5-3 victory that made real the Impossible Dream and gave Boston the pennant by one game over those same Twins.

771 Dennis Eckersley and Dutch Leonard both struck out (771) batters while pitching for Boston. Eck and Leonard were both successful starters for the Red Sox, and they share a strikeout total that is among the top 15 in franchise history.

772 Wade Boggs scored (772) runs from 1983-89. He surpassed the century mark seven consecutive seasons, led the league twice (1988, 1989), and was among the top seven league leaders every year. Boggs played ten more seasons but never surpassed the century mark in runs again.

773 The number of RBI (773) for shortstop Rico Petrocelli. His career high 103 RBI in 1970 was the only time he surpassed the century mark—but after 12 seasons in Boston he closed out his career with a total that remains among the top ten in franchise history.

774 Cy Young gave up (7.74) hits per nine innings from 1901-08. That ratio still ranks among the ten best in franchise history.

775 Boston gave up (775) runs in 1934. It was the fourth lowest total out of eight teams in the league—but it was a huge improvement over the past decade when the team was selling players instead of focusing on winning games. The offense was up as well, scoring 820 runs for the third highest total in the league. The result was a much improved 76-76 club. The fans could enjoy the games more too, and not just because the team was improved. Owner Tom Yawkey spent $750,000 to renovate Fenway—which had been damaged by two separate fires—and play began at the "new" Fenway Park on April 17, 1934.

776 Johnny Pesky scored (776) runs for the Red Sox. He surpassed the century mark for Boston during six consecutive seasons to begin his career, including a high of 124 runs in 1948 that was the third highest total in the league. Pesky's career total with the club remains among the ten best in franchise history.

777 Hideo Nomo gave up (7.77) hits per nine innings of work in 2001. His no-hitter helped, of course, as Nomo's ratio was the best on the club and the fifth best among league leaders.

778 The winning percentage (.778) for Boston during May, 1946, after posting a 21-6 record. Boston won 15 consecutive games beginning on April 25, and won 21 of 25 games to start the season. The Red Sox were up seven games when June began, and led by 16.5 games in early September. It took owner Tom Yawkey 13 seasons, but with a record of 104-50 he finally got a pennant.

779 The average on-base plus slugging percentage (.779) for American League players in 1998. Boston's high-powered offense was paced by Mo Vaughn and Nomar Garciaparra, who both were well above the league average. Vaughn hit 40 homers and posted a team high .993 OPS, while Nomar hit 35 homers and posted a .946 OPS.

780 Boston scored (780) runs in 1956. Nobody hit the century mark, as the club was led by Billy Klaus and Jim Piersall who each scored 91. Boston's offense was only third best in the league, and with just 84 wins the club was fourth in the pennant race.

781 The winning percentage (.781) for Mel Parnell in 1949. He led the league in wins after posting a career best 25-7 record. He is tied with Wes Ferrell and Dave Ferriss for the sixth highest season win total in franchise history, but only Cy Young (four times) and Smoky Joe Wood (once) have surpassed 25 victories in a season. Parnell's winning perentage from 1949 was second best in the league, but it remains one of the top 20 in franchise history.

782 The on-base plus slugging percentage (.782) for Chick Stahl in 1904. He led the club with a .366 on-base percentage and a .416 slugging percentage, so obviously his OPS was a team high as well. Stahl hit .290 with three home runs—and he was also fifth in the league in OPS.

783 The winning percentage (.783) for Tex Hughson in 1944. He was third in the league with a 2.26 earned run average, but his 18-5 record gave him the best winning percentage in the league—and earned him a third consecutive All-Star selection.

784 The number of putouts (784) for All-Star catcher Jason Varitek in 2005. He made only eight errors in 824 chances—picked up 32 assists—and threw out 21 runners trying to steal. Varitek posted a .990 fielding percentage, and earned the first Gold Glove of his career.

785 Ernie Shore gave up (7.85) hits per nine innings from 1914-17. His best season was 1915, when he posted a 19-8 record and gave up just 207 hits in 247 innings of work. Shore's ratio of hits per nine innings with Boston remains among the top 15 in franchise history.

786 The winning percentage (.786) for Tex Hughson in 1942. He led the league in wins after posting a 22-6 record, and his winning percentage remains one of the top 15 in franchise history.

787 The number of batters (787) faced by Pedro Martinez in 2002. He gave up only 144 hits and 40 walks, but he struck out 239 batters in 199-plus innings. Martinez led the league with a .923 WHIP, the same ratio he led the league with in 1999. He posted three of the top ten ratios in franchise history during a four-year span from 1999-2002.

788 The number of RBI (788) as a member of the Red Sox for Jimmie Foxx. He only played six full seasons in Boston, and he surpassed the century mark in RBI during every one of them—including a career high and league leading 175 RBI in 1938. His career RBI total with Boston is among the top ten in franchise history.

789 The winning percentage (.789) for Lefty Grove in 1939. In his final All-Star season the Hall of Fame pitcher was 15-4, and he led the club with the second best winning percentage in the league.

790 Tim Wakefield struck out (7.90) batters per nine innings in 2001. He notched 148 strikeouts in only 168-plus innings on the mound for the second best ratio on the team, and the seventh best ratio in the league. His teammate Hideo Nomo struck out ten batters per nine innings pitched for the best ratio in the league that season.

791 The number of hits (791) for Ellis Burks as a member of the Red Sox. He spent parts of seven seasons with Boston where his highest hits total was 174 in 1990, when he made his first All-Star appearance. Burks' career hits total remains among the top 50 in franchise history.

792 The winning percentage (.792) for Dutch Leonard in 1914. He was 19-5 during his sophomore season and he led the club with a winning percentage that was second best in the league. Leonard only gave up 24 earned runs in 224-plus innings of work that season.

793 The winning percentage (.793) for Ellis Kinder in 1949. He was 31 years old when he made his big league debut for the St. Louis Browns in 1946. He came to Boston in a trade after 1947, and in 1949 he was fifth in league MVP balloting after posting a 23-6 record. He was named *The Sporting News* A.L. Pitcher of the Year after leading the league with a winning percentage that remains one of the ten best in franchise history.

794 The number of strikeouts (794) for Ray Culp from 1968-73. Culp struck out a career high 197 batters in 1970, and his career total for Boston remains among the top ten in franchise history. He also made history with Boston, along with teammates Dave Morehead, Jim Lonborg, and Dick Ellsworth, as they were the starters in a four-game series against the White Sox in August, 1968, during which no Boston pitcher issued a single walk. It was the first time since baseball's expansion era began in 1961 that a team did not walk a batter in a four-game series. It took a while for another team to replicate that feat, as the next time it occurred was when Oakland did it vs. Tampa in 2000.

795 Jacoby Ellsbury was successful on (79.5) percent of his minor league stolen base attempts. He stole 105 bases for Red Sox farm teams, but was caught only 27 times. He got off to a quick start for the big club as well. Ellsbury was 9 for 9 in 2007, and then he was 16 for 16 to start 2008. Only two players since baseball began tracking caught steals in 1951 began their careers with more than 25 successful attempts: Tim Raines (27 for 27) and Mitchell Page (26 for 26). Ellsbury was gunned down by Jason Kendall on May 18, 2008, ending his own streak at 25. He did, however, finish the season with a league best 50 steals.

796 Boston scored (796) runs in 1978. That total was the second highest in the league, led by Jim Rice and Carlton Fisk, who scored 121 and 94 respectively. Boston's offense only scored 112 runs during the final month of the season, however—the lowest output for the club during any month that year—as the Red Sox went 14-15. New York, of course, rallied from 14 games back on July 19 to win a one-game playoff for the division title, leading many fans and members of the media to question manager Don Zimmer's decision to not rest starters like Butch Hobson in preparation for the stretch run.

Zimmer, by the way, has always maintained that fatigue did not cause the collapse.

797 The offensive winning percentage (.797) for Wade Boggs in 1988. Boston won the East with an 89-73 record, good for a .549 winning percentage—but statistical models predict that a lineup consisting of nothing but the 1988 version of Wade Boggs would have won 129 games. Boggs' offensive winning percentage estimate was the highest in the league—followed closely by teammate Mike Greenwell, who got a .767 prediction for the second highest in the league.

798 Lefty Grove faced (798) batters in 1939. He only let 54 of them get on base and score an earned run as he posted a league best 2.54 earned run average. It was the ninth and final time of his career that Grove led the league in ERA.

799 Roger Clemens struck out (7.99) batters per nine innings in 1991. The Rocket struck out 241 batters in 271 innings. His total led the league, and his ratio led Boston but was only the third best in the league. Clemens owns eight of the top 25 ratios in franchise history— and of those, his ratio from 1991 is the *lowest* one.

800 The number of RBI (800) for outfielder Manny Ramirez from 2001-07. Manny surpassed the century mark in RBI during his first six seasons in Boston—and it took only seven seasons for Manny to move into sixth place in the franchise record book.

Boston Red Sox Career Saves Leaders

Player	Career Saves	Seasons
Jonathan Papelbon*	188	6
Bob Stanley	132	13
Dick Radatz	104	5
Ellis Kinder	91	8
Jeff Reardon	88	3
Derek Lowe	85	8
Sparky Lyle	69	5
Tom Gordon	68	4
Lee Smith	58	3
Bill Campbell	51	5

*still active in 2011

Boston Red Sox Single Season Saves Leaders

Player	Saves	Year
Tom Gordon	46	1998
Derek Lowe	42	2000
Jonathan Papelbon	41	2008
Jeff Reardon	40	1991
Ugueth Urbina	40	2002
Jonathan Papelbon	37	2007
Jonathan Papelbon	37	2010
Jonathan Papelbon	35	2006
Jeff Russell	33	1993
Bob Stanley	33	1983

"It took all 25 of us to get the job done. It's just phenomenal."
— *Jonathan Papelbon, after closing out Colorado to win the 2007 World Series*

Chapter 9

The Closers

JONATHAN PAPELBON MADE his big league debut in 2005 as a towering righty with a live fastball and unlimited potential. He made three starts that season but the majority of his innings came out of the bullpen—and it was in the pen where the fourth-round pick out of Mississippi State made an enormous impact during his full-fledged rookie season in 2006. Papelbon was 35 for 41 in save opportunities and placed second in Rookie of the Year balloting.

There was talk about moving him back to the rotation in 2007.

It is safe to assume that the vast majority of Red Sox Nation is grateful that move never materialized. Papelbon was 37 of 40 in save chances in 2007, and 41 of 46 in 2008.

Prior to Papelbon it was Keith Foulke who led the team with 32 saves in 2004, but his team leading total fell to only 15 games in 2005. Byung-Hyun Kim led the team with just 16 saves in 2003. Ugueth Urbina led Boston with 40 saves in 2002, his only full season with the club. It was Derek Lowe in 2001, leading the club with 24 saves. Lowe also led the club with 42 saves in 2000. The year before that it was Lowe and Tim Wakefield who shared the team lead with 15 saves. And the year before that was Tom Gordon's magical 46 save season.

The role of closer, however, was a carousel of sorts—until Papelbon came along.

He's dominated the late innings for Boston from 2006-10, and was on the mound to clinch the 2007 World Series vs. Colorado. Papelbon is the first true power closer to emerge from Boston's farm system since, well, ever.

There have been a handful of guys who led the league in saves while closing for Boston since saves became an official statistic: Derek Lowe (2000), Tom Gordon (1998), and Bill Campbell (1977). Saves were not an official statistic back in 1964, but you can go back and add them up—and if you do, you'll find that The Monster, Dick Radatz, notched 29, a total that would have led the league. You can also find totals for Radatz (1962), Mike Fornieles (1960), Ellis Kinder (1951, 1953), and Bob Klinger (1946) that would have led the league.

Any conversation about Boston's closers must also include Bob Stanley, who saved a franchise record 132 games from 1977-89.

He saved a career high 33 games in 1983, and five times he was among the league's top ten leaders.

It took only three years, however, for Jonathan Papelbon to surpass Bill Campbell, Lee Smith, Tom Gordon, Sparky Lyle, Derek Lowe, Jeff Reardon, Ellis Kinder, and Dick Radatz as he climbed the franchise leader board into second place all-time for saves. Papelbon closed out 2008 with 113 career saves—and on July 1, 2009, with his 20th save of the season he surpassed Bob Stanley to become the all-time franchise leader in saves.

Today's game requires a dominant presence on the mound in the late innings—and that is never truer than it is when your team is the Boston Red Sox, a perennial playoff contender.

Not only did Papelbon close out the 2007 World Series, but it was his third save of the series and his fourth of the 2007 postseason. In the 2008 Division Series vs. Anaheim he earned a win and a save in three games, pitching five innings but allowing only two hits, no runs, and one walk, while striking out seven.

Papelbon, however, is not the only Boston reliever to be clutch in the postseason.

Keith Foulke gave up only seven hits and one earned run in 14 innings during the 2004 postseason—earning a save vs. Anaheim, a save vs. New York, and a win and a save vs. St. Louis. Foulke will forever be an historic footnote because he was on the mound for the final out of the 2004 World Series. He got the save on a comebacker from Edgar Renteria that ended 86 years of heartache for Red Sox Nation.

Papelbon, Foulke, and Lowe are all here in the ninth.

Look for more of our favorite clutch performances as well: Pedro Martinez vs. Roger Clemens in the Bronx, Bill Mueller in the 2004 World Series, Ted Williams' final at bat, a pitching Triple Crown for Pedro Martinez, and El Tiante shutting out the Big Red Machine in the 1975 World Series.

It's the ninth, closer time . . .

801 Roger Clemens gave up (8.01) hits per nine innings in 1996. That ratio was the second best in the league behind Juan Guzman of the Toronto Blue Jays. The Rocket gave up 216 hits during 242-plus innings of work. He also led the league with 257 strikeouts, but despite all that he posted a subpar 10-13 record.

802 The number of games (802) for Tony Conigliaro as a member of the Red Sox. More than three decades after his final game his total remains among the top 50 in franchise history—and the Fenway Faithful still lament what might have been if not for the fateful pitch that struck him in the face.

803 The on-base plus slugging percentage (.803) for Johnny Damon from 2002-05. Damon played 597 games for Boston, during which time he posted a .362 on-base percentage and a .441 slugging percentage. That ranks him just inside Boston's top 30 for OPS.

804 The on-base plus slugging percentage (.804) for Rick Ferrell from 1933-37. The Hall of Famer posted a .394 OBP for Boston, while collecting 144 extra-base hits for a .410 slugging percentage. He was pretty good behind the dish, too. Ferrell was the starting catcher for the inaugural 1933 All-Star Game, where Hall of Fame manager Connie Mack left him in for the entire game. Ferrell caught 1,806 career games for a record that lasted better than 40 years. His brother and teammate, Wes Ferrell, said, "Brother or no brother, he was a real classy receiver."

805 The official game time (8:05) for the ESPN Sunday night matchup on May 28, 2000, that featured Pedro Martinez vs. Roger Clemens. Boston took on the Yankees in the Bronx, with both aces going the distance, and both hurling shutout ball for eight innings. Trot Nixon hit a two-run home run off Clemens in the ninth—and Martinez closed out the Yankees with a four-hit shutout in what was easily one of the best regular season games all year.

806 The winning percentage (.806) for Dave Ferriss in 1946. Better known as Boo by the Fenway Faithful, Ferriss won 21 games as a rookie in 1945 (including eight consecutive starts to begin his career), and then he came back in 1946 to post a 25-6 record and make his second consecutive All-Star team. His winning percentage in 1946 was the best in the league, and it remains one of the top ten in franchise history.

807 The number of strikeouts (8.07) per nine innings for Curt Schilling in 2006. Schilling struck out 183 batters in 204 innings of work for the best ratio on the club, and the fifth best ratio in the league.

808 The offensive winning percentage (.808) for Wade Boggs in 1987. In the year of Boggs' power surge, the Red Sox struggled to a 78-84 record—which equates to a paltry .481 winning percentage. Statistical models predict an all-Boggs lineup would have posted 131 wins. Boggs' predicted rating was the highest in the league that season.

809 The number of times (809) Bobby Doerr walked. He posted more walks than strikeouts during 11 of 14 seasons in his career—and only five players in franchise history have drawn more free passes: Ted Williams (2,021), Carl Yastrzemski (1,845), Dwight Evans (1,337), Wade Boggs (1,004), and Harry Hooper (826).

810 Boston scored (810) runs in 1984. Three players surpassed the century mark: Tony Armas (107), Wade Boggs (109), and Dwight Evans (121). The offense was the second highest scoring in the league after posting the best team average (.283), on-base percentage (.341), and slugging percentage (.441) among 14 A.L. teams.

811 The on-base plus slugging percentage (.811) for Bill Mueller in 2004. That was down a lot from his .938 mark the season before when Mueller won the batting title. His average fell from .326 to .283, and his homers fell from 19 to 12. Mueller did, however, improve where it counts the most—in the postseason. In 2003, he hit only .222 when Boston lost a tough seven-game series to the Yankees, but in 2004, he hit .429 as Boston swept St. Louis in the World Series.

812 The on-base plus slugging percentage (.812) for Jason Varitek in 1999. It was the first season that Tek was the fulltime catcher for Boston, and he responded by hitting 20 home runs with 76 RBI. He reached base at a .330 clip while posting a .482 slugging percentage.

813 Boston scored (813) runs in 1988. Led by Wade Boggs, who scored 128 runs, Boston's offense was the highest scoring in the league—and they rode that offense to a division title.

814 Charley Hall gave up (8.14) hits per nine innings of work from 1909-13. He tossed 690-plus innings during that span, dividing his time between the rotation and the pen. Hall won a career high 15 games in 1912, but his best ratio of hits per nine innings was 6.77 in 1910. His career ratio with the Red Sox is among the top 20 in franchise history among pitchers with at least 500 innings.

815 The number of games (815) started by Cy Young during his Hall of Fame career. That total is a major league record. Young made 297 of those starts for Boston—and won 192 of his record 511 games for the Red Sox.

816 The number of extra-base hits (816) for Jose Canseco. In parts of 17 seasons he hit 462 home runs and twice led the league in homers—juiced or otherwise. Canseco spent two seasons in Boston, playing 198 games and hitting 47 doubles, two triples, and 52 home runs.

817 The number of batters (817) faced by Pedro Martinez in 2000. He gave up only 128 hits and 32 walks—and that gave him a major league record ratio of .737 walks plus hits per innings pitched. Martinez struck out 284 batters in 217 innings on his way to an 18-6 record, a 1.74 earned run average, and a second consecutive Cy Young Award.

818 Roger Clemens struck out (8.18) batters per nine innings in 1987. That ratio led the club and was third in the league behind Mark Langston and Teddy Higuera. Clemens was second in the league in total strikeouts with 256 and third in the league with a 2.97 earned run average, but he led the league with 20 wins and earned the Cy Young Award.

819 The on-base plus slugging percentage (.819) for Tony Conigliaro as a member of the Red Sox. That mark still ranks among Boston's top 30.

820 Buck Freeman hit 90 triples during (820) games for Boston. Fewer than 50 players have played more games for the Red Sox, and only Hall of Fame legends Harry Hooper and Tris Speaker have hit more triples.

821 Keith Foulke converted saves at a (.821) rate in 2004. He saved 32 of 39 chances, and Boston was 59-13 during the 72 games he appeared in. Boston signed him as a free agent prior to 2004 because the team expected to be back in the postseason—and it turned out to be a great move all around. In the 2004 postseason, Foulke tossed three scoreless innings vs. Anaheim, six scoreless innings vs. New York, and got a win and a save vs. St. Louis as Boston won the World Series.

822 The on-base plus slugging percentage (.822) for Dustin Pedroia in 2007. He got on base at a .380 clip and 48 of his 165 hits went for extra-bases during his rookie campaign—and there was no sophomore slump for this Rookie of the Year recipient either. Pedroia improved his stats in nearly every category in 2008, and in the process he became the first player in franchise history to have a five hit game, a five run game, and a five RBI game in the same season.

823 Denny Doyle got (823) career hits. He got 313 of those hits during three seasons in Boston, after being traded to the club from California on June 14, 1975. Doyle was hitting .067 for the Angels at the time of the trade, but he hit .310 the rest of the way and he solidified the Red Sox infield by playing stellar defense at second base. Doyle also put together a 22-game hitting streak in 1975, and he had at least one hit during every game of the 1975 World Series.

824 The number of batters (824) faced by Orioles' pitcher Jack Fisher in 1960. He is an historical footnote because of one of those batters—Ted Williams. It was Fisher who Williams faced in the final game of his career, September 28, 1960. Williams hit a 380 foot drive that was caught just short of the right field bullpen in the bottom of the fifth, and when he got back to the dugout he told Vic Wertz, "If that one didn't go out, none of them will today." The game was being played in a dense fog with heavy air—but in his next at bat, and the last of his career, Williams hit one 420 feet off the roof of the Red Sox bullpen. The *Boston Herald* wrote the next day, "His greatness as a hitter demanded no less . . . Ted Williams has been incapable of the mediocre."

825 The number of hits (825) for Pete Runnels from 1958-62. In five seasons with Boston the All-Star infielder hit .320, and his hits total with the club still ranks among the top 50 in franchise history.

826 The number of times (826) Harry Hooper walked from 1909-20. His career high was 89 walks in 1915, and though he never surpassed the century mark or led the league in any one season, he was among the top six leaders nine times during 12 seasons with the club. His career total of 1,136 walks is among the top 75 in baseball history, and the 826 he got for Boston is among the ten best totals in franchise history.

827 Luis Tiant gave up (8.27) hits per nine innings of work from 1971-78. He was a three-time 20-game winner in Boston, and four times his ratio of hits per nine innings was among the league's top ten leaders. His career ratio with Boston remains among the top 20 in franchise history.

828 The number of games (828) for Fred Lynn as a member of the Red Sox. That total remains among the top 50 in franchise history. In those games, Lynn collected 944 hits with 523 runs, 217 doubles, 29 triples, 124 home runs, and 521 RBI. He hit .308 with a .520 slugging percentage.

829 The number of at bats (829) for Billy Conigliaro as a member of the Red Sox. The kid brother of Tony Conigliaro, they briefly played together, combining to hit 54 home runs for Boston in 1970. Billy spent parts of three seasons with the club, hitting a total of 33 home runs in 247 games. He later won the 1973 World Series with Oakland, but that was his last season before injuries forced him from the game as well.

830 The number of batters (830) faced by Vern Ruhle in 1975. The Tigers' rookie pitcher hit seven of those batters—and unfortunately for Boston, that total included Jim Rice. Boston's rookie slugger was hit by Ruhle on September 21, with only five games left on the schedule. The pitch broke a bone in his left hand and Rice missed the entire 1975 postseason.

831 Tex Hughson gave up (8.31) hits per nine innings of work. He pitched parts of eight seasons from 1941-49, all of them for Boston, and three times he placed among the top ten league leaders in fewest hits per nine innings. Hughson's career ratio is among the top 25 in franchise history.

832 The number of hits (832) for Phil Todt from 1924-31. The first baseman led the club with 153 hits in 1926 to set a career high, and his overall total with Boston remains among the top 50 in franchise history.

833 The winning percentage (.833) for Pedro Martinez in 2002. Martinez was 20-4 with a 2.26 earned run average, but narrowly missed a fourth Cy Young Award after Barry Zito (23-5) took top honors for Oakland. He led the league in winning percentage, however, with a mark that remains among the top ten in franchise history.

834 The number of extra-base hits (834) for Jim Rice. He led the league with 86 extra-base hits in 1978, and he was among the top ten league leaders six times. His career total is among the top 100 in baseball history, and it is the fourth highest in franchise history.

835 Pedro Martinez faced (835) batters in 1999. It was not a good year to bat against Martinez—he led the league in wins, strikeouts, and earned run average—and won both the Cy Young Award and the pitching Triple Crown. He also started the All-Star Game, and the best hitters in the N.L. could do no better than their A.L. counterparts who faced Martinez on a regular basis. Pedro set down all six batters he faced—five of them on strikes—picked up the win, and earned MVP honors for the game.

836 The number of hits (836) Jesse Tannehill gave up from 1904-08. He was on the mound for 885-plus innings, which works out to a very nice ratio of 8.50 hits per nine innings of work—one of the top 30 such ratios in franchise history.

837 The number of batters (837) faced by Earl Wilson in 1962. He posted some good numbers, allowing only 163 hits in 191 innings—but it helped, of course, that Wilson tossed nine of those innings and faced 31 of those batters without giving up a hit in a game against the Los Angeles Angels on June 26. His no-no was the first of two on the season by the Red Sox staff, with Bill Monbouquette getting his on August 1. It was the third time in franchise history that the pitching staff recorded two no-hitters in a single season. Dutch Leonard and Rube Foster were the hurlers who did it for the club back in 1916, and Cy Young and Jesse Tannehill did it back in 1904.

838 The number of hits (838) for Jim Tabor from 1938-44. The third baseman played 806 games for Boston, hitting .273 with 393 runs, 162 doubles, 27 triples, 90 home runs, and 517 RBI—and his hits total for the club remains among the top 50 in franchise history.

839 Tim Wakefield gave up (8.39) hits per nine innings in 2005. That ratio was the best on the club and seventh best in the league. Wakefield, who was 16-12, gave up 210 hits in 225-plus innings.

840 The number of runs (840) the Cincinnati Reds scored in 1975. They were the Big Red Machine—the best offense in the N.L. and the best team in baseball with 108 wins. No one bothered to tell Red Sox pitcher Luis Tiant, apparently—that or he just flat out didn't care. Tiant tossed a tidy five-hit shutout against Cincinnati in Game 1 of the 1975 World Series.

841 The on-base plus slugging percentage (.841) for Carl Yastrzemski. In 23 seasons the Hall of Famer hit 452 homers while reaching base at a .379 clip. Yaz led the league in OPS four times and eight times he was among the league's top ten leaders. His career mark ranks among the top 20 in franchise history.

842 The on-base plus slugging percentage (.842) for Dwight Evans as a member of the Red Sox. Dewey led the league twice, five times he was among the league's top ten leaders, and his career OPS with the club ranks among the top 20 in franchise history.

843 Roger Clemens struck out (8.43) batters per nine innings in 1986. He led the league in almost everything and won Most Valuable Player and Cy Young Award honors—but his ratio of strikeouts per nine innings was only third best in the league, and believe it or not, it was only the second best on the club. Bruce Hurst posted a ratio of 8.62 strikeouts per nine innings to best Clemens that season.

844 The on-base plus slugging percentage (.844) for Trot Nixon as a member of the Red Sox. Nixon was fourth in the league with a career high .975 OPS in 2003, and his career mark with the Red Sox ranks among the top 20 in franchise history.

845 The on-base plus slugging percentage (.845) for Mike Stanley in 1998. He began the season with Toronto, but Boston traded for the catcher to strengthen the club for their postseason push. Stanley had been hitting just .240 for Toronto with a .825 OPS, but after rejoining Boston (who had traded Stanley the year before to New York) he posted a .888 OPS the rest of the way—hitting .288 with seven home runs and 32 RBI in only 47 games as Boston won the Wild Card.

846 Dutch Leonard faced (846) batters in 1914. Only 24 of those batters reached base and scored an earned run against him. Leonard posted a 19-5 record—but of greater significance, his 0.96 earned run average is a major league record for baseball's modern era.

847 The offensive winning percentage (.847) for Tris Speaker in 1913. The Hall of Famer hit .363 with a .441 on-base percentage—and statistical models predict that a lineup consisting of nothing but the 1913 version of Speaker would have won games at an unprecedented .847 rate.

848 The earned run average (8.48) for Tom Gordon during nine losses in 1996. He was 12-9 on the season with an overall 5.59 ERA, but in his 12 victories he posted a much healthier 3.22 ERA. In case you are wondering how Gordon could post a winning record, much less win 12 games, in a season where he obviously gave up a ton of runs, well, the answer is his teammates scored seven or more runs in all 12 of his victories.

849 The offensive winning percentage (.849) for Ted Williams in 1960. In his final season, the Hall of Fame legend hit .316 with 29 home runs in only 310 at bats. Statistical analysis suggests the Red Sox club that won only 65 games that season could have won 131 games if only they could have penciled in the 41-year-old veteran for all nine spots on the lineup card.

850 The on-base plus slugging percentage (.850) for Tony Conigliaro in 1965. That gave him the seventh highest mark in the league on the strength of 32 home runs, 58 extra-base hits, and 267 total bases.

851 Boston scored (851) runs in 1997. Nomar Garciaparra led the team with 122 runs, but despite leading the league in team average the offense was only fourth in the league in scoring—and won just 78 games.

852 The winning percentage (.852) for ace Pedro Martinez in 1999. He led the league with the fourth best winning percentage in franchise history. Martinez posted a league best 23-4 record and won his first of back-to-back Cy Young Awards for Boston.

853 The ratio (8.53) of hits per nine innings pitched for Joe Dobson during nine years and two stints with the club from 1941-54. That ratio is one of the top 35 in franchise history. Dobson's record with Boston was 106-72, placing him in the top ten for wins and the top 20 for winning percentage in franchise history.

854 The number of batters (854) faced by Derek Lowe in 2002. He only let 63 of those batters score an earned run against him, and his 21 wins and 2.58 ERA were both the second best numbers in the league. Lowe, who for his efforts placed third in Cy Young balloting, was the closer for Boston the previous season—posting 24 saves in 2001. His victory total in 2002 made him the first big league pitcher since 1971 to post 20 victories after saving 20 or more games the previous season. Wilbur Wood did it for the White Sox in 1970-71.

855 The on-base plus slugging percentage (.855) for Nick Esasky in 1990. Boston traded for him in the off-season, and it was a great deal as he posted the best numbers of his career: .277 average, 30 home runs, and 108 RBI. He was among the top ten league leaders in OPS, slugging, total bases, home runs, extra-base hits, and RBI—but of those categories, the only one he led the club in was slugging percentage. In fact, his OPS was only third best on the club behind Wade Boggs and Dwight Evans. Esasky played just the one season in Boston and then cashed in on his big numbers for a three-year $5,550,000 contract with the Atlanta Braves—but a severe case of vertigo brought his career to an end and he only played nine games in Atlanta.

856 Roger Clemens walked (856) batters from 1984-96. He left Boston having walked the most batters in franchise history, to go along with his franchise record 2,590 strikeouts—but Tim Wakefield is the current leader in walks. The knuckleball artist surpassed 960 career walks for Boston in 2008.

857 The winning percentage (.857) for Roger Clemens in 1986. He dominated opposing teams with a 24-4 record for a league best winning percentage, a feat he accomplished three times in his career. Clemens was so strong that he earned both the Most Valuable Player Award and the Cy Young Award.

858 The on-base plus slugging percentage (.858) for Wade Boggs during his 18-year Hall of Fame career. In 11 seasons in Boston, Boggs was above a .800 OPS in all but the last one—in seven seasons with New York and Tampa at the end of his career, Boggs was above a .800 OPS only twice.

859 Boston scored (859) runs in 2002. Johnny Damon paced the club with 118, and Nomar Garciaparra scored 101 as the Red Sox offense was second in average and second in runs among 14 teams in the league. Boston won 93 games—but in 2002 it took 99 wins just to get the Wild Card (won by eventual world champion Anaheim).

860 The on-base plus slugging percentage (.860) for Jason Varitek in 2001. Tek was 1 for 2 vs. Detroit on June 7, hitting a home run and drawing three walks. It was his seventh homer of the season and he raised his average to .293, to go along with his .371 on-base percentage and a .489 slugging percentage, as Boston held a one-game lead on the Yankees for first place in the East—but that same game Varitek cracked his elbow while going into the stands after a foul ball. He missed the rest of the season, and Boston was only 48-55 the rest of the way, falling 13 games back of New York.

861 The on-base plus slugging percentage (.861) for Dwight Evans in 1989. Dewey led the league in OPS twice, but 1989 was the last of his five seasons during which he placed among the top ten league leaders. He hit .285 with 20 big flies on the season.

862 Bruce Hurst struck out (8.62) batters per nine innings in 1986. Hurst struck out 167 batters during 174-plus innings of work for the second best ratio in the league. His ratio that season is also among the top 15 in franchise history, but it set a franchise record for lefties.

863 Tim Wakefield gave up (8.63) hits per nine innings in 1997. He gave up 193 hits while tossing 201-plus innings of knuckleballs at opposing batters—who did not have much success against the Red Sox hurler. Wakefield's ratio was second on the club behind Tom Gordon, but it was among the top ten ratios in the league.

864 The winning percentage (.864) for Boston against the St. Louis Browns and the Washington Senators in 1950. Boston was 38-6 against the two clubs, but only 56-54 against the rest of the league. The Red Sox closed out the season 94-60, but after posting a 19-25 record against New York and Detroit, Boston placed third in the league behind those same two clubs.

865 Boston scored (865) runs in 1941. That total led the league, thanks to Ted Williams, his .406 average, the 135 runs he scored, and the 120 runs he drove home. He had plenty of help, of course: Dom DiMaggio scored 117 runs, and Jimmie Foxx had 105 RBI, while Jim Tabor had 101 RBI. Despite all of that run support the club won only 84 games, while New York scored 830 runs, yet won 101 games—of course Boston's pitchers gave up 119 more runs than did New York's.

866 The number of batters (866) faced by Tim Wakefield in 1997. The knuckleball artist led the team with 201-plus innings that season, as well as pitching a team high four complete games and two shutouts.

867 The number of runs (867) Boston scored in 2007. The offense was the third highest scoring in the league, and the pitching staff gave up just 657 runs—the lowest total in the league. That adds up to success, but it especially helped that both the offense and pitching started strong. Boston was 28-12 through 40 games, and gave up just 136 runs during that stretch. Only two other teams since the advent of the DH in 1973 previously had won 28 or more games while giving up fewer runs during the season's first 40 games: Detroit (35 wins, 120 runs, 1984), and Oakland (28 wins, 130 runs, 1990). All three teams won the pennant.

868 The number of RBI (868) for Manny Ramirez as a member of the Red Sox from 2001-08. Manny's 144 RBI in 2005 was his best total in Boston—and his career total with the club ranks among the top ten in franchise history.

869 It took only (869) games for Nomar Garciaparra to amass 2,000 total bases—a number he surpassed in 2003 in fewer games than any player in baseball history. His record lasted only until 2006 though, when Cardinals' slugger Albert Pujols surpassed 2,000 total bases in only 854 games.

870 Josh Beckett struck out (8.70) batters per nine innings in 2007. That ratio was the seventh best in the league, and the second best on the team behind Daisuke Matsuzaka. Beckett struck out 194 batters, which set a new career high, in only 200-plus innings of work—and his ratio that season ranks among the top 15 in franchise history.

871 The number of hits (871) for Chick Stahl as a member of the Red Sox from 1901-06. His best season was 1904 when he got 170 hits—but he also got ten hits for the club during the 1903 World Series, not too bad either. Stahl's career total with Boston is among the top 50 in franchise history.

872 The winning percentage (.872) for Smoky Joe Wood in 1912. He was 34-5, and he led the league with a winning percentage that became the franchise standard for 66 years. Wood only placed fifth in league MVP balloting that season. Tris Speaker, his teammate, won the award—but two pitchers actually placed ahead of Wood: Ed Walsh (27-17) and Walter Johnson (33-12).

873 The number of batters (873) faced by Jim Bagby in 1938. He was a 21-year-old rookie who led the club with 15 wins. Bagby also led the club with 43 games and 198-plus innings.

874 The number of batters (874) faced by Daisuke Matsuzaka in 2007. That total was the highest on the staff. Dice-K gave up 191 hits and opponents scored 100 earned runs against him, but after posting a 15-12 record he placed fourth in Rookie of the Year balloting.

875 The winning percentage (.875) for Jamie Moyer after going 7-1 for Boston in 1996. The crafty lefty signed a free agent contract worth $825,000 prior to the season, but the Red Sox were sellers at the trade deadline and so they unloaded Moyer on the Seattle Mariners in exchange for outfielder Darren Bragg. Moyer went 6-2 down the stretch in 11 starts with Seattle, but the Mariners did not make the playoffs. Bragg hit .252 with three home runs the rest of the way for Boston, and he played just two additional seasons with the club.

876 The number of games (876) for Tony Conigliaro. He was on the path to greatness through 493 career games—but one pitch from Jack Hamilton on August 18, 1967, changed everything. Conigliaro fought his way back and played two more seasons for Boston and one season for California, but he was out of baseball from 1972-74. He made one last comeback attempt with Boston in 1975. He hit a home run in his third game back, but he was hitting just .123 after 21 games so the club sent him to the minors and later released him—ending his career for good.

877 The number of batters (877) faced by Gene Conley in 1961. Boston's pitching staff gave up 167 home runs that season—the seventh highest total out of ten teams in the league—and unfortunately, Conley is the man who gave up the most homers on the staff. He gave up 33 home runs in 33 games. Not that its any consolation, but the next season Conley led the staff with 15 wins—but he also repeated as gopher champ, giving up 28 long balls in 1962.

878 The on-base plus slugging percentage (.878) as a member of the Red Sox for Joe Cronin. The Hall of Fame infielder was selected for the All-Star Game five times during his tenure with the club from 1935-45, and his OPS during that span is among the top ten in franchise history.

879 The on-base plus slugging percentage (.879) for Wade Boggs in 1989. He hit only three home runs—but a .430 on-base percentage, 205 hits, and 51 doubles helped his cause. His OPS was the best on the club and fifth best in the league.

880 The number of innings (880) for Dave Ferriss. He tossed 538-plus innings and won 46 games during his first two seasons in 1945-46, but he only played in parts of six seasons total—all with Boston—and he was just 19-14 in 341-plus innings from 1947-50. Ferriss did not win a game after 1948, but his career record of 65-30 gives him the second best winning percentage (.684) in franchise history.

881 The on-base plus slugging percentage (.881) for Wade Boggs in 1991. Boggs hit .332 but lost the batting title to Julio Franco of the Texas Rangers, who hit .341 that year. Boggs was third in the league in on-base percentage, and his team leading OPS was also among the top ten league leaders.

882 The winning percentage (.882) for Bob Stanley in 1978. The relief pitcher was 15-2 with a 2.60 earned run average. Stanley's winning percentage was second best in the league, but it broke the franchise record held by Smoky Joe Wood since 1912.

883 The number of innings (883) for Eddie Cicotte as a member of the Red Sox from 1908-12. Knuckles, a nickname that was a reference to the knuckleball and occasional spitball that were mainstays in his arsenal of pitches, was 51-46 for the club and gave up just 265 earned runs during those innings—which works out to a 2.70 earned run average that ranks among the top 15 in franchise history. Cicotte was sold to the White Sox in 1912, and so he missed that championship season. He did win the 1917 World Series with Chicago, but later he was one of the players implicated in the Black Sox Scandal surrounding the 1919 World Series, and he was subsequently banned from baseball.

884 The number of strikeouts (8.84) per nine innings for Daisuke Matsuzaka in 2007. The Japanese star enjoyed a great start to his career in Boston, striking out 201 batters in 204-plus innings of work. Dice-K led the club in total strikeouts, and his ratio per nine innings also led the club and was the sixth best in the league.

885 The number of batters (885) faced by Herb Pennock in 1922. It was his last season prior to being sold to the Yankees, and the only stat he led the club in was losses—17. Well, that and his seven wild pitches. He got to New York just in time for Yankee Stadium to open in 1923, just in time to win the first World Series in the history of the Evil Empire, and apparently just in time to get his career on track for the Hall of Fame.

886 The ratio (.886) of walks plus hits per innings pitched for Dutch Leonard in 1914. He was a 22-year-old lefty who won 19 games in record fashion. Leonard set a modern era major league record with a 0.96 earned run average, and his .886 WHIP at the time was the second best in franchise history. Today it remains the third best behind Pedro Martinez and Cy Young.

887 The number of games (887) Hall of Fame legend Jimmie Foxx played for the Red Sox. Double-X, as he was often referred to, played 2,317 major league games—a total that ranks among the top 100 in baseball history—and the 887 he played in Boston places him among the top 50 in franchise history.

888 Boston gave up (8.88) hits per nine innings in 2000. The pitching staff led the league in earned run average, saves, shutouts, fewest hits allowed, and fewest runs allowed. It helped, of course, that Pedro Martinez set a franchise record by giving up just 5.31 hits per nine innings (a ratio that ranks among the top five in baseball history), and that he also led the league with a 1.74 ERA and four shutouts.

889 The ratio (8.89) of hits per nine innings pitched for Derek Lowe as a member of the Red Sox from 1997-2004. Lowe was a big-time pitcher, saving 42 games one season, winning 21 games in another, and of course, going 3-0 during the 2004 postseason. He was 70-55 for the club—and after giving up 1,024 hits in 1,037 innings of work, he left Boston with one of the top 40 ratios in franchise history.

890 The on-base plus slugging percentage (.890) as a member of the Red Sox for Wade Boggs. He was among the top ten league leaders for OPS seven times from 1983-91, but the only time he cracked the top ten for slugging percentage was in 1987 when he hit a career high 24 home runs. He led the league in OPS that season, and again in 1988, but it was his ability to consistently get on base that allowed Boggs to post a career OPS that ranks among the top ten in franchise history.

891 Jonathan Papelbon converted saves at a (.891) rate in 2008. The hard throwing Mississippi State product was third in the league with 41 saves and he failed to convert only five opportunities.

892 The on-base plus slugging percentage (.892) for Mike Easler in 1984. Boston got their new DH from the Pirates in exchange for lefty John Tudor. Easler responded by posting the finest offensive numbers of his career: a .313 average, 27 home runs, and 91 RBI. His extra-base hits total was ninth highest in the league—and his OPS was seventh highest.

893 The ratio (.893) of walks plus hits per innings pitched for Cy Young in 1908. He was a 41-year-old veteran who gave up just 230 hits and 37 walks in 299 innings of work. It was the sixth time in his career he posted a WHIP that was under 1.000. Young's ratio from 1908 is also the fourth best in franchise history.

894 The number of hits (894) for Jake Stahl during a nine-year major league career. Stahl began with Boston in 1903, and then spent time with Washington and New York before ending his career back where he started, in Boston. He was briefly a player-manager for Boston, where he also got the majority of his career hits—456. Stahl, by virtue of playing in the dead ball era, has the distinction of having placed among the league's top ten leaders in home runs three times (including winning a home run title) despite hitting only 31 home runs in his career.

895 The number of games (895) for Phil Todt as a member of the Red Sox from 1924-30. The left handed first baseman led the club in home runs and total bases in 1928, and he was a solid player for the better part of a decade. Despite a games total that ranks among the top 50 in franchise history, Todt never made it to the postseason with Boston. He did get one shot at a World Series. With Philadelphia in 1931, Todt got just one at bat against the Cardinals. It was the last at bat of his career. He drew a walk, but his team lost the series.

896 The on-base plus slugging percentage (.896) as a member of the Red Sox for Tris Speaker. In six full seasons with the club from 1909-15 he was among the top six league leaders in OPS every time. The Hall of Fame outfielder only led the league in OPS once—in 1916, after Boston traded him to Cleveland—but his career mark is among the top 50 in baseball history, and his percentage with Boston is among the top ten in franchise history.

897 The ratio (8.97) of hits per nine innings pitched for Mike Boddicker from 1988-90. Boston traded away a young Curt Schilling and Brady Anderson to get Boddicker from the Orioles during the stretch run in 1988. It didn't work out that postseason, but Boddicker was a solid addition to the club. In parts of three seasons he was 39-22, and he gave up 527 hits in 528-plus innings of work for one of the top 50 ratios in franchise history.

898 The number of times (898) the Oakland Athletics struck out in 2003. That was the second lowest total in the league, and they also boasted the best pitching staff in the A.L. When Oakland took the first two games of the 2003 Division Series vs. Boston many thought the superior team was clearly in control of the series—they were wrong, of course. Boston stormed back to win the best-of-five series in dramatic fashion, winning the final three games by a total of four runs.

899 The fielding percentage (.899) for Butch Hobson in 1978. Boston's third baseman had a knack for making wild throws on a pretty frequent basis, and he made an unheard of 43 errors that season. His fielding percentage was so bad that the next time a major league player was beneath .900 in a season of at least 100 games was Ryan Braun for the Milwaukee Brewers in 2007.

900 The winning percentage (.900) for Boston vs. Anaheim in 1999. The Red Sox went 9-1 against the Angels while outscoring the club 63-31. Anaheim was easily Boston's favorite opponent that season. Boston's least favorite, surprisingly, was the Montreal Expos, who swept all three games against Boston during inter-league play and outscored the Red Sox 26-4.

Postseason Walk-offs for the Boston Red Sox

October 11, 1915 – World Series Game 3
Duffy Lewis singled to right field against Pete Alexander with two outs in the ninth, scoring Harry Hooper for a 2-1 victory vs. the Philadelphia Phillies.

October 9, 1916 – World Series Game 2
Del Gainer singled to left field with one out in the 14th against Brooklyn's Sherry Smith, scoring Mike McNally for a 2-1 victory.

October 21, 1975 – World Series Game 6
Carlton Fisk homered to left leading off the bottom of the 12th against Pat Darcy, giving Boston a 7-6 victory and forcing a Game 7 vs. Cincinnati.

October 4, 2003 – Division Series Game 3
Trot Nixon hit a two-run 11th inning homer against Oakland's Rich Harden, giving Boston a 3-1 win and setting the stage for a dramatic come-from-behind series victory after dropping the first two games in Oakland.

October 8, 2004 – Division Series Game 3
David Ortiz hit a two-run tenth inning homer against Jarrod Washburn, giving Boston a sweep of Anaheim and setting the stage for a showdown with the New York Yankees.

October 17, 2004 – League Championship Series Game 4
David Ortiz hit a two-run 12th inning homer against Paul Quantrill, giving Boston a 6-4 win and its first victory of the series against the Yankees.

October 18, 2004 – League Championship Series Game 5
David Ortiz hit a two-out single in the bottom of the 14th against Esteban Loaiza, scoring Johnny Damon for a 5-4 victory and sending the series back to New York.

October 5, 2007 – Division Series Game 2
Manny Ramirez hit a two-out three-run home run in the ninth against Angels closer Francisco Rodriguez, scoring Julio Lugo and David Ortiz for a 6-3 victory.

October 6, 2008 – Division Series Game 4
Jed Lowrie singled to right against Scot Shields with two outs in the ninth, scoring Jason Bay for a 3-2 victory over the Angels and setting up a showdown vs. Tampa Bay in the League Championship Series.

"Ortiz into deep right field. Back is Sheffield! We'll see ya later tonight!"
— Joe Buck, FOX broadcaster calling David Ortiz's walk-off homer in Game 4 of the 2004 ALCS

Chapter 10

Walk-off

DAVID ORTIZ HIT his first career walk-off home run as a member of the Minnesota Twins. It came on September 25, 2002, and it was also his last home run with Minnesota. Big Papi signed with Boston in the off-season, but when the Red Sox began play on April 27, 2003, with 25 games already in the books, Ortiz was hitting just .188 with no home runs. His last blast for the Twins was a walk-off shot in extra-innings, and his first blast for the Red Sox was just as dramatic. Ortiz hit a pinch homer that day against Anaheim. It came in the fourteenth inning and proved to be the decisive blow in a 6-4 victory.

It was not a walk-off shot because Boston was on the road. It was clutch, however, and it was also indicative of the kind of play Boston fans soon came to expect from him.

Ortiz was 22 for 72 on the season, a .306 average, with 14 extra-base hits and 22 RBI when batting in "late and close" situations—meaning at bats that came in the seventh inning or later of one-run games, or games where the potential tying or go-ahead run was at least in the on-deck circle. In extra-innings he hit .364 with three homers—including a walk-off blast on September 23. His first game-ending homer for Boston, it kept the club ahead of Seattle in a Wild Card race that the Red Sox eventually won by a two-game margin.

Ortiz is now synonymous with walk-off homers. After all, he hit a total of nine game-ending blasts from 2002-07.

And that was just in the regular season.

It was his blasts in the 2004 postseason that cemented his legacy in Boston. On October 8, 2004, Ortiz clinched the Division Series vs. Anaheim with a Game 3 walk-off homer against Jarrod Washburn and set up a showdown with the Yankees in the League Championship Series. Nine days later, Ortiz hit a walk-off twelfth inning homer against Paul Quantrill in Game 4 of that series to keep Boston's postseason alive. The very next day he got a walk-off fourteenth inning single against Esteban Loaiza to send the series back to New York. Okay, so only two of his three walk-off hits that postseason were homers—but Ortiz *did* become the first player in baseball history to record three postseason walk-off hits, let alone three in the same year.

And since Boston also won the 2004 World Series, the impact of his performance against Anaheim and New York cannot be overstated.

Boston has won several postseason games via walk-off hits, of course, and not just those provided by Big Papi. Duffy Lewis won Game 3 of the 1915 World Series vs. Philadelphia with a two-out single that scored Harry Hooper. Del Gainer won Game 2 of the 1916 World Series vs. Brooklyn with a walk-off single that scored Mike McNally. Boston won both of those series in five games.

Boston's third postseason walk-off hit remains one of the most enduring images in baseball history—Carlton Fisk, Game 6 of the 1975 World Series.

Boston then suffered through a long string of postseason walk-off hits from their opponents—Bobby Grich (1986), Tony Pena (1995), Travis Fryman (1999), Bernie Williams (1999), and Ramon Hernandez (2003)—before getting another of their own. Trot Nixon won Game 3 of the 2003 Division Series vs. Oakland with an eleventh inning homer against Rich Harden. Boston rallied to win that series, only to suffer one of the most devastating walk-offs in franchise history in the form of Aaron Boone just ten days later.

Manny got into the walk-off act in 2007. He hit a game-ending homer against Angels' ace closer Francisco Rodriguez during Game 2 of the Division Series. Rodriguez got beat by a late Boston homer in Game 2 of the 2008 Division Series as well. It was not a walk-off shot, but J.D. Drew continued Boston's flair for the dramatic when he hit a two-run ninth inning homer that gave the Red Sox a 7-5 road victory and a two-game advantage over Anaheim.

It was Ortiz, however, who brought redemption to all of Red Sox Nation with his heroic walk-offs in the 2004 postseason.

And for that it is Ortiz who closes out chapter ten. Who else would you want at the plate in extra-innings with the game on the line?

On to the tenth . . . free baseball!

901 The slugging percentage (.901) for Ted Williams in 1953. Williams, a twice-tested war hero who recently had cheated death in the skies above a war-torn Korea, came back to the Red Sox in time to play 37 games that season after playing only six games in 1952. Incredibly he hit .407 in 91 at bats, including six doubles, 13 home runs, and 34 RBI.

902 The ratio (9.02) of hits per nine innings pitched for Ike Delock as a member of the Red Sox from 1952-63. He gave up 1,211 hits while working 1,207-plus innings. Twice he was among the league's top ten leaders in games, three times for saves, three times for winning percentage, and once for wins—and his ratio of hits per nine innings with the club still ranks among the top 50 in franchise history.

903 The on-base plus slugging percentage (.903) as a member of the Red Sox for Fred Lynn. He led the league in OPS twice and was among the top ten league leaders four times from 1975-80. Lynn, who became a member of the Boston Red Sox Hall of Fame in 2002, ranks among the top ten in franchise history for career OPS.

904 The ratio (9.04) of hits per nine innings pitched as a member of the Red Sox for Joe Bush from 1918-21. He was 46-39 during that time, giving up 783 hits while pitching 779-plus innings. Bullet Joe, as he was called, was just good enough to be sold to the Yankees by owner Harry Frazee.

905 The winning percentage (.905) for Boston against the New York Highlanders in 1912. The next season the Highlanders became the Yankees, but in 1912 they were simply known as the worst team in baseball. Boston was 19-2 against New York; 9-2 at home in the brand new Fenway Park, and 10-0 on the road. Boston was in second place on June 9, when Tris Speaker hit for the cycle and led the club to a 9-2 victory over the St. Louis Browns. Boston won again the next day, moving closer to first, while looking ahead to a five-game series in New York. Boston swept that series with scores of 5-2, 15-8, 11-3, 13-2, and 10-3, left town all alone in first place, and never looked back on their way to winning the 1912 World Series.

906 The number of games (906) for Rich Gedman as a member of the Red Sox from 1980-90. He was the runner-up in Rookie of the Year balloting after just 62 games in 1981, and despite playing more than 100 games in a season just three times, the likeable catcher still ranks among the top 40 in franchise history for career games.

907 The ratio (9.07) of hits per nine innings pitched for Charlie Wagner. He began his career in Boston back in 1938, and he posted a 32-23 record during parts of six seasons with the club. Wagner gave up 532 hits while pitching 527-plus innings for a ratio that remains among the 50 best in franchise history, but he is best known for the close association he kept with his teammates and the organization after his career ended. Wagner was teammates with some of Boston's biggest names: Williams, DiMaggio, Doerr, Cronin, and Foxx. He later became a Boston scout, and he was a part of the Red Sox family in some capacity—scout, coach, consultant—until his death in 2006.

908 The number of batters (908) faced by Earl Wilson in 1963. Only 88 of those batters reached base and scored an earned run against Wilson, giving him a team best 3.76 earned run average—but unfortunately, Wilson also led the club with 16 losses. Wilson struggled for the next couple of years until he was traded to the Tigers. He was 5-5 for Boston in 1966, but he went 13-6 for Detroit the rest of the year. Wilson then went 22-11 in 1967, and he won the World Series with Detroit in 1968.

909 The on-base plus slugging percentage (.909) for Carlton Fisk in 1972. The Hall of Famer got his career off to a great start by winning Rookie of the Year honors. Fisk was seventh in the league in on-base percentage, second in slugging, and second in OPS.

910 The number of batters (910) faced by Curt Schilling in 2004. He was 21-6, and placed second in Cy Young balloting after just 82 of those batters reached base and scored an earned run against him. That was nothing compared to what he did during Game 6 of the League Championship Series. He was seriously injured with an open surgical wound on his ankle—but he tossed a gutsy seven innings, facing 25 batters but giving up just four hits and one run, bloody sock and all. Boston won 4-2 to force the unthinkable—Game 7.

911 The ratio (9.11) of hits per nine innings pitched for Earl Johnson as a member of the Red Sox from 1940-50. He only played parts of seven seasons, however, because after going 4-5 as a 22-year-old lefty in 1941 he left the club to serve in the military. Johnson won a Silver Star, a Bronze Star, and a battlefield commission for acts of heroism during the Battle of the Bulge. Johnson returned to the club in 1946 and earned a win during Game 1 of the World Series—and although he never became a star for the club, like many players of his era he maintained close ties with the organization until his death.

912 The ratio (9.12) of hits per nine innings pitched as a member of the Red Sox for John Tudor from 1979-83. He was 39-32 for the club, giving up 645 hits in 636-plus innings of work. Tudor was traded to Pittsburgh in 1983, who then traded him to St. Louis in 1984, where in 1985, two years after he left Boston, Tudor gave up just 6.84 hits per nine innings and won 21 games for the Cardinals.

913 Boston struck out (913) batters in 1985. That total was third best in the league, and that was with Roger Clemens being limited to just 15 games in his sophomore season. Bruce Hurst led the club with 189 Ks, Oil Can Boyd struck out 154, and Bob Ojeda was third with

102. The team total increased to 1,033 with a healthy Clemens in 1986, who struck out 238.

914 The offensive winning percentage (.914) for Ted Williams in 1941. Williams was so good during his .406 campaign that statistical models predict an all-Williams lineup could have won games that year at a .914 clip.

915 The on-base plus slugging percentage (.915) for Mo Vaughn in 1993. He hit .297 and placed among the top ten league leaders in on-base percentage, slugging percentage, and OPS. He was also the team leader in ten major offensive categories, including home runs (29), RBI (101), extra-base hits (64), and times on base (247).

916 The number of games (916) Joe Cronin lost as Boston's manager—he won 1,071. The Hall of Famer led the club for 13 seasons and posted a .539 winning percentage, while securing one pennant in 1946.

917 The ratio (9.17) of hits per nine innings pitched as a member of the Red Sox for Mike Fornieles from 1957-63. Boston traded former batting champ Billy Goodman to get Fornieles from the Baltimore Orioles. In 1960, his best season, Fornieles led the league in both games and saves, and was fourth in winning percentage. His ratio with the club remains just inside the top 50 in franchise history.

918 Boston struck out (918) batters in 1972. That total was the fourth highest among 12 teams in the league, led by the 168 strikeouts for Marty Pattin. An All-Star the previous season with Milwaukee, Pattin came to Boston in the blockbuster trade that sent Jim Lonborg, Ken Brett, Billy Conigliaro, Joe Lahoud, George Scott, and Don Pavletich to the Brewers. Pattin also led Boston with 17 wins and 13 complete games. His final two victories came on September 30, and October 4, which would have been great except the club lost all three games in between those dates—and as a result placed second in the division a half-game back of the Tigers.

919 The ratio (9.19) of hits per nine innings pitched as a member of the Red Sox for Bob Ojeda from 1980-85. The crafty lefty was a product of the Red Sox farm system, but he was traded to the New York Mets after the 1985 season in a deal that brought Calvin Schiraldi to Boston. I think everyone knows how that worked out. Ojeda was among the top ten N.L. leaders in 1986 after giving up just 7.66 hits per nine innings and posting an 18-5 record for the Mets—

and he also was 1-0 with a 2.08 earned run average against his former club during the 1986 World Series. The same series, of course, during which Schiraldi was 0-2 with a 13.50 earned run average against his former club.

920 The on-base plus slugging percentage (.920) for Dwight Evans in 1984. It was the second time he led the league in OPS. Dewey was among the top ten league leaders that season in several important offensive categories: on-base percentage (.388), slugging percentage (.532), runs (121), hits (186), total bases (335), doubles (37), triples (8), home runs (32), and RBI (104). He was only 11th in MVP balloting.

921 Boston gave up (921) runs in 1996. That total was the third highest in the league, with the staff posting a ridiculously high 5.00 earned run average. Team leaders included Rogers Clemens with a 3.63 ERA and Tim Wakefield with 14 wins.

922 Boston gave up (922) runs in 1925. It really hurts when your best players are sold to your biggest rival—and it shows up in the stats, too. Boston's total was by far the highest among eight teams in the league. The Red Sox gave up 6.07 runs per game but only scored 4.20 runs per game. The franchise that won 105 games in 1912 lost 105 games in 1925—but if there was any consolation to be found that season, it was that New York was actually the second worst team in the league, having lost 85 games.

923 The on-base plus slugging percentage (.923) as a member of the Red Sox for Nomar Garciaparra. Nomar placed among the top ten league leaders in hits and extra-base hits during the same season six times during his tenure with the club. That rare combination of average and power contributed to an OPS that is among the ten best in franchise history.

924 The on-base plus slugging percentage (.924) for Carlton Fisk in 1975. He was limited to just 79 games in the regular season, but he did plenty of damage. Fisk hit .331, belting ten home runs and 52 RBI. He reached base at a .395 clip while posting a .529 slugging percentage. He also hit a pretty important home run that October.

925 Jonathan Papelbon converted saves at a (.925) rate in 2007. He was 37 for 40 in the regular season and made his second consecutive All-Star team—and he struck out 84 batters in only 58-plus innings. Papelbon also made seven appearances in the 2007 postseason. He got a victory vs. Anaheim in the Division Series, earned a save vs. Cleveland in the League Championship Series, and earned three saves vs. Colorado in the World Series. Papelbon did not give up a single earned run in the postseason—and he was on the mound to clinch the World Series, striking out Seth Smith for the final out.

926 The number of times (926) shortstop Rico Petrocelli struck out. Only four players struck out more times for Boston: Dwight Evans (1,643), Jim Rice (1,423), Carl Yastrzemski (1,393), and Mo Vaughn (954).

927 Boston averaged (9.27) hits per game in 1990. The Red Sox offense tallied 1,502 hits on the season, easily the highest total in the league. Wade Boggs (187), Mike Greenwell (181), Ellis Burks (174), and Jody Reed (173) were all among the top ten league leaders in hits.

928 Boston scored (928) runs in 1996. That total was fourth best in the league, led by the big stick of Mo Vaughn, but the Red Sox offense, good as it was, could do nothing to compensate for the lack of pitching that season—seeing as they barely scored more than the staff allowed.

929 The fielding percentage (.929) for Freddy Parent in 1904. He made 63 errors at shortstop in 155 games—which explains why the *Boston Herald* wrote of Athletics catcher Ossee Schreckengost, "He almost gave the anxious fans heart disease when he hit a grounder toward Parent. There was no one that had the courage to stir until Parent had sent the ball straight into LaChance's glove, and then a roar even louder than before emitted from the throats of the onlookers." The reason the fans were so anxious was because Red Sox ace Cy Young was only two outs from a perfect game when Schreckengost hit the grounder. Young was perfect that day, of course, and he later told reporters, "Happy, I should say I was."

930 The on-base plus slugging percentage (.930) for Vern Stephens in 1949. He was second in slugging and OPS behind Ted Williams for a Red Sox offense that dominated the league leader boards. Boston placed four players among the top ten for batting, three for OBP, three for slugging, three for OPS, five for runs, four for hits, five for doubles, two for triples—and Stephens and Williams were the top two for home runs and RBI.

931 The number of games (931) for Jim Piersall during eight seasons with the Red Sox from 1950-58. He scored 502 runs, got 919 hits, 158 doubles, 32 triples, 66 home runs, 366 RBI, and he hit .273. Piersall was a two-time All-Star in the outfield for Boston, and his games total remains among the top 50 in franchise history.

932 Tom Gordon converted saves at a (.932) rate for Boston from 1997-99. He saved 68 of 73 chances and set a team record by notching 54 straight over a two-year period from 1998-99. Gordon blew a save on April 14, 1998, but did not blow another one until June 5, 1999.

933 The on-base plus slugging percentage (.933) for Kevin Youkilis at the 2008 All-Star break. Youk was hitting .314 with 15 home runs and 63 RBI. The fantasy baseball staff on MLB.com wrote, "History says power production won't last." Well, they got that one wrong. Youk finished the season fourth in the league with a .958 OPS and 115 RBI, and he hit 29 home runs.

934 The on-base plus slugging percentage (.934) for one-time Bash Brother Jose Canseco in 1995. He hit .306 with 24 home runs in only 102 games—but once Boston made it to the Division Series vs. Cleveland, whatever juice he was using had little effect. Canseco was 0 for 13 in the series and Boston got swept.

935 Boston struck out (935) batters in 1969. Bill Lee was a 22-year-old rookie who struck out 45 of those batters while working 52 innings. The team leader was Ray Culp, who struck out 172 batters while posting a team best 17-8 record. The club total was the fourth highest among 12 teams in the league, as Jim Lonborg and Sonny Siebert also hit the century mark in Ks.

936 The on-base plus slugging percentage (.936) as a member of the Red Sox for Mo Vaughn. He never led the league in on-base or slugging percentage, but he was among the top ten leaders in OPS six times. His career OPS is also among the top 60 in baseball history, and his OPS for Boston is among the ten best in franchise history.

937 The ratio (.937) of walks plus hits per innings pitched for Cy Young in 1904. His WHIP was the best in the league, a feat made more impressive still when you consider how it got so low—Young tossed 24 consecutive hitless innings. His streak began on April 25, when he did not give up a hit in his final two innings of work. It continued on April 30, when he tossed seven hitless innings in relief.

The high point was May 5, when he tossed the first perfect game in baseball's modern era—and then six days later he held Detroit hitless for six innings before the streak ended.

938 The on-base plus slugging percentage (.938) for Bill Mueller in 2003. He won the league batting title and was fourth on the club in OPS—but he was also eighth in the league in OPS, meaning four of the top eight players in the league at combining power with average played for the Red Sox.

939 The on-base plus slugging percentage (.939) for Wade Boggs in 1986. It was the second highest ratio in the league behind Don Mattingly of the New York Yankees. Boggs led the league in average and on-base percentage, but failed to crack the top ten in slugging after hitting only eight home runs.

940 The number of hits (940) for Doc Cramer during five seasons with Boston from 1936-40. He was a four-time All-Star during that stretch and he led the league with 200 hits in 1940, his last year with the club. Cramer, who batted .302 for Boston, still ranks among the top 40 in franchise history for career hits.

941 Pedro Martinez struck out (9.41) batters per nine innings of work in 2004. He fanned 227 batters in 217 innings, but was second in the league for both total strikeouts and ratio of strikeouts per nine innings (Johan Santana led both of those categories for the Twins). Martinez signed with the Mets as a free agent after 2004, but during seven seasons with Boston he led the club in strikeouts and ratio of strikeouts per nine innings six times. The only exception was 2001, when Martinez was limited to just 18 games due to injuries.

942 The number of at bats (942) for Wally Schang during three seasons with Boston from 1918-20. He hit .291 during 323 games, scoring 137 runs while hitting four home runs. Schang hit only .244 for Boston during 225 at bats in 1918, however, but he came alive at the perfect time and hit .444 in the 1918 World Series vs. the Chicago Cubs. He won a total of four World Series titles in his career—one each with Boston and New York, and two with the Philadelphia Athletics.

943 The fielding percentage (.943) for Philadelphia Athletics rookie outfielder Hal Peck in 1945. He made 12 errors on the season but he also picked up nine assists—including one of the most bizarre assists in the history of Fenway Park. Boston infielder Skeeter Newsome got a base hit that was fielded cleanly by Peck, who then aired out a throw back to the infield to try and hold Newsome to a single. The thrown ball, however, hit a low flying pigeon and then ricocheted directly to the Athletics second baseman. Newsome was trying for two all the way, but the second baseman got the tag down—and Peck got the assist.

944 The number of hits (944) for Fred Lynn during seven seasons with Boston from 1974-80. Lynn hit .308 with 217 doubles, 29 triples, 124 home runs, and 521 RBI for the Red Sox. He got 177 hits in 1979 to set a career high, and his overall total for the club still ranks among the top 40 in franchise history.

945 The on-base plus slugging percentage (.945) for 23-year-old rookie Sam Horn in 1987. He hit 14 home runs in only 46 games after making his debut on July 25. Horn displayed tremendous power in BP and at the minor league level, but he had a great deal of difficulty putting the ball in play against major league pitching—hence, only two homers for Boston after 1987, and only 62 for his career.

946 The fielding percentage (.946) for Butch Hobson in 1977. Honestly, no disrespect intended, but that was the highest fielding percentage during five full seasons in Boston for the error prone third baseman.

947 The on-base plus slugging percentage (.947) for Mike Greenwell in 1988. He hit .325 with 22 home runs, and if there was a guy who you wanted up in the clutch that season, it was Greenwell. On July 16, however, Kevin Romine pinch-ran for Greenwell in the sixth inning of a game against the Royals. Greenwell would have led off the bottom of the ninth in a 6-6 ballgame, but it was Romine who batted instead. Romine hit only .192 all season, but he picked that moment to hit his first major league home run. It gave Boston a thrilling 7-6 walk-off win for their third straight victory at Fenway, and the club went on to record 20 consecutive home wins as they rallied from nine games back to claim the division title.

948 The on-base plus slugging percentage (.948) for Troy O'Leary after going 1 for 5 vs. Texas on July 13, 1995. O'Leary went into the All-Star break having a career year—he was hitting .345 with seven home runs, 35 RBI, a .570 slugging percentage, and a .962 OPS in only 48 starts. He made 58 starts after the break beginning with the Texas game on July 13, and from there his numbers began to drop off. He hit just .271 in the second half with three home runs, 14 RBI, a .412 slugging percentage, and a .730 OPS.

949 Boston scored (949) runs in 2004. That total was the highest in baseball—either league. Manny Ramirez scored 108 runs and Johnny Damon led the club with 123, while Manny and David Ortiz drove home 130 and 139 runs respectively.

950 The slugging percentage (.950) for David Ortiz after 57 plate appearances in 2008 during which he was ahead in the count 3-0. Big mistake on the part of opposing pitchers to fall behind Big Papi, who went 9 for 20 with a double, three home runs, 37 walks, an astounding .807 on-base percentage, and a 1.757 on-base plus slugging percentage.

951 The number of batters (951) faced by Pedro Martinez in 1998. Martinez logged more innings and faced more batters that first season in Boston than in any of his subsequent six campaigns. He gave up just 188 hits, however, in 233-plus innings of work. That gave him a ratio of 7.24 hits per nine innings that was second best in the league—and that led to a team best 19-7 record.

952 The on-base plus slugging percentage (.952) for Dustin Pedroia in June, 2008. He hit only .260 for the month of May, but Pedroia got hot in June, hitting .356 with a .407 on-base percentage and a .545 slugging percentage. He did even better in August, scoring 33 runs while getting 43 hits, a .374 average, and a 1.060 OPS.

953 Roger Clemens struck out (9.53) batters per nine innings of work in 1996. He was only 10-13 during his final season in Boston, but the Rocket led the league in both strikeouts and strikeouts per nine innings. He fanned 257 batters in just 242-plus innings for a ratio that ranks among the top ten in franchise history.

954 The fielding percentage (.954) for third baseman Frank Malzone in 1957. He made 25 errors on the season, but still posted a higher fielding percentage than the league average for third basemen. Malzone won the 1957 Gold Glove—the first year the award was handed out—and he went on to win three consecutive Gold Gloves from 1957-59.

955 The number of times (955) Mickey Vernon walked from 1939-60. He was a patient hitter who struck out only 869 times while batting .286 for his career. Vernon also hit 172 home runs—not bad at all—and he was a seven-time All-Star and a two-time batting champion. Late in his career he spent two seasons with Boston. He hit .310 with 15 home runs and 57 walks in 1956—but that club came in fourth in the pennant race, and unfortunately, above all else, that is what Vernon's career was defined by. He played 2,409 games but never played in the postseason. Only Ernie Banks and Luke Appling, both Hall of Famers, are ahead of him on that list.

956 The number of batters (956) faced by Mike Boddicker in 1990. The veteran teamed with Roger Clemens to form a great one-two punch in the rotation, as only 85 of those batters reached base and scored an earned run against him. He posted a 17-8 record and a 3.36 earned run average that contributed to Boston's first place finish in the division. Boddicker pitched a complete game six-hitter against Oakland during Game 3 of the League Championship Series, but fell victim to three Red Sox errors in a 4-1 loss.

957 The number of singles (957) for Mike Greenwell. That total ranks among the top 15 in franchise history, but that does not mean you should confuse Greenwell for a Punch-and-Judy kind of guy. Gator, as the Kentucky native was often called, got 1,400 hits for Boston—and the other 443 all went for extra-bases.

958 The fielding percentage (.958) for Boston's pitching staff in 1940. Ten out of 17 players who took the mound that season fielded cleanly for a 1.000 percentage—including Ted Williams. That's right, Williams was a 21-year-old budding superstar who tossed two innings in relief. He gave up three hits and one earned run for a 4.50 earned run average (which incidentally, was below the 4.51 league average . . .) and he even got two assists while on the mound.

959 The fielding percentage (.959) for outfielder Duffy Lewis from 1910-21. On April 20, 1912, the Red Sox began their first season at the brand new Fenway Park—and Lewis was one of the premier outfielders on that team. His fielding percentage might seem low when compared to players from today's era, but he was consistently above the league average during his era and he is a permanent part of Fenway lore because of the original contour of the outfield that endured from 1912-33. There was a ten foot high mound that created an incline along the fence, running from the left field foul pole all the way to the center field flag pole. The left fielder was forced to play that area of the park while running uphill almost all the time—and because no one excelled at it the way Duffy Lewis did, the Fenway Faithful dubbed the hill as Duffy's Cliff.

960 The number of batters (960) faced by Gary Peters in 1970. Peters won the 1963 Rookie of the Year Award for the Chicago White Sox after posting a 19-8 record. The lefty was a 33-year-old veteran, however, in 1970, his first season in Boston, when he gave up 221 hits, 100 earned runs, and made 16 wild pitches—all team highs. Yet, he also won 16 games, and he led the club with four shutouts (the third highest total in the league).

961 The on-base plus slugging percentage (.961) for David Ortiz in 2003. Big Papi posted a .369 on-base percentage and a .592 slugging percentage during his first season in Boston, which combined to give him the fifth best OPS in the league. Ortiz was only third on the club, however, in OPS—because Manny Ramirez posted a 1.014 OPS that was second in the league and Trot Nixon posted a .975 OPS that was fourth in the league.

962 The number of games (963) for Troy O'Leary during seven seasons with the club from 1995-2001. He hit .276 for Boston, scoring 490 runs while collecting 954 hits, 209 doubles, 37 triples, 117 home runs, and 516 RBI. Fewer than 40 players have taken the field more times for Boston than did O'Leary.

963 The number of batters (963) faced by Matt Young as a member of the Seattle Mariners in 1990. The Mariners were a terrible team, so bad that the fine folks at ESPN used to quip on SportsCenter that there was no team in Seattle—only made up box scores to fill space in the local sports section. Young toiled on that "team" and posted a respectable 3.51 earned run average—allowing just 88 of those batters to score an earned run against him. He was only 8-18, but he pitched so well that Boston gave the hard-throwing lefty a $9,000,000 free agent contract. The big things expected by the Fenway Faithful never materialized, however, as Young went 3-11 in two seasons with the club. He was so bad that Dan Shaughnessy of the *Boston Globe* dubbed him "Door Matt" and "Sigh Young."

964 The on-base plus slugging percentage (.964) for Joe Cronin in 1938. The shortstop led the league with a career high 51 doubles— and he was also among the league's top ten leaders for average, on-base percentage, extra-base hits, times on base, and OPS.

965 The on-base plus slugging percentage (.965) for Wade Boggs in 1988. It was the second year in a row that Boggs led the league in OPS, despite the fact he hit 19 fewer home runs than he did in 1987. Boggs set career highs with 24 home runs and a 1.049 OPS in 1987, but came back down to his more routine clip of five home runs in 1988.

966 The number of games (966) as a member of the Red Sox for shortstop Nomar Garciaparra. Nomar banged out 507 extra-base hits during his tenure with the club and posted a .553 slugging percentage that ranks among the top ten in franchise history.

967 The fielding percentage (.967) as an outfielder for Leon Culberson in 1946. Culberson lives in infamy as the guy who pinch-ran for Dom DiMaggio after Boston's starting center fielder pulled a hammy while tying Game 7 of the 1946 World Series at 3-3 with an eighth inning double. Culberson took over in center field, where DiMaggio was one of the best in the game—Culberson, well, not so much. What followed was Enos Slaughter's "Mad Dash" for the Cardinals, as he raced home and scored from first on a two-out single to center field (it was ruled a double, but . . .) and the Cardinals won the World Series. DiMaggio later said, "Culberson had to back up on the ball. Had he been positioned correctly, it would have made a big difference. I maintained from the beginning that I might have even had a play on Slaughter at third base." Most news reports were not so kind—suggesting the batted ball was routine enough that DiMaggio almost certainly would have caught it and retired the side.

968 The fielding percentage (.968) for shortstop Luis Aparicio from 1971-73. The Hall of Famer won his ninth and final Gold Glove in 1970, the year before he came to Boston. In his prime, Aparicio was once described by Phil Rizzuto as, "The only guy that I ever saw go behind second base, make the turn and throw Mickey Mantle out. He was as sure-handed as anyone." He might have been past his prime when he came to Boston, but he did play the final 362 games of his career with the Red Sox, where he still turned 178 double plays and gave the fans plenty of dazzling defensive gems to cheer about.

969 The ratio (.969) of walks plus hits per innings pitched for Roger Clemens in 1986. It was the first of three times that Clemens posted the best WHIP ratio in the league. He gave up only 179 hits and 67 walks, but struck out 238 batters in 254 innings—and his ratio from that season remains among the top ten in franchise history.

970 The number of batters (970) faced by lefty Mickey Haefner for the Washington Senators in 1946. He was a decent pitcher who posted decent numbers—but in Red Sox lore he lives in infamy because he faced one batter too many in a meaningless game. Boston ran away with the pennant that year, but the N.L. race was a dogfight between Brooklyn and St. Louis—and when they tied with identical 98-58 records at season's end, a best-of-three playoff series was held to determine who would meet Boston in the World Series. To stay sharp, Boston played an exhibition game against an assortment of A.L. players. In that exhibition game, Mickey Haefner drilled Ted Williams with a pitch on his elbow. The Red Sox star required extensive treatment and therapy for two days prior to the start of the World Series, but in the only Fall Classic of his career the obviously injured Williams hit just .200 with no home runs.

971 The fielding percentage (.971) for Wade Boggs in 1988. He made 11 errors in 151 games for his highest fielding percentage during a full season at third base with Boston. Gary Gaetti won the Gold Glove that year, a feat Boggs never accomplished until he left Boston for New York, where he won the award twice—in 1994 and 1995.

972 The ratio (.972) of walks plus hits per innings pitched for Cy Young in 1901. It was the fourth of seven seasons that he led the league in WHIP, and he did so with one of the top ten ratios in franchise history. Young actually owns five of the top ten WHIP ratios in the Red Sox record book—and his career .970 ratio with the club is a franchise record.

973 The fielding percentage (.973) for shortstop Spike Owen during 248 games from 1986-88. Owen came to the club along with Dave Henderson in a trade with Seattle on August 19, 1986. He hit only .183 the rest of the season but he did well on defense—and he did come alive on offense during the playoffs. Owen was 15 for 41 against the Angels and Mets in the postseason.

974 The number of hits (974) Babe Ruth gave up as a pitcher. He gave up 934 of those hits while pitching for Boston, but only nine of them left the yard. Ruth also gave up just 290 earned runs while pitching for Boston—despite taking the mound for 1,190-plus innings. He posted a 2.19 earned run average with the club over the course of six seasons, a mark that remains among the top five in franchise history.

975 The number of batters (975) faced by Sonny Siebert in 1971. He faced 33 of those batters in a highly anticipated match-up vs. Vida Blue and the Oakland Athletics on May 28. Oakland and Boston led their respective divisions and were the best teams in the league through the first two months of the season—and Blue came into the game with a 10-1 record, while Siebert was 8-0 for Boston. It was Siebert who won that day, tossing eight-plus innings of solid work for a 4-3 victory that ran his record to 9-0. Siebert was streaky the rest of the year, losing his next four, winning five straight, then losing five straight. He closed out the season 16-10, and Boston fell to a distant third in the standings by season's end.

976 The on-base plus slugging percentage (.976) for Manny Ramirez in 1998. Manny hit 45 homers with 145 RBI for Cleveland, and he placed among the league's top ten leaders in OPS and almost every other significant offensive category as well. Manny also hit .357 with two home runs and a .929 slugging percentage vs. Boston during the 1998 Division Series. Manny defeated Boston twice in the postseason while playing for Cleveland, while losing once—but he never got a ring until he signed that free agent contract with the Red Sox.

977 The on-base plus slugging percentage (.977) for Jim Rice in 1979. Rice was second in the league in slugging and third in OPS after he hit 39 home runs and amassed 369 total bases. Not to mention he hit .325 that season. The 1978 MVP, Rice was only fifth in MVP balloting in 1979, partly because, despite the prodigious rate at which he abused pitchers around the league, his numbers were not even the best on the Red Sox. Those belonged to Fred Lynn, who hit .333, with a .423 on-base percentage, a .637 slugging percentage, a 1.060 OPS, and he tied Rice with 39 home runs.

978 The fielding percentage (.978) for second baseman Doug Griffin in 1972. He made 15 errors in only 129 games—the highest total of his career—but he still won his first Gold Glove. He never won another one.

979 The fielding percentage (.979) for John Valentin in 1994. He was solid defensively during 83 games at shortstop, but against the Seattle Mariners on July 8, he was flat out in the right place at the right time. Seattle led 2-0 in the top of the sixth, and they had runners on first and second with no outs against Red Sox pitcher Chris Nabholz when designated hitter Marc Newfield came to the plate. With the runners moving on the pitch, Newfield hit a line drive right at Valentin—who caught it and turned an unassisted triple play.

980 The fielding percentage (.980) for shortstop Rick Burleson in 1979. He turned 109 double plays and won the only Gold Glove of his career. Burleson, Dwight Evans, and Fred Lynn all won Gold Gloves in 1979—marking only the second time in franchise history that three teammates won the award in the same season.

981 The fielding percentage (.981) for all A.L. second basemen from 1982-91. In that same span, Red Sox second sacker Marty Barrett posted a .986 fielding percentage—and though he never won a Gold Glove, he did hit the trifecta with his "hidden ball trick." The play that "only" works in Little League, Barrett got big leaguers Jim Traber, Doug DeCinces, and Bobby Grich.

982 The fielding percentage (.982) for Jackie Jensen in 1959. He made 311 putouts and recorded 12 assists from right field—and he became the first outfielder for Boston to earn a Gold Glove. Jensen is also a member of the Red Sox Hall of Fame, and each year the Boston Chapter of the Baseball Writers Association of America (BBWAA) gives the Jackie Jensen Award to a major league player who best personifies "spirit and determination." Kevin Youkilis won the award in 2007.

983 The fielding percentage (.983) for Carlton Fisk from 1971-80. Pudge won his Gold Glove during his 1972 Rookie of the Year campaign—but the 15 errors he made that season was the second highest total of his career.

984 The fielding percentage (.984) for Fred Lynn in 1978. He made 408 putouts and recorded 11 outfield assists—and won the first of three consecutive Gold Gloves. Lynn, Carl Yastrzemski, and Dwight Evans combined to give the Red Sox at least one Gold Glove outfielder every season from 1975-85. Evans won the most with eight overall, Yaz won seven, and Lynn won four.

985 The fielding percentage (.985) for outfielder Reggie Smith in 1968. He made 390 putouts and eight assists as the Red Sox center fielder—and he earned the only Gold Glove of his career.

986 The fielding percentage (.986) for Don Baylor during 13 games at first base in 1986. He was the designated hitter in 143 games, but in 70 chances at first he made only one error—and the Red Sox Faithful actually *cheered* when he made it. The reason?—well, it was April 29, and Roger Clemens already had eight strikeouts when the Mariners Gorman Thomas came to bat with two outs in the fourth inning. Thomas hit a foul pop that Baylor should have caught—but he dropped it for his only error of the season, and the fans tacking red K signs on the wall in back of the bleachers could not have been happier. They cheered because it gave Clemens another shot at a strikeout—and he got Thomas looking. He went on to strikeout the next seven batters—eight in a row overall—to tie a league record. Then in the ninth—and thanks to Baylor's error—Clemens became the first player in baseball history to strikeout 20 batters in a nine inning game.

987 The career fielding percentage (.987) for Dave Stapleton. He played a little bit of everywhere and was good defensively no matter where he was at—but he was especially good at first base, which is relevant for #989.

988 Hall of Fame outfielder Harry Hooper scored (988) runs as a member of the Red Sox. He hit the century mark for the club only once, in 1913, but his career total for the club is among the ten best in franchise history.

989 The fielding percentage (.989) for first baseman Bill Buckner in 1986. He made 14 errors but was right at the league average in terms of fielding—and in all fairness, with all the injuries he battled that season it was rather routine late in the year for Dave Stapleton (who was a perfect 1.000 during 29 games at first) to enter late in the game as a defensive replacement for Buckner. John McNamara chose to not make that move when Game 6 of the 1986 World Series went extra-innings, even after Boston took a two run lead in the top of the tenth. Buckner's error in the bottom of the tenth lives on in infamy because it gave the game to the Mets—but it is worth noting that Dwight Evans, the man with more Gold Gloves than any other player in franchise history, made an error in the fifth inning of that same game that let Ray Knight advance from second to third. Knight subsequently scored when Danny Heep hit into a double play.

990 The number of games (990) caught as a member of the Red Sox for Carlton Fisk. His total is the second highest in franchise history, and his career total of 2,226 games behind the dish is a major league record.

991 On July 18, 2006, Jason Varitek was behind the plate for game number (991) of his Red Sox career—breaking the previous club record of 990 games caught by Hall of Fame icon Carlton Fisk. On September 19, 2006, Varitek and his record were honored during a pre-game ceremony that included Fisk.

992 The fielding percentage (.992) for first baseman George Scott in 1971. He won his third Gold Glove in five seasons, but it was his last as a member of the Red Sox. Scott won six consecutive Gold Gloves—five of them for Milwaukee—from 1971-76. He was the only first baseman in franchise history to win a Gold Glove until Kevin Youkilis earned his first in 2007.

993 Pedro Martinez struck out (9.93) batters per nine innings in 2003. It was the fourth time he led the league in that category for Boston and the fifth time overall. Martinez, who struck out 206 batters in just 186-plus innings of work in 2003, recorded six of the top ten strikeouts per nine innings ratios in franchise history during a seven-year stretch from 1998-2004.

994 The fielding percentage (.994) for All-Star center fielder Ellis Burks in 1990. He made 324 putouts and recorded seven outfield assists, but made only two errors, and won his only career Gold Glove.

995 The fielding percentage (.995) for All-Star catcher Tony Pena in 1991. He was behind the dish for 140 games but made only five errors in 929 chances. Pena earned his fourth career Gold Glove, but it was his first for Boston. It was also the first Gold Glove for a Red Sox catcher since Carlton Fisk in 1972.

996 The fielding percentage (.996) for Jason Varitek in 2002. Tek made only four errors in 127 games behind the plate, but Bengie Molina won the Gold Glove for Anaheim after making just one error in 121 games. Boston's captain finally got his first Gold Glove in 2005—but he made twice as many errors as he did in 2002. He made eight errors in 130 games and his fielding percentage dropped to .990, but he got the hardware.

997 Roger Clemens faced (997) batters in 1986. He led the league in wins and earned run average, and picked up both Cy Young and Most Valuable Player honors—but he also faced nine additional batters during the All-Star Game. He got the start during his first appearance in the mid-Summer Classic, and Clemens did not disappoint. He tossed three perfect innings—nine up, nine down—picked up the win, and earned MVP honors for the game.

998 The number of total bases (998) for Pokey Reese during his eight-year big league career. Reese was a first-round pick of the Cincinnati Reds who first made it to the majors in 1997, and though he won a pair of Gold Gloves and stole a few bases in the N.L., he never became a star. After five seasons with the Reds and two with the Pirates, Reese signed as a free agent with the Red Sox prior to 2004. He got 74 total bases in limited duty in his only season with the club—and as it turned out, his final season as a big league player. Great timing on his part, however, because Reese was there for the sweep over Anaheim, the comeback against New York, and the title in

St. Louis. He hit .000 after going 0 for 1 in the 2004 World Series—the only one of his career—but who cares, he got a ring.

999 The number of batters (999) faced by Frank Viola in 1992. Viola won a Cy Young Award and a World Series while pitching for the Twins, and Boston expected big things when they gave him big bucks in the free agent market prior to the 1992 season. Viola posted a 13-12 record, but it was hard for fans to be down on him because pitching was not Boston's problem. Viola and Roger Clemens anchored a staff that posted the second best earned run average in the league—but Boston's offense scored only 599 runs all season, the second lowest total out of 14 teams.

1000 The number of sleepless nights (1000) for Yankees' fans on account of Kevin Millar, Dave Roberts, Bill Mueller, David Ortiz & Co., the Fenway Faithful, and Mariano Rivera after the 2004 American League Championship Series. If there are any curses left in baseball, they are all on the north side of Chicago.

About the Author

Tucker Elliot is a Georgia native and a diehard baseball fan. A former high school athletic director and varsity baseball coach, he's now a fulltime writer and has authored or contributed to more than two dozen baseball books, to include the following Black Mesa titles:

- *Atlanta Braves IQ: The Ultimate Test of True Fandom*
- *New York Yankees IQ: The Ultimate Test of True Fandom*
- *Major League Baseball IQ: The Ultimate Test of True Fandom*
- *Tampa Bay Rays IQ: The Ultimate Test of True Fandom*
- *San Francisco Giants: An Interactive Guide to the World of Sports*

Acknowledgements

On August 25, 1986, I saw my first Red Sox game in person. It was Boston vs. Texas in Arlington, and I remember it being exceptionally hot—and I also remember not caring about the weather because the game was being aired on Monday Night Baseball and Roger Clemens was going for his 20th win of the season.

I'd like to thank my mom and dad for taking my brothers and I to that game. I'd also like to thank John McNamara, who reached up into the stands before that game and gave my kid brother a baseball.

And then the Rocket struck out ten while carrying a 2-0 shutout into the eighth inning—and if it's possible to include someone in an acknowledgement section for the express purpose of *not* thanking him, I should mention Geno Petralli. It was his pinch-hit homer that tied the game and kept us from seeing history—the Rocket's first 20-win season.

Later that fall we watched Boston take on the Mets in the World Series from our grandparent's house in Charleston, South Carolina, and our grandfather told us stories about the Red Sox that I remember to this day.

I'm inspired to write these books from these childhood memories. A game on the radio while shooting hoops with dad, sandlot baseball with our brothers while our parents sat under shade trees in lawn chairs, and of course, the countless hours spent driving us to practices and games, consoling us when we lost, cheering us when we won—and for all of this, I am grateful to my family. Any success I experience as an adult I believe in my heart is a direct result of the time my parents invested in me as a kid.

I have many friends and colleagues who continue to show their support daily, too many to list them all here—but you know who you are, and please know that you have my sincere gratitude.

I have been exceptionally lucky in my travels to interact with the many great men and women who serve our country overseas. And big surprise, there are a *huge* number of men and women serving overseas in the military that absolutely love the Boston Red Sox.

My world is a better place for having crossed paths with two such families who are quite special, for they serve their country selflessly on a daily basis and I am honored to call them my friends: Mark Sewell, who is a military doctor and a little league coach to his sons Jack, Charlie, and Harry (all future Red Sox players!), and his wife Natasha—Dr. Sewell has served his country both in Europe and Afghanistan but never failed to keep tabs on his beloved Red Sox; and the Waltman family, Gary and Selena, their two youngest Erin and

Tyler, and their two oldest, Taylor and Casey, who have impacted my life more than they possibly know.

Tucker Elliot
Tampa, FL
March 2011

References

I do extensive research for every book. My preferred method of research is actually to dig through piles and piles of old, dusty copies of *Sports Illustrated* and *Baseball Digest* magazines—and I did that, a lot—but technology being what it is today, I also made good use of LexisNexis to cull through decades of *New York Times*, *Boston Herald*, *Boston Globe*, and Associated Press articles via the Internet.

I also made use of some other valuable websites. Major League Baseball at mlb.com has done an amazing job of making statistics available to fans. The individual team sites offer detailed franchise histories, and a virtual clearinghouse of player information from past and present. I also used espn.com and baseball-reference.com extensively, but verified all statistics through the MLB site, and when discrepancies arose I always defaulted to the numbers put out by Major League Baseball.

My personal library is filled with books on baseball. *The Team by Team Encyclopedia of Major League Baseball*, written by Dennis Purdy, is one of the best. It proved to be a valuable resource. I also used *The 2005 ESPN Baseball Encyclopedia*, edited by Pete Palmer and Gary Gillette; *100 Years of the World Series*, by Eric Enders; and *Baseball, an Illustrated History*, by Geoffrey C. Ward and Ken Burns.

Two additional books that proved to be valuable resources in my research are *The 50 Greatest Red Sox Games*, by Cecilia Tan and Bill Nowlin, and *The Boston Red Sox*, by Milton Cole and Jim Kaplan.

Of course, any mistakes found in these pages are my own.

I also recommend the following reading list for Red Sox fans: *Faithful*, by Stewart O'Nan and Stephen King; *Big Papi: My Story of Big Dreams and Big Hits*, by David Ortiz and Tony Massarotti; and *Now I Can Die In Peace: How ESPN's Sports Guy Found Salvation, With a Little Help From Nomar, Pedro, Shawshank and the 2004 Red Sox*, by Bill Simmons.

About Black Mesa

Black Mesa is a Florida-based publishing company that specializes in sports history and trivia books. Look for these popular titles in our trivia IQ series:

- *Mixed Martial Arts (Volumes I & II)*
- *Boston Red Sox (Volumes I & II)*
- *Tampa Bay Rays*
- *New York Yankees*
- *Atlanta Braves*
- *Major League Baseball*
- *Milwaukee Brewers*
- *St. Louis Cardinals*
- *Boston Celtics*
- *University of Florida Gators Football*
- *University of Georgia Bulldogs Football*
- *University of Texas Longhorns Football*
- *University of Oklahoma Sooners Football*
- *New England Patriots*

For information about special discounts for bulk purchases, please email:

black.mesa.publishing@gmail.com

www.blackmesabooks.com

Also in the Sports by the Numbers Series

- *Major League Baseball*
- *New York Yankees*
- *San Francisco Giants*
- *University of Oklahoma Football*
- *University of Georgia Football*
- *Penn State University Football*
- *NASCAR*
- *Sacramento Kings Basketball*
- *Mixed Martial Arts*

Coming in 2011:
- *Texas Rangers*
- *Los Angeles Dodgers*
- *Boston Celtics*
- *Dallas Cowboys*

www.ingramcontent.com/pod-product-compliance
Lightning Source LLC
Chambersburg PA
CBHW071453040426
42444CB00008B/1315